MY HEART WILL TRIUMPH

MY HEART WILL TRIUMPH

MIRJANA SOLDO

My Heart Will Triumph Copyright ©
2016 CatholicShop Publishing

Written by Mirjana Soldo

Co-authors: Sean Bloomfield and Miljenko "Miki" Musa

Cover Photograph: Foto ĐANI

Cover Art: Damon Za

My Heart Will Triumph

ISBN-10: 0-9978906-0-6

ISBN-13: 978-0-9978906-0-0

www.MyHeartWillTriumph.com

CatholicShop Publishing

317 Riveredge Blvd, Ste 208

Cocoa, FL 32922 USA

www.CatholicShop.com

info@catholicshop.com

1-800-565-9176

For Father and Mother

In a special way, I wish to thank Miki Musa and Sean Bloomfield. It is because of their love, patience and help that this book has come among you.

INTRODUCTION

MY NAME IS Mirjana. I've experienced visions of the Virgin Mary for more than 35 years. I cannot say it more directly than that.

I understand that it might be difficult to imagine such a thing happening in modern times. Even to some believers, miracles are things of the past. But I doubt that anyone was more shocked than I was when it all began. I did not even know such things *could* take place, especially in Međugorje, a small village in former Yugoslavia.

You should know that I've been tested by doctors and scientists from all over the world, and they all agree on one thing: I am perfectly normal. I even have that in writing.

So, before you question my mental health, with a smile on my face I simply ask: Do *you* have an official document validating your sanity?

I did not write this to persuade you to believe me. I am just a messenger, and I wish to share my story with the hope that it might bring some comfort to a world in which peace is becoming increasingly scarce.

Saying that my life changed on the afternoon of June 24, 1981 hardly conveys the gravity of what transpired.

Until that day, I lived under the heavy hand of communism and stomached the many aggravations that went along with it, but the worst suffering began after I and five other children experienced something extraordinary.

What we saw radically changed us, our families, and millions of people around the world, but it also provoked the wrath of the Yugoslav regime. Fearing that my testimony was a threat to their rule, the communists declared me an *enemy of the state* when I was just 16 years old.

Perhaps their fears were warranted, because I had come to know something far greater than the communist government—far greater, in fact, than anything on Earth...

I had come to know God's love.

The six of us in the first days of the apparitions. From left to right: Ivan, Marija, me, Ivanka, Vicka and Jakov.

CHAPTER 1

"I thank you, Father, Lord of heaven and earth, because you have hidden these things from the wise and the intelligent and have revealed them to infants."

— *Jesus (Matthew 11:25)*

IN THE BEGINNING, among the six of us, I was the outsider.

Unlike the others, I had grown up in Sarajevo. With its busy streets and tall buildings, everything about my city was a stark contrast to the fields, dirt roads, and stone houses of Međugorje.

But even greater than the physical differences of these two places were the cultural ones.

Međugorje was populated mostly by the Croats, a proud people who had endured countless hardships throughout history. Whether facing Turkish conquerors or communist oppressors, the residents of Međugorje stayed true to their Catholic faith. Still, even in 1981, those who lived in Međugorje had to be discreet about their beliefs so as not to draw the scrutiny of the government.

The population of Sarajevo, on the other hand, was a colorful blend of all the people who inhabited the rest of Yugoslavia. Sometimes called "the Jerusalem of Europe," Sarajevo's population of roughly

400,000 people included Bosnian Muslims (about 45%), Serbian Orthodox Christians (30%), a scattering of us Catholic Croats (8%), and even a small community of Jews. The dominant ideology in those days, however, was atheistic communism.

Sarajevo's diverse history was especially obvious in its architecture. It looked as if pieces of different puzzles had been tossed together to make a city. On the periphery, the red tile roofs of traditional Bosnian homes shone bright against drab concrete monoliths built by the communists, while closer to *Baščaršija*—Sarajevo's charming "Old Town" and the heart of the city—ornate mosques and Ottoman citadels competed for the eye with extravagant remnants of the Austro-Hungarian Empire.

Throughout my childhood, I had many friends from varying religions and backgrounds. In fact, out of all my friends in Sarajevo, only a few were Catholic. Muslims and Orthodox were far more prevalent there, and the city's skyline was dominated by minarets and Byzantine church spires. I had friends from both faiths, but we never worried about our differences. I would sometimes even celebrate my friends' holy days, and they would celebrate mine. I learned to respect people of other faiths even before the Virgin Mary taught us that it was right to do so.

As I grew up, I was continually drawn to spend my summers in Međugorje, even though the houses there lacked running water and I spent most of my time working beneath the scorching sun. My aunt, uncle and cousins lived in Međugorje, and my parents allowed me to stay with them year after year. Međugorje was my second home.

Uncle Šimun and Aunt Slava treated me like their own child, so I never felt like I was merely a guest in their home. Their two oldest daughters, Milena and Vesna, were more like sisters to me than cousins. I slept in their room and we talked every night until their little brother Vlado asked us to be quiet or when our giggles accidentally woke their little sister, Jelena.

Sandwiched between scrub-covered mountains, the parish of

Međugorje was comprised of five small hamlets. Founded on May 15, 1892, the parish was placed under the protection of Saint James, the patron saint of pilgrims—a choice which, 90 years later, would seem almost prophetic. The first church of St. James was inadvertently built on unstable ground, so a new one was completed in 1969. At first, no one understood why the priests built such a big church, but after the events of 1981, it often seemed too small.

My aunt and uncle lived in Bijakovići, a hamlet near the base of a hill called Podbrdo. Like everyone in Međugorje, they made a meager living by growing tobacco, grapes, and other crops. While traditional Herzegovinian houses featured stone walls and orange tile roofs, Šimun and Slava lived in a more modern home built with bricks and stucco.

No one in Sarajevo understood what I loved so much about Međugorje, not even my parents. At home, I had all the comforts of city life, which my parents worked hard to provide. By comparison, life in Međugorje was far more difficult. The villagers had to grow most of their own food, ration water, and work just to survive. Yet it was this simplicity that drew me there every summer.

For the first nine years of my life in Sarajevo, my parents treated me like a princess. My father was especially doting. If my mother asked me to do the laundry or wash the dishes, he would do it for me. My parents even brought me my breakfast in bed sometimes, and they always cooked what I liked because I was thin and they wanted me to eat more. To encourage me, my mom and dad applauded if I finished everything on my plate. This led to some embarrassing moments, though. When I was about seven years old, I visited my relatives and the family had prepared a special meal for my aunt's father-in-law. I didn't know that it was only for him and I ate all of it.

I sat there proudly, expecting applause, but instead everyone looked at me with surprise. Thankfully, my aunt's father-in-law laughed about it.

For a picky eater like me, the food in Međugorje was different from what I was used to. But my mother always warned me before I went there so I never complained.

"If I hear that you refused to eat something," she said, "then you'll come back home that very second."

Despite the contrasts, I loved Međugorje. While my family was vacationing on the coast of the Adriatic Sea for summer holidays, I was going to an obscure farming village in the Herzegovina highlands.

Međugorje was not entirely foreign to me, though. From as early as I can remember, my family and I occasionally visited the village to see our relatives. As a little girl, I relished playing with my cousins and their friends. We raced through open fields and played hide-and-seek in vineyards. During those visits, I came to know a rural freedom that the city could not offer.

One little boy was especially kind to me. His name was Marko. A year older than I was, he had thick black hair and eyes the color of Turkish coffee. Marko's uncle on his father's side was married to my aunt on my mother's side, so we often saw each other at my aunt's house throughout the years. His parents and my parents enjoyed spending time together, so when they visited us in Sarajevo, Marko would come along as well. My memories of him are as old as my earliest memories of myself. I even recall sleeping in the same room as him when we were little.

Marko was different from the other boys. He had a peace about him—a quiet and gentle stoicism that I admired—and he was always smiling. I attributed his kindness to his strong belief in God, something his parents had instilled in him from an early age.

When we were teenagers, Marko's fondness had developed into more of a romantic attraction, but he was too shy to tell me about it. His feelings were clear to everyone, though. Every time I came to Međugorje for the summer, he always happened to show up under the guise of visiting my uncle and aunt. My cousins often teased me about him.

There was not much opportunity for that kind of socializing in

Međugorje, though. I worked hard when I was there, like everyone else. On most days, my cousins and I woke before dawn to pick tobacco in the fields, and later we strung the tobacco leaves to dry.

When I first started visiting, my uncle and aunt did not wake me to go work with them. They thought I needed more sleep since I was not accustomed to their lifestyle. But it did not feel right for me to sleep while my cousins worked, so I started getting up on my own and going with them. At first, everyone was surprised, but my uncle soon began waking me up at 4 am with the rest of the family.

We usually had some free time after finishing our work. We had fun with simple things like taking walks on the outskirts of the village or sitting and talking on the stone walls. The kids in Međugorje were always eager to hear about city life, and I was just as enamored with their tales of living in the country.

One of my closest friends was a tall, dark-haired girl named Ivanka. Her home in Mostar was not far away, and she spent summers and weekends in Međugorje with her grandmother, so she was more of a local than I was. We connected on our appreciation for city life and she particularly enjoyed talking about fashion—and sometimes about her fondness for a local boy named Rajko.

I felt exhausted at the end of every day, and my hands were always sticky from picking tobacco, but I was always joyful. In fact, my hands were the only things I was ashamed of when I returned to school in Sarajevo. My classmates came back from summer holidays with beautiful sunbathed hands while mine were yellowish-black from tobacco residue, so I hid my hands under my school desk.

But that was only a minor inconvenience. I felt wonderful when I was in Međugorje. I felt *alive*. And I always looked forward to the end of each school year so that I could return.

In 1981, towards the end of my sophomore year of high school, I began to feel unusual. It was more intense than mere excitement about my upcoming trip to Međugorje, and, even stranger, it manifested into a strong desire to be alone in prayer.

I withdrew and prayed in silence, refraining from my usual adolescent routines like taking walks with friends and hanging out in cafes. My mother became increasingly worried because my behavior seemed abnormal for a 16-year-old girl.

At the time, I was attending one of the best high schools in Sarajevo. During breaks between classes—when the other kids mingled in the hallways—I began going alone to an old Orthodox church near the school. Most of my fellow Catholics avoided Orthodox churches, but, to me, this one felt like a peaceful refuge.

The church was always empty. The air inside was cool and dark and smelled of old wine and incense. Each day, I lit a candle and prayed. Basking in the silence, I tried to comprehend what was happening to me. The strange feeling continued to intensify every day, and by the time the school year ended, I was praying more than I ever had before.

When I finally departed for Medugorje, it did not seem like it was *me* who was going. It was like watching someone else's life in a movie. Why did I feel so peculiar?

When my father dropped me off at the station to catch the train to Mostar, he could sense my confusion. As always, he cried—but this time he also begged me to change my mind about going.

I hugged him. "I'll be fine, Dad. Don't worry."

Taking my seat on the train, a vague anticipation grew within me. Anticipation for what? I did not know. I always looked forward to seeing my friends and family members in Medugorje, but this was a different and more intense feeling, like I was standing on the edge of the unknown, about to dive in. I gazed through the window as the train passed the urban sprawl of Sarajevo and continued along the Neretva River, a ribbon of turquoise twisting through the Dinaric Alps. What was happening to me? And why did I suddenly want to pray all the time?

Misty cliffs gave way to the wider expanse of Jablaničko Lake, and a series of tunnels and arched bridges finally deposited the train at the Mostar station where Uncle Šimun waited to pick me up.

Within a few days of arriving in Međugorje, all my questions were answered in a way I never could have imagined.

I woke with a smile on the morning of June 24, 1981. It was the feast day of St. John the Baptist, the prophet described in the Bible as *"the voice that cries out in the wilderness to prepare the way of the Lord."* But my joy had less to do with St. John than with the fact that we did not have to pick tobacco that day. Holy days in Međugorje were non-working days, which meant that I had plenty of free time.

It was the perfect opportunity to catch up with Ivanka. Her family's home was next door to my uncle's house, and when I found her, she and I decided to take a walk on the outskirts of Bijakovići. Setting out on the narrow road, we stopped at a neighboring house to see if a local girl named Vicka wanted to join us. She was taking a nap, but her mother promised to tell her that we had come by.

At that time, people in Međugorje never locked their doors and it was normal for neighbors to walk into each other's houses unannounced. The most common pastime in the village was simply talking to each other, and as we continued our walk, we heard "Where are you going?" from nearly every home. But everything got quiet as we passed the last house of the village.

Strolling down an unpaved road in the shadow of Podbrdo Hill, we talked about the terrible thunderstorm that had recently hit the area. The phone lines were still down after lightning struck the main telephone switchboard. We also talked about everyday things—what we had done in school, new friends we had made, the latest fashions, and other things teenaged girls usually talk about.

But lurking behind our lighthearted conversation was a heavy subject which neither of us wanted to acknowledge—Ivanka's mother, Jagoda, had passed away less than two months before after a long illness. A saintly woman, she embraced her suffering without complaint, even in the last moments of her life. As was the custom in Herzegovina, Ivanka wore black mourning clothes on the day of her mother's funeral and would continue to do so every day for another year.

I could hear the sadness in Ivanka's voice as we walked, and grief lingered in her eyes. I hoped the fresh air would bring her some temporary joy. Indeed, Ivanka began to smile as we talked and shared.

Tired of walking, we sat down in a shady spot below the hill at around 5 or 6 pm. In the middle of our conversation, Ivanka suddenly blurted, "I think I see Our Lady on the hill!"

She was gazing up at Podbrdo, but I thought she was kidding so I did not look.

"Yeah, sure it's Our Lady!" I said. "She came to see what the two of us are up to because she has nothing better to do."

But as Ivanka continued to tell me what she saw, I got upset at her. Our parents had taught us to respect faith and never take God's name in vain, so when I thought Ivanka was joking about the Blessed Mother, I felt uncomfortable and afraid.

"I'm leaving," I said, and I headed home. But when I reached the village, a powerful sensation seized my heart. *Something* was calling me back—a feeling so strong that it forced me to stop and turn around.

I found Ivanka in the same place, gazing at the hill and jumping up and down. I had never seen her so excited, and chills went through my body when she turned to look at me. Her normally-tanned skin looked as pale as milk, and her eyes were radiant.

"Look now, *please!*" she begged.

I slowly turned and looked up at the hill. When I saw the figure, my heart whirled with fear and wonder but my brain struggled to process it.

No one ever climbed that hill, but what I saw was unmistakable— there, among the rocks and brambles, was a young woman.

Class photograph from my school in Sarajevo. I'm the blonde-haired girl in the middle row.

CHAPTER 2

"*I am coming among you because I desire to be your mother—your intercessor.*"

— *From Our Lady's message of March 18, 2012*

A M I DEAD *or alive?* That's what I asked myself when I first gazed upon the beautiful woman on the hill. My heart was in such turmoil that I could hardly identify one emotion before another took over.

Pinch yourself, I thought. *You must be dreaming!*

In those frantic first moments, I did not dare approach the woman. At a distance of a hundred or more meters, the woman's face was difficult to discern, but I could see that she wore a bluish-gray dress and held something in her arms. I soon realized that the *something* in her arms was an infant.

A mother would never *climb such a hill with a baby in her arms,* I thought.

I was too fixated on the woman to pay attention to what else was happening, but I vaguely recall some other local children gathering around us. A boy named Ivan came by carrying apples, and when he saw what we saw, he dropped them all and ran away. And when Vicka came to find us, she was so terrified that she kicked off her slippers and fled.

Ivanka and I looked at each other after Vicka ran away. Without saying a word, we bolted down the road.

I burst into my uncle's house and screamed, "I think I saw Our Lady!"

My Grandma Jela, who was alone inside, looked at me in shock. She studied me for a moment.

"Let Our Lady be where she is, in Heaven. Take the rosary, go to your room, and pray to God."

I was too excited to explain to my grandmother that I really *had* seen something, so I did exactly what she told me to do—I ran into the bedroom and prayed.

Eventually I stopped trembling, but sleep eluded me that night. Every time I closed my eyes, all I could see was the woman on the hill. I was certain it had been Our Lady, more because of what I felt than what I saw. But wasn't the Virgin Mary supposed to be in Heaven? I searched my memories for anything that might help me comprehend what I had just witnessed.

Until that moment, I never imagined that a person could see *Gospa*—the Croatian name for the Blessed Virgin Mary—on Earth. I had never heard of other so-called "apparitions," and I assumed that this was the first time she had appeared to *anyone*. In communist Yugoslavia, religious books were practically contraband, so our knowledge of miracles was limited to the measured homilies of our priests who were always aware that government spies lurked in the pews. Anything misconstrued as an attack on the regime, the priests knew, could send them to prison—or worse.

Although my hometown of Sarajevo was a communist stronghold, I had a relatively peaceful childhood. My parents, Jozo and Milena, were originally from Bijakovići, but they went to live in Sarajevo after they got married. I was born there on March 18, 1965.

Even in my earliest memories, I was always a little different from other children.

From the time I was a baby up until I was four or five years old, I barely had any hair, and what I did have was wispy and almost stark white. One day, tired of waiting for my hair to grow in, my mom took the advice of a neighbor and shaved my head before my dad came home from work. She left me bald. I looked strange to other girls, so I wore a cap and played soccer with the neighborhood boys. I was their goalkeeper. Eventually, as my mom had hoped, better hair grew back, and I rejoined the world of girls.

I used to play with a little girl named Minka. During the Muslim calls to prayer that echoed through the city, Minka would suddenly stop playing, kneel down and bow to pray. I watched her with wonder. One time, I did exactly as she did. My mother saw me and quickly called me inside, explaining that Minka and I belonged to different religions. Still, our friendship taught me not to focus on the differences among people.

Playing with friends was nice, but I usually preferred to spend time alone. In the quiet seclusion of our apartment, I wrote poetry, painted, and sketched. I was especially good at drawing figures of women and girls, and my classmates often asked me to draw pictures for them. One of my drawings was chosen to represent my elementary school in an international art competition in Japan.

I also loved to read. One book in particular, *The Little Prince* by Antoine de Saint-Exupéry—or *Mali Princ* in my Croatian language—deeply moved me. The story of a stranded pilot who meets a boy prince from another world left me with the sense that something greater lay hidden beyond what I could see, and it led me to ponder the big question:

What is the meaning of life?

As the Little Prince said, "Only the children know what they are looking for."

The geographer, the lamplighter and other characters from *The*

Little Prince literally lived on their own little worlds. They reminded me of the residents of our apartment building—people of many backgrounds living in little concrete boxes stacked upon one another, so close to each other and yet still so far away.

There were not many Catholic children in Sarajevo. The small number of us who came from practicing families had to go to catechism classes almost secretly at the Church of St. Anthony of Padua, in the historic neighborhood of Bistrik. With its distinctive maroon-colored exterior, the church somehow transcended ethnic division. Muslims and Orthodox also came there to pray, and the Franciscans who lived in the adjoining monastery served the poor of every faith.

My catechism classes taught me to fear God more than to love Him. I was left with the image of an angry ruler who watched from Heaven to judge and punish me for every mistake. But I also developed a devotion to the church's namesake, St. Anthony, whose compassion and love whispered of a different version of God.

One parent from the local Catholic community would always lead four or five of us on foot to the church. Before I left, my mother told me, "If someone along the way asks where you're headed, tell them that you're going to have ice cream or to a playground or something."

One day, on our way to catechism class, we passed my elementary school teacher. Like most teachers in Sarajevo, she was a member of the Communist Party.

"Mirjana!" she said, stopping.

I stopped as well. "Um, hello Comrade Teacher." We had to address every teacher as comrade—*drug* for males and *drugarica* for females in our language.

"Where are you headed?" asked my teacher.

I froze in fear.

"I have no idea," I told her, and then I quickly turned and hurried after the others. She was probably more confused than suspicious.

Under the leadership of President Josip Broz Tito, the government sought to indoctrinate its citizens early by controlling the education system. Our classroom history books praised the "heroic" ideologies of Karl Marx, Friedrich Engels and Vladimir Lenin. Teachers repeatedly told us that God was a fable and that religion, as Marx once said, was "the opiate of the masses." I was often confused about what to believe.

The government automatically enrolled children entering the first grade of primary school into the *Savez Pionira Jugoslavije*, or *Union of Pioneers of Yugoslavia*. As new *pioniri*, barely seven years old, we received the official uniform: a red bandana and a *Titovka*, or "Tito hat," emblazoned with the red communist star. Through the pioneer oath, we pledged to love the *Socialist Federal Republic of Yugoslavia* and promised to "spread brotherhood, unity, and the principles for which comrade Tito fought."

The indoctrination continued through the grades. Every year on May 25, Yugoslavia celebrated President Tito's birthday as a national celebration known as Youth Day. Leading up to Youth Day, our curriculum glorified Tito for bringing communism to the country. Teachers asked every student to write a poem or essay praising the president and the state-run media circulated the best ones. I always looked forward to the writing contest, and some of my submissions were even selected.

Thousands gathered at government rallies on Youth Day. The ceremonies included sports presentations in Tito's honor and dance routines by the *pioniri*. Orchestras performed bombastic partisan songs like *Uz Maršala Tito*, with lyrics calling Tito *the heroic son* and boasting that *not even Hell shall stop us* and that whoever disagrees *will feel our fist*.

"Education is a weapon," Joseph Stalin once said, "whose effects depend on who holds it in his hands and at whom it is aimed."

Living in a cultural crossroads like Yugoslavia gave me a diverse and sometimes complicated education. The government required us to learn both the Latin alphabet and the Cyrillic alphabet, with the former used by Croats and the latter by Serbs. Learning to read in two alphabets taught me the difference between 'Yugoslavia' and

'Југославија,' for example. I also learned English through a curriculum from the United Kingdom, giving me a slight British accent when I practiced the language.

More than anything, I enjoyed being home with my family. Dad was easygoing and full of joy. My mother was a little stricter and more susceptible to the stresses of life, but she worked hard to provide a happy, loving home for us. As a little girl, I was always more attached to my father.

Sometimes I asked him, "Why do we even need Mom?" He smiled.

My father's big green eyes always looked vibrant against his black hair, and his slight chubbiness complimented his personality. When my cousins visited from Herzegovina, he usually woke early and asked them what they wanted for breakfast. Then he'd go buy the ingredients and come back to prepare it for them, all before he had to leave for work.

Although I could not see it at the time, life in Sarajevo was difficult for my parents. Dad worked during the day and spent most nights studying and taking classes to be able to work at a radiology ward. Mom worked as a cook at a large company. She left our apartment every day at 5 am and came home exhausted every afternoon. They were unable to pay someone to babysit me in the years before I could be enrolled in school. So, by the time I turned five, I stayed home alone, which was stressful for Mom and Dad. A few times a day, my dad walked back to our apartment to check on me through the window, always careful not to let me see him, and then he hurried back to work.

For eight years I was their only child, their "little princess"—that is, until July 16, 1973, when my brother, Miroslav, entered the world.

After Mom gave birth, I waited nervously until they returned from the hospital. Even then, I was more concerned about my father than anyone else. I remember everything he wore that day—his brown sports jacket, neatly-ironed gray slacks, a white collared shirt—and how his eyes were full of love when he looked at the new baby. I wanted my father's love all to myself. I took Dad aside and said, "You just love me, and I'll love the baby."

My mom got dangerously sick after my brother was born. The doctor had instructed her to rest, but she immediately began working when she came home. She developed an infection and an extremely high fever. I did not understand what was happening, but I noticed that my dad was worried; he did not joke with me like normal. He divided his time between being at my mother's bedside and taking care of Miroslav, or Miro as we called him.

My mom eventually recovered, but the experience of seeing her so sick made me vow to never take her for granted again. From then on, I tried to make sure she always knew how much I loved her.

I took it upon myself to help take care of Miro, and it was not long before my hesitation about him disappeared. Since I was almost nine years older than him, the role I naturally assumed was more like a second mother. Our parents had to work, so I was often responsible for him. I changed his diapers, bathed him, and fed him, and when he learned to walk, I took him with me through Sarajevo. My friends called us "Mirjana and the trailer" because of the way I held his hand and led him around.

In 1976, after my father started working as a senior technician at a radiology ward, we moved to a different apartment on the top floor of an 8-story building, close to the heart of the city. With only two rooms and one bathroom, our new home was snug for a family of four, but we never felt cramped. Entering through the front door, a hallway divided the apartment into two parts. The kitchen and living room were on one side. We ate meals at a table in a small dining area connected to the kitchen. Our living room was furnished with two couches, two armchairs, and a TV. During the day, we gathered there to talk, watch television, and pray as a family, but at night, Miro and I used the living room as our bedroom. The couches pulled out to make our beds and we stored our clothes in a large cabinet that ran along the wall. My parents' bedroom and the bathroom were on the other side of the hallway.

From such a high vantage, I felt like I could see the entire world from our apartment windows.

When fog poured over the distant mountains and covered Sarajevo, only the tips of the highest towers, minarets, and steeples pierced through, like signposts on a thoroughfare of cloud. On clear evenings, the city lights in the valley looked like a bowl of stars. Sometimes I watched airplanes take off from Sarajevo Airport, and I shivered at the notion of riding in one. *I'll never do that,* I thought.

Miro played in the park adjacent to the complex and I enjoyed the tree-lined path beside the *Miljacka River.* If our family needed to go anywhere, a public tram stop was only a few blocks away. Sometimes we took walks together through the cobblestone streets of Baščaršija, stopping to feed pigeons near the historic *Sebilj* fountain, or to light a candle at the Sacred Heart Cathedral.

An older Muslim woman named Paasha lived alone in the apartment below ours. She did not have any family nearby so my parents treated her like she was part of ours. If something broke in her apartment, my father fixed it, and when we invited Paasha over for dinner, my mom prepared the meal according to Islamic law.

"The food most beloved to God," Paasha would say, "is food shared among many people."

Paasha became quite fond of me, and she started calling me *Mala Plavuša,* or "little blonde." Sometimes when I was outside in the park, she opened her window and shouted, "My Little Blonde! Will you go buy me some bread?"

Even if I had to leave my friends, I never said no. Buying things for Paasha gave me the opportunity to chat with her. Although she probably could have gone shopping herself, I think she enjoyed the company, and with Grandma Jela so far away, she became like my surrogate grandmother. Paasha loved to speak about God and she admired our Catholic beliefs.

"Hold on to your faith," she used to tell me. "And when you get married, choose someone who shares your beliefs. It's best for your children."

I laughed. "Children? Marriage? That's a long way off!"

"Ah, but one day, my dear, you'll be saying 'that was a long time ago'."

Strong believers like Paasha were rare in Sarajevo, though. The communists had been quite successful at secularizing the local culture. Even Christmas was a working day and children had to go to school. The government paid special attention to anyone who was absent from work or school on that day.

My family and I celebrated Christmas as best we could in the privacy of our apartment. Leading up to Christmas, we decorated a little Christmas tree, prayed together and sang holiday songs. On Christmas day, we went to work and school like everyone else, but later we'd all meet for Mass and then go home to share a big meal. The next day, my uncle and his family came to visit.

Despite the difficult circumstances, we always had a wonderful Christmas.

When I was 12, my father got a job training radiography technicians in Libya. It was difficult for him to be so far away from home, but the wage was higher and he wanted to provide a better life for us. When he sent me a cassette player one day, I assumed he had gotten rich—but electronic goods were just much cheaper in Libya. During the two years Dad was away, I took even more responsibility for Miro. But as he grew and became more independent, he often accused me of being annoying. "I don't need a second mother," he'd say.

I usually tried to clean the house before Mom came home from work. To make it especially nice, I liked to put flowers in a vase for her. I would ask Miro to go out and buy the flowers, but naturally, as a little boy, he was always ashamed to buy something so "girly." After some coaxing, he would angrily march down to the flower shop and come back ducking between buildings so his friends wouldn't see him with a bouquet. I always took the flowers at the door and barred him from entering until Mom came home, because otherwise he would make a mess and undo all my cleaning. Miro was never happy about that.

Despite our little disagreements, our home was always full of love.

My parents hardly talked to me about faith, at least not with words. Instead, they were living examples of it, and, through their example, they showed me the importance of prayer.

We practiced our faith in relative secrecy, but most of our neighbors knew we were Catholic. It was impossible to hide our beliefs. A girl named Gordana and her family lived nearby. They were Serbian and Orthodox by birth, but they did not practice any religion. Like many people in Sarajevo, Gordana's parents saw no value in it. But Gordana watched my family closely when she visited us. She saw how we went to Mass, how we prayed together, and how our home was always full of something special—something invisible to her eyes but evident to her heart.

"Why don't we belong anywhere?" Gordana asked her mom one day.

"How do you mean?" said her mom.

"It would be so nice to live like Mirjana's family. Why don't we pray and go to church like they do?"

At first, Gordana's parents dismissed the idea, but Gordana was so insistent that her parents finally gave in. They started going to the nearby Orthodox church and praying together as a family.

Growing up, I was never exceptionally devout or pious, but I always believed. Like other Catholics, I felt great reverence for the Virgin Mary, but I had a deeper relationship with Jesus. I talked to Him often. With my childlike faith, I thought of Jesus as an older brother in whom I could confide every little concern, from playground disagreements to difficult school exams. I also asked Him questions about life, especially one that was constantly on my mind… *Why do people have to suffer?*

From as early as I can remember, I sympathized with anyone who suffered. As a little girl, if I saw a sick or depressed person, I cried for him. I constantly wondered why a loving God allowed them to suffer. Grownups told me that instead of worrying about sad things, I should have fun and be happy like other children. But how could I be happy when someone was hurting?

My mother was already aware of my sensitivity when I began hiding away during the spring of 1981, but it still worried her. My insistence on spending the entire summer in Međugorje exasperated her concerns.

"Do you have some kind of prayer book I can read?" I asked her one night.

"A prayer book?" she said. "Why?"

"I don't know. I just really feel like I should pray."

She hesitated, but then she went into her bedroom and came back with her and my father's marital prayer book.

"This is all I have," she said.

Prayer books were rare in Yugoslavia. The communists discouraged the printing and importation of religious materials. In keeping with tradition, however, they allowed each couple to have a prayer book at their wedding. My parents cherished theirs.

I retreated to a quiet place and pored through the book. I felt like she had given me a priceless treasure. With each prayer that I recited, my heart swelled with joy.

On the other side of our apartment, however, my mother lay in bed, overcome with anxiety. To her, my strange behavior seemed like some sort of omen. She wept all night, convinced that something was going to happen to me.

And she was right—something did.

Five of us in the first days of the apparitions. From left to right: me, Vicka, Ivanka, Jakov and Marija.

CHAPTER 3

"My children, do not be afraid to open your hearts to me. With motherly love, I will show you what I expect of each of you, what I expect of my apostles. Set out with me."

— *From Our Lady's message of March 18, 2011*

I CANNOT SAY that I woke on the morning of June 25, 1981, because I don't think I ever fell asleep the night before, given my state of mind. Regardless, I left early to pick tobacco with my cousins as if it was any other day in Međugorje.

Vesna and Milena reminded me about our plans to visit our aunt's house that evening, adding that Marko would be there. I nodded, but I only wanted to think about the woman on the hill.

As I worked in the fields, I did not see any of the others—the ones who, like me, would later be known as "the visionaries." Lost in the monotony of picking and stringing tobacco, I replayed the events from the previous afternoon in my mind. Had I truly seen what I thought I saw?

As it got closer to the time of the previous day's vision, a strange feeling began to consume me. Something within was calling me back to the hill. It soon became too strong to ignore.

"Uncle Šimun," I said, "I feel like I need to go back to the hill. May I?"

My uncle looked at me and pondered for a moment. "Okay," he finally said, "but your aunt and I will go with you. We want to see what's going on."

We left right away. When we reached the base of Podbrdo, it seemed like half the village was already there. News always spread quickly in Bijakovići. When I found Ivanka, Vicka and Ivan in the crowd, three flashes of white light drew our eyes to the hill. We were all amazed to see the same figure we had seen the day before. This time she was a little farther up the hillside.

Two other children who had not been with us the previous day— 16-year-old Marija and 10-year-old Jakov, one of my cousins—joined us, and together we all ran up towards the lady.

The onlookers below were baffled as they watched us scale the steep slope at an impossible speed, seemingly coasting over boulders and thorn bushes. Some people tried to run after us, but they could not keep pace. I was a city girl and not particularly athletic, but it felt effortless. It was as if I simply glided—or like something carried me—to the place where the woman was standing.

"It takes at least 12 minutes to get up there," my uncle later said, "and yet the children did it in two. Seeing that terrified me."

The first time I gazed upon the woman up close, I realized she was not of this world. Immediately—and involuntarily—we fell to our knees. Not sure what to say or do, we began to pray the *Our Father*, *Hail Mary*, and *Glory Be*. To our astonishment, the woman prayed along with us, but she remained silent during the *Hail Mary*.

A beautiful blueness encompassed the woman. Her skin was imbued with an olive-hued radiance, and her eyes reminded me of the translucent blue of the Adriatic. A white veil concealed most of her long, black hair, except for a curl visible near her forehead and locks hanging down below the veil. She wore a long dress that fell past her feet. Everything I saw seemed supernatural, from the unearthly blue-gray glow of her dress to the breathtaking intensity of her gaze. Her very presence brought with it a feeling of peace and maternal love, but I also felt intense fear because I did not understand what was happening.

"Djeco moja, ne bojte se," she said in perfect Croatian. *My Children, be not afraid.* With a resonant, melodic tone that no human could ever replicate, her voice was like music.

Ivanka found the courage to pose a question, one that had obviously been burning within her. "How is my mother?" she asked.

Our Lady looked at Ivanka with tenderness. *"She is with me."*

One of the others asked Our Lady if she would come again the next day, and she gently nodded in affirmation. Overall, though, little was said in our first meeting. It seemed that the intent was for everyone to get comfortable with what would become a regular occurrence.

I had always been extremely shy. As a child, when visitors came to our home, I ran into another room and shut the door. If my mother made me come out, I stood in the background and remained silent until the guests departed. That's how it was for me during the first apparition. I was simply awestruck. My only desires were to gaze at her beauty and bask in the tremendous love I felt when she looked at me.

When the villagers finally reached us on the hillside, no one among them could see what we saw, but later they said that our facial expressions shocked them. And although we could hear our own voices during the apparition, they said that our lips moved without making any sounds. They could only hear us speak when we prayed, or sometimes when we answered questions.

Later, hearing other people describe the apparition unsettled me, almost as if strangers had been watching me sleep. But what the villagers saw convinced them that we were experiencing something incredible. Here were six children, only a few of whom had been friends before that day, kneeling on sharp rocks and briars, faces aglow and eyes transfixed onto something unseen. Scientists, I later learned, categorized our experience as being in a *state of ecstasy*. I called it being in Heaven.

"Will you leave a sign," said Vicka, "so that people will believe us?"

Our Lady simply smiled, but then Vicka asked me to tell her what time it was. It seemed like a strange request at that moment, and I was too mesmerized to even consider looking at my watch. I hoped the encounter would never end, but it eventually had to.

"Go in God's peace," Our Lady said. Then, quite suddenly, she began to ascend, fading into the blueness. Simultaneously, I felt myself come back to this world, a transition accompanied by a great amount of pain and sadness. I longed to be with Our Lady forever.

Wiping my tears, I looked at the other visionaries. They, too, appeared to be struggling with the shift back to "reality." Ivanka was especially emotional, and with good reason—she now knew that her mother was with the Virgin Mary.

Bystanders claimed that our vision lasted ten to fifteen minutes, but that seemed impossible. It felt like so much longer. I looked at my watch to check the time, but what I saw perplexed me. The numbers and hands of my watch had completely turned backward. The 2 o'clock mark was in the place of the 10 o'clock mark, and so on, and the hands were ticking backwards. I recalled how Vicka had asked me to tell her the time. It all seemed so strange.

Onlookers peppered us with questions as we descended the hill, but we were still too stunned to give detailed answers. Together we had experienced something extraordinary—a glimpse of the divine, and a meeting with the Mother of God—and yet, for each of us, the encounter had been an intimate and personal one.

Fr. Slavko, a priest who would later serve in Međugorje, once got frustrated because he could never get all six of us visionaries together in one place. "If I were Our Lady," he said, "I never would have chosen the six of you. You're all so different, and that's a sign for me that it's true."

Most of us never would have spent time together had it not been for the apparitions. When everything began, observers probably shared my first impressions of the others. None of us were particularly pious compared to other children in the village, and we each had our own unique strengths and weaknesses. In spite of this, or perhaps *because* of it, Our Lady chose us and brought us together.

With brown, curly hair and a persistent smile, 17-year-old Vicka Ivankovic was a joyful and vivacious girl. She was always first to take initiative in the group. *Vicka* is a nickname; her real name, *Vida*, is the Croatian word for *vision*.

I had never spent time with 16-year-old Ivan Dragićević before the apparitions. Tall, with black hair, Ivan seemed shy and quiet. The name Ivan is the Croatian equivalent of *John*, a common name in the New Testament meaning "God is gracious."

Neither did I know 16-year-old Marija Pavlovic, a thin girl with short, brown hair. In Croatian, the letter *j* is pronounced like a *y*, so her name is the Slavic version of *Maria* or *Mary*. In the same way, my first name is pronounced *meer-yana*, and derives from the original Hebrew form of the name Mary—*Miriam*.

The youngest and by far the smallest member of the group was 10-year-old Jakov Colo. Although Jakov was my cousin, I had not associated with him much. He lived alone with his mother, Jaka. With his youthful innocence, Jakov—whose name was the Croatian version of *James*—always entertained us and made us laugh.

And of course there was my dear friend, Ivanka Ivankovic. At 15-years-old, she was the youngest of us four girls. She had a penchant for being late and always seemed to be the last one to show up when we all met.

We were all so different, but the extraordinary gift of seeing Our Lady bonded us together. Our interpretations of the experience were and would remain as varied as our personalities, but, through the years, we have always agreed on one thing...

No words can describe the beauty of Our Lady and the feeling that comes with seeing her.

The Franciscans of Herzegovina.

CHAPTER 4

"I am calling you to be my apostles of light who will spread love and mercy through the world. My children, your life is only a blink in contrast to eternal life."

— *From Our Lady's message of August 2, 2014*

"THAT BLONDE GIRL from Sarajevo must have started it."

In those first days, I was the prime target of the regime's suspicions and I often overheard such statements. Some even accused me of bringing drugs from the city, when, in truth, all I knew of drugs were the ones used for illnesses.

The accusations hurt my feelings, but I understood why the skeptics singled me out. In a village where everyone knew everyone, I was the "foreigner." I even spoke differently. The people of Yugoslavia shared a common language, but the Serb-dominated dialect I grew up with in Sarajevo was noticeably different from the Croat vocabulary of Medugorje.

Overall, though, the local people supported us and stood up for us. I did not think it could be any different, because I assumed that everyone simply *knew* that we saw Our Lady. It was even strange to me that people near us during the apparition could not see any of what we saw. I would never lie about something so sacred, so it seemed equally impossible for anyone to doubt me. Still, all I cared about was seeing her again. In those days, I lived more in Heaven than I did on Earth. I did not care what my parents said, what the priests said, what the police said—I lived solely for the one moment every day when Our Lady came. Nothing else seemed important.

On the evening of June 25, Marko left his home in Mostar with his parents and two brothers and headed to the same family gathering that I planned to attend. He had big plans for that night; he was finally going to ask me to be his girlfriend.

As their car passed through Čitluk, one of Marko's aunts saw them from the side of the road and waved them down. His father stopped the car and his aunt ran to the window, giddy with excitement.

"Do you know what happened in Međugorje?" she said.

"No," said Marko's mother. "Tell us."

"Well, six children claim to see Our Lady!"

Marko leaned forward. "Which children?"

His aunt listed the seers, and when she said my name, Marko felt an instant pain in his stomach.

That's it, he thought. *It's over.*

Knowing that I would never lie, he believed immediately. But he feared that my experience would drastically change me somehow, and he was certain that his dreams of a future with me had suddenly become impossible. I was too overwhelmed by my experience the previous afternoon to attend the family gathering, so Marko was left to wonder.

Uncle Šimun, Aunt Slava, and my cousins had spent enough time with me over the years to know that I was telling the truth. They had never seen me so excited, afraid, or prayerful. My cousins and aunt asked me numerous questions about Our Lady and listened intently as I described her. Uncle Šimun gave me his full support but tried not to be intrusive, knowing that I needed a little extra privacy to process everything happening to me.

Grandma Jela believed me, too. She noticed how much I had been praying as well as other things.

"Your face looks different somehow," she told me one day.

"How so, grandmother?"

She squinted her eyes and leaned closer. "As if something illuminates it."

Faith meant everything to my grandmother. Many years before, it was tested in unimaginable ways.

In the days after World War II, she and her husband, Mate—my grandfather on my mother's side—lived in the parish of Medugorje with their five children. Like most families at that time, they worked the land and struggled to survive in the harsh conditions.

Although I never met him, I grew up hearing stories about Grandpa Mate. My mom and Uncle Šimun loved their father dearly. Amiable and generous, people in the village respected Mate for his wisdom and sought his advice on important matters. Back then, a Herzegovinian man had to struggle to feed his family, but even toughness could not have helped my grandfather in the chaotic days when the communists seized power.

At that time, young men were often taken to so-called "voluntary work actions," which, in truth, were labor camps—and they were anything but voluntary. When the government took Jela and Mate's son, Niko, he looked at his mother and said, "I won't be coming back alive."

Sadly, Niko's fears were validated. One day, government workers brought his body to my grandmother, saying that he'd been killed in an accident. Most mothers would have collapsed in throes of grief, but somehow she suppressed her pain and walked 15 kilometers to where my grandfather was working. She did not want him to find out from someone else.

Not long after losing Niko—the uncle I would never know—the government falsely accused my grandfather of being an enemy of the state. Without warning or justification, the communists came one night and took him.

Such horrors were all too common at that time. The government had spies in every village. Reporting an "enemy" to the government—whether it was true or if the spy just wanted someone gone—ensured a strong future in the Communist Party. Many innocent people were killed and dumped in unmarked graves.

When months passed and Mate did not return, it became painfully clear to Jela that he, too, was dead. She never found out where they buried him.

My mother was only nine years old when her father disappeared. Afraid of provoking the communists after seeing their brutality firsthand, she rarely spoke about him. When she moved to Sarajevo, Communist Party officials made sure she knew they were watching. They warned her that they knew who her father was, and that she would have serious problems if she ever spoke about him, her faith, or any other "inappropriate" subjects at her workplace.

My grandmother was a hero to me. After losing her husband, she endured the countless hardships that went along with being a destitute widow. She raised five children in extreme poverty, a feat she attributed solely to God's grace.

Grandma Jela was in her eighties when I experienced the first apparition. Her faith had been tested by fire and purified by a life of prayer, so I took solace in the fact that she believed me when I told her what I had seen. She knew that I would never lie, especially not about something as sacred as the Blessed Mother.

My grandmother was not alone in her strong beliefs. The great majority of people in the parish of Medugorje lived for God.

Even before the apparitions began, most families recited the rosary together every evening, with the oldest person leading the prayer. We gathered in my uncle's house after dinner. My grandmother took her role seriously—after leading the rosary, she continued praying for priests, the sick, expectant mothers, and everyone else she could think of. For us children, it seemed like the prayers would never end.

But expressions of faith extended far beyond the rosary—most of daily life in Međugorje revolved around religion. People never worked in the fields on holy days, which says much about their beliefs because the fields were their only source of sustenance.

Even the mountain overlooking the village, with its huge cement cross, was a constant reminder of the strong faith. In 1933, parish priest Fr. Bernardin Smoljan, together with the parishioners, decided to build the cross to commemorate the 1900th anniversary of Christ's crucifixion. The name of the mountain was changed to *Križevac*, meaning *Cross Mountain*. A decade later, the communists killed Fr. Smoljan and other local priests.

Close to Međugorje is the town of Široki Brijeg, home to a large monastery and a church dedicated to the Blessed Mother's Assumption into Heaven. The priests and brothers who live there—members of the Franciscan order, which began with St. Francis of Assisi—have been ministering in Herzegovina for hundreds of years. Despite periods of intense persecution, they never abandoned the local people, and it's still common to see Franciscans in their long, brown robes throughout the region. In fact, Franciscans run the parish of Međugorje.

Locals remember the Franciscans who lived at the Široki Brijeg monastery in 1945 with particular admiration.

In the chaotic days after World War II, the communists were eager to seize power and impose their atheistic ideologies on the people of Yugoslavia. To them, religion was more than a mere annoyance; given the strong faith of the people, it was a clear obstacle to their plans.

On February 7, 1945, a group of communist soldiers arrived at Široki Brijeg with vicious plans—they would cut off the faith of the people at what they perceived to be its source. For communism to flourish, they had to silence the priests. As Stalin once said, "Death is the solution to all problems. No man—no problem."

It was said among people here that the soldiers rounded up the monastery's Franciscans, and then the commanding officer began shouting at the friars. "There is no God! There is no pope! There is no Church!"

He glared into their eyes as he moved down the line. "And there is no need for priests! All of you must now go out into the world and work like every other man. Remove your robes at once."

Refusing to comply, the Franciscans stood there stoically. One of the soldiers allegedly ripped a crucifix off the monastery wall and threw it at the Franciscans' feet. "You each get to choose," said the soldier. "Life or death."

One by one, each of the Franciscans knelt down and embraced the crucifix. The soldiers took them out, shot them, and dumped twelve of them in a small cave on the monastery grounds. Their bodies lay in the cave for many years, but today they're entombed in places of honor inside the church.

According to another account, the first soldier ordered to shoot the Franciscans refused. He, too, was shot and killed at the monastery. A second soldier suffered the same fate, so the commanding officer gave the orders to a third soldier.

That man later confided in someone and recounted his experience. Seeing no way out, he went to perform the order. But when he saw the peaceful Franciscans gathered in prayer, he suddenly realized why his two colleagues were unable to finish their work.

At that point, however, the soldier could not think clearly, and the fear of dying like the other two soldiers overwhelmed him. He reasoned that the Franciscans were going to be killed anyway. If he carried out his order, he thought, then at least one person would stay alive.

He killed the priests.

Decades later, his decision still tormented him. "It is such a terrible image permanently imprinted before my eyes," he reportedly said. "At first I tried to forget it, but all my efforts have been in vain. Since then, I cannot sleep. Every night is a hell from which there is no exit."

In total, the communists murdered 34 Franciscan priests at Široki Brijeg, and over 500 priests were killed in the Yugoslav republics of Croatia and Bosnia-Herzegovina around that time.

Their deaths, however, were not in vain. The Široki Brijeg massacre had the opposite effect than the one desired by the communists—it strengthened the faith of the local people and confirmed their suspicions that the new regime posed a real threat to everything they held true.

It was in this volatile environment that I grew up.

"If you die for God, you'll live forever," my mom once told me. "But if you say 'no' to God, you will die forever."

At the time, I was confused and bothered by her statement, but when I got older, I finally understood what she had been trying to say—that I should never let anything take precedence over faith, and that nothing in this life is more important than earning the *next* life with God.

It made me wonder—if I were faced with the unthinkable, would I stand up for my beliefs?

I never imagined that I would have to answer such a question, but when the apparitions began, I became the target of the same government that killed my uncle, my grandfather, and the 34 Franciscans at Široki Brijeg.

The six of us "visionaries" in the early days. From left to right: Ivan, Marija, Ivanka, me, Jakov and Vicka

CHAPTER 5

"I desire to be a mother to you, a teacher of the truth—so that in the simplicity of an open heart, you may become cognizant of the immeasurable purity and of the light which comes from it and shatters darkness, the light which brings hope."

— *From Our Lady's Message of May 2, 2014*

ON THE THIRD day—June 26, 1981—we were stunned to find hundreds of people waiting on the hill when we came for the apparition. News had spread throughout the region.

The afternoon was swelteringly hot, and the air became suffocating as the crowd pushed in on us. But no amount of discomfort could prevent us from being there.

Again we scaled the hill at an impossible speed and fell to our knees upon reaching Our Lady. Witnesses later told us that our apparition lasted for thirty minutes.

She greeted us with the words *"Praised be Jesus,"* which we all recognized as part of the traditional Croatian greeting *Hvaljen Isus i Marija,* or *Praised be Jesus and Mary.* Later I understood why Our Lady only said the first part—as a most humble servant of God, she would never praise herself.

Vicka's grandmother had suggested that she "test" the vision by sprinkling holy water on it. If it was something diabolical, her grandmother reasoned, then holy water would disperse it. But instead of merely sprinkling the water, Vicka emptied the glass.

"If you're Our Lady, stay with us," she said. "If you are not, then be gone!"

Our Lady smiled. One of us asked her why she had chosen to appear in Međugorje and not somewhere else.

"I have come because there are many true believers here," she replied. *"I have come to convert and reconcile the whole world."*

Another asked, "Why are you appearing to us? We are no better than others."

"Because I need you the way you are," she replied.

After the apparition ended and everyone was descending the hill, Marija suddenly went off to the side and knelt, experiencing another apparition. Marija later told us that Our Lady tearfully said, *"Peace, peace, peace, and only peace! Peace must reign between God and men, and between all men."*

As soon as the telephone lines were repaired, my aunt called my mother. A delicate woman who avoided drama, Aunt Slava didn't know how to inform her. How do you tell a mother that her daughter claims to see the Blessed Mother?

"Something has happened to Mirjana," said Aunt Slava.

My mom got worried. "What? Is she okay?"

"Well, uh, how do I say this?"

My mom feared it was something so horrible that my aunt could not even utter it.

Slava continued, "She says she sees the Blessed Mother."

My mom was silent for a moment, but then she asked, "Well, does she seem normal to you?"

"She looks the same to me as before. There's nothing abnormal about her."

My mom recalled how strange I was acting in Sarajevo. "Then she must be experiencing something. She wouldn't lie or joke about such things."

My parents came to Međugorje immediately. They were troubled when they saw me during an apparition for the first time, especially by the extreme emotions on my face and the tears flowing down my cheeks. Knowing me as well as they did—and fully aware that my shyness should have made it impossible for me to be the center of attention in such a large crowd—they never expressed any doubts.

Miro was only seven years old when the apparitions began. He believed right away. For him it was simple—if his big sister claimed to see Our Lady, then it was so.

When my parents had to return to Sarajevo, they asked me to come back with them. They were worried about my safety; every day seemed increasingly chaotic, with bigger crowds and more police. I politely told them that I was not ready to go back. In truth, I wanted to stay forever—I assumed that Our Lady could only appear in Međugorje, and nothing was more important to me than seeing her.

My mother later told me that my father cried in the car when they left without me.

"What will happen to her?" he said repeatedly as they drove.

The next day, June 27, the six of us met at Marija's house to rest and talk before the apparition.

Vicka and I lay in the cool shade underneath a large, covered table and the others sat on a couch.

A policeman suddenly barged in. "Where are the ones who claim to see Our Lady?" he said.

We looked out from beneath the table. He must have thought it strange to find us there.

"Get in the car," he said.

As we left the house, Marija's family pleaded with us. "Don't let them give you any pills or injections!"

The man drove us to the police station in the neighboring town of Čitluk. The local authorities, it seemed, were getting pressure from the Yugoslav government to "put out the fire." But this was a flame that no one could extinguish.

The officers interrogated us and accused us of lying. When we continued to insist that we were telling the truth, they yelled and cursed at us. It was the first time I had ever heard such vulgar language. Naturally, we were frightened, but our persistence began to confuse and soften them. Some of them may have even believed us, but they never could have shown it. In Međugorje and Čitluk, many of the policemen secretly baptized their children and even got married in churches under the cover of night. On the job, however, they had to follow orders.

After the interrogation, they took us to a clinic to be examined. We all sat nervously in the waiting room. The doctor called Ivan in first, followed by Vicka. Through the thin walls, I could hear her refusing to let him examine her.

By the time he summoned Ivanka, it was fifteen minutes to 6 pm. I worried that we'd be late for the apparition, so I went in with her.

The doctor glared at me. "Who called you?" he said.

"We're in a hurry," I said. "We need to go back."

"No. You all need to stay."

He lit a cigarette and offered me one.

"No," I said.

"What's your name?" he asked.

"Mirjana."

"Where are you from, Mirjana?"

"Sarajevo."

"Ah, Sarajevo," he said. "So you're the one. Hold out your hands."

He checked to see if my hands trembled, but they were steady.

"We *really* need to go back," I said.

In that moment, the phone rang. There was a sense of urgency in the doctor's voice after he took the call. He came to us and said, "Now you'll be examined by a psychiatrist in Mostar."

"No," I said.

"No?" he said.

"Maybe you think we're all crazy, but what more do you want from us?" I opened the door. "Goodbye. We have to leave."

And we left. We asked at a nearby inn for someone to drive us to Bijakovići. A local man offered to take us, so we piled into his car. With the time of the apparition fast approaching, we were distraught to find police blocking the road leading into Međugorje. Hundreds of parked cars lined the roadside; people who came for the apparition had parked and walked. The police were ticketing the cars and writing down the registration numbers.

We hopped out of the car and ran to the hill. As soon as we arrived, three flashes lit the hillside.

In addition to being harassed by the authorities, we also had to face the doubts of the person who we thought would support us the most: the parish priest.

40-year-old Fr. Jozo Zovko was new to Međugorje. A Franciscan priest known for his long sermons, he started working as the pastor of St. James Church just a few months before everything started. He was away at a religious retreat in Zagreb when the apparitions began. On June 27, he headed back to Međugorje, stopping briefly at the hospital in Mostar to visit his ill mother. Near the hospital entrance, he encountered a woman he knew from Međugorje who had injured her arm.

"Where have you been?" she cried out when she saw him. "Our Lady appeared in Međugorje and you weren't there!"

"What are you talking about?" he said. "Listen, those who see, let them see. And those who do not see, let them go to church and pray."

Continuing on to Međugorje with another priest, Fr. Jozo told him what the woman had said, adding, "I think she hit her head, not her arm!"

But when he saw the huge numbers of people going to the hill, he could not ignore it. At first, he suspected the worst: lies, hallucinations, or a deception by the communists meant to discredit his work. Seeing all the people streaming past St. James Church on their way to the hill troubled him. If the Blessed Virgin Mary was appearing, then why wouldn't she appear in the church?

I was in Sarajevo when Fr. Jozo started working in Međugorje earlier that year, so I had never met him before. For my entire life, I had always felt an enormous awe and respect towards priests, so I was a little nervous when he summoned me to the parish office on the evening of June 27. Fr. Jozo's dark brown eyes matched the color of his hair, and his face might have looked friendly if he was not trying so hard to be stern. Without even the hint of a smile, he asked me to sit and describe the previous evening's apparition.

"We went to the hill," I said, "and then we saw the sky light up three times. I looked at the hill and said, 'There she is!' This time, she was even farther up than she had been before."

"And what did you do?" said Fr. Jozo.

"We ran up as if it were nothing. When we reached Our Lady, we immediately knelt down in front of her. A lot of people came up the hill. As we were kneeling, some people stepped on our legs and some put children in front of us. I fainted because of all that, and from all the emotions."

"You fainted?"

"Yes, Ivanka and I fainted, probably because of the humid air and all. Everybody wanted us to ask Our Lady something. I asked her, 'How is my grandfather?' I loved him very much. She said, 'Grandfather is fine.'"

Grandpa Ilija, my dad's father, passed away just months earlier. My dad's mother died when I was small and I hardly remember her, but Grandpa Ilija was dear to me. His name—the Croatian form of Elijah—means "the Lord is my God." A tender man, he always gave me a big hug and kiss when I visited him. I remember him sitting and smoking in front of his house, a peaceful smile on his wrinkled face. He rolled his own cigarettes, so I always brought his favorite rolling paper from Sarajevo.

When Grandpa Ilija was dying, my father was with him in Međugorje. It was during the school week and he passed away before I could get there. In his final moments, my grandfather called out for me so that he could kiss me one last time. I regretted not getting the chance to say goodbye to him, so it was beautiful to hear Our Lady say that he was well.

Fr. Jozo then asked me to describe what Our Lady did during the apparitions. No words could truly describe what it was like to be with her, but I tried.

"She often looked around at the people," I said. "We asked her to leave us a sign so that the people would believe us, so they don't laugh at us. But she did not answer. She simply said, 'I will come tomorrow.'"

"Is she beautiful?" asked Fr. Jozo.

"Oh! Incredibly! She has black hair, a little bit pulled back, and blue eyes."

"Have you ever seen a girl like her?"

"Never."

"How tall is she? Is she smaller than you?"

"Like me, but she's slimmer. She's *really* beautiful."

I wanted to describe what made her so beautiful, but I couldn't pinpoint anything specific. When people speak of physical beauty, they often highlight someone's eyes, hair, or other distinguishing feature. But Our Lady's beauty was different. Every feature was beautiful, and everything was harmonized. A white veil framed her oval face. The color of her skin was similar to the sun-glazed complexion of most Mediterranean people, and, paired with her black hair, she resembled a person from the Middle East. Her diminutive nose was perfectly aligned with her almond-shaped eyes, and the slight rosiness on her cheeks was similar to the color of her lips, which were small, full, and tender-looking.

But her "appearance" was also a feeling, one best described by the word *maternal*. Her expression conveyed the qualities of motherhood—care, compassion, patience, tenderness. Her eyes held such love that I felt like she embraced me every time she looked at me.

"And how was she holding her hands?" Fr. Jozo continued.

"She opened her arms in different ways," I said. "They don't remain in one place."

"You weren't afraid at all to look?"

"Not at all. I was really happy. I wouldn't mind if she took one of us with her, so the people can see that it's really her."

Fr. Jozo looked at me questioningly. "*Takes* one of you? Would you like it if she took *you?*"

"I would."

"Seriously, you wouldn't regret it?"

"I wouldn't."

I was serious. The immense feeling of love I felt during the apparitions was like nothing I had ever experienced on Earth, and my only desire whenever I saw Our Lady was to stay with her forever.

"It hurts me," I continued, "that they're saying I brought drugs from Sarajevo."

Concern filled Fr. Jozo's face. "Who says that?"

"The policemen. Two of them called me over and asked me to show them my watch. I showed them and told them how it happened, and then I left. But I overheard them saying 'That one from Sarajevo, maybe she brought some drugs from the city,' and so on. Other people said the same, too."

"What do they mean by drugs?"

"As if we were drug addicts, that we took drugs and that's why we see Our Lady."

"What do you think about that?"

"I would like to tell them straight in the eyes: let a doctor examine me to see if I'm on drugs."

In the coming years, I would be examined by more doctors than most people ever see during their entire lives, but instead of finding what they all suspected—drugs, epilepsy, mental illness, or deception—it was my normality that left them all baffled.

Pilgrims head towards St. James Church, with
Cross Mountain in the background.

CHAPTER 6

"An impure heart cannot do correct and just things; it is not an example of the beauty of God's love to those who surround it and to those who have not come to know that love."

— *From Our Lady's Message of July 2nd, 2011*

"**M**Y CHILDREN, THERE has always been injustice in this world."

That was Our Lady's answer during the apparition of June 28, 1981 when I told her that people were accusing us of using drugs or having some medical condition that caused our visions.

During the same apparition, we asked for her name. *"I am the Blessed Virgin Mary,"* she replied.

We asked her if she had a message for the priests. She said, *"Let them believe strongly."*

One of us asked, "Will you appear to the crowd so they can see you?"

"Blessed are those who believe without seeing," she said, and then she looked at the people. *"Let them believe as if they see me."*

Then, as we always did, we asked her to leave some kind of sign so that everyone would believe. And, just like before, she simply said that she would come back the next day.

Earlier that day, the six of us had gone to Sunday Mass at St. James Church. It was overflowing with people, many of whom had come from distant parts of Herzegovina. It was clear that many of them had come out of curiosity, not devotion, as they mostly talked about signs and miracles. Few of them prayed or made the sign of the cross during Mass.

Even more distressing, Fr. Jozo's sermon seemed to be aimed at the six of us. "It's true that God can reveal Himself and has done so before," he said. "And, indeed, Our Lady has appeared on Earth before. But why do we need such wonders when we have the Eucharist, the Bible, and the Church? Jesus is *here!*

"My friends, we are only human beings, and human beings can be manipulated so easily. We live in challenging times and we have to always be prudent. More than anything, we must constantly pray to the Lord."

After hearing his homily, I dreaded having to meet with Fr. Jozo that evening.

A day or two earlier, a local man gave me a book about the apparitions in Lourdes, France and suggested that I read it to see if there were similarities to what we were experiencing. I was fascinated to learn that someone else had once seen Our Lady. In 1858, a peasant girl named Bernadette was out gathering firewood along a riverbank. She suddenly heard a gust of wind and looked up to see a beautiful woman in a grotto. The woman remained silent, but in the coming days, Bernadette continued to see her in the same place and they began to communicate.

"I do not promise to make you happy in this world," the woman told Bernadette, *"but in the next."*

Villagers gathered around Bernadette when she experienced the apparitions, but Fr. Peyramale never went to the grotto to see for himself, choosing instead to interview Bernadette in the rectory. He doubted her story.

"I am not asked to make you believe," Bernadette said. "I am just asked to tell you."

One day, Bernadette asked the woman her name and she replied, *"I am the Immaculate Conception."*

When Bernadette relayed that to Fr. Peyramale, he realized that she was telling the truth. Such a simple, impoverished child never could have known about the relatively new dogma of the Immaculate Conception.

Our Lady left a sign that can still be seen in Lourdes: a miraculous spring appeared out of the ground in the grotto. Today, ailing people from all over the world go there to bathe in the water and pray for healing.

When I read that Our Lady had appeared to Bernadette 18 times, I assumed it would be similar in Međugorje. Something kept telling me that she'd appear for just a few more days, and I related this to the other visionaries. At some point, we began believing it was true. With the communists terrorizing us and the apparitions rousing our emotions, we'd barely ate or slept and it was easy to get confused. But deep down, I desperately wanted the apparitions to continue. How would I go back to living a normal life after experiencing Heaven?

Those days were marked by contrasts—joy and fear, solitude and suffering, the love of Heaven and the animosity of the police. I had been an ordinary teenaged girl, living in peace with my family, when everything suddenly changed. I grew up overnight.

It took Marko a few days to visit me in Međugorje. When he arrived on his little scooter, he was too uncomfortable to enter my uncle's house, so he stood outside and paced back and forth. When I opened the door and invited him in, he looked at me with surprise and relief.

"Oh, thank God," he said.

"What?" I said.

"You're normal!"

"More than you, it seems. What did you expect?"

"Well, I didn't know what you'd be like now. I was afraid to come. I envisioned you looking somber and your hair standing up like you'd stuck your finger in an electrical outlet or something. But you're the same."

I laughed. "Well, thanks, I guess."

Perhaps I would have changed more had I been younger, although certainly not as drastically as Marko imagined. As I got to know the other visionaries and observed our different personalities, I began to think that Our Lady wanted us just the way we were, with all of our quirks and flaws included.

Later, when I learned more about Lourdes, Fátima, and other apparitions of the past, I saw how Our Lady usually visited young people and I wondered why. Was it because we were not yet burdened by plans and obligations? Were the hearts of children purer than those of adults?

If I had been older, perhaps I would have comprehended everything faster, but her messages don't require lengthy commentary or theological interpretation. She speaks to all of us, and she does so with simple words.

On the evening of June 28th, Fr. Jozo had more questions for me. He seemed concerned that I did not know enough about the Catholic faith.

"Tell me, Mirjana," he said. "Will you read the Bible more now?"

"I'd like to read the Bible more," I said.

"I know you'd like to, but *will* you?"

I hesitated. "Well—"

"Do you even have a Bible?"

I looked down. "No. My godmother in Sarajevo has it. Sometimes I visit her and I read it there."

I could see the frustration on Fr. Jozo's face. Here in front of him was a girl who claimed to be visited by the Mother of God, and she did not even own a Bible. The closest thing we had at home was an illustrated children's book of Bible stories.

"Do you feel the need to learn something now?" he said. "For instance, to pray to Our Lady?"

"I'd love to do that," I said, and I meant it. I had even recently asked people to write down some prayers for me because I wanted to learn them. The experience of seeing Our Lady had inspired me to embrace the faith with all my heart.

"You know," said Fr. Jozo, "the people say they haven't seen what you see."

"I can't help them," I said. I thought about Fr. Peyramale and Bernadette, and I wanted to ask Fr. Jozo why he still had not come to the hill to observe for himself. But I had far too much respect for him as a priest to question him.

"Some have started doubting. Some of the old people are saying that your apparition serves no purpose. People are disappointed."

I thought for a moment, unsure of how to answer. "Not everyone can see."

"And why can't they see? Do you have any opinion about that? Any doubt?"

"If everyone saw her then everyone would say that God exists. Everyone would believe. I can't explain it. God doesn't appear to everyone. You should believe even if you don't see Him."

But even though they did not *see*, many *believed*, and the sleepy farming village of Međugorje was rapidly transforming into a place of pilgrimage.

Since the early days of Christianity, believers have embarked on journeys of faith to the Holy Land, Rome, and Marian shrines like the *Basilica of Our Lady of the Pillar* in Zaragoza, Spain, where tradition contends that St. James the Apostle experienced the first apparition of Mary. Also in Spain, people trek a medieval pilgrimage route known as the *Camino de Santiago*, or the Way of St. James, to strengthen their faith and pay homage to the patron saint of pilgrims. In fact, our word for pilgrimage, *hodočašće*, stems from the word *hodati*, which means *to walk*.

Most pilgrims trying to reach Međugorje came by car or bus, but the police blockade on the main road to town turned most of them into *hodočasnici* anyway. As the flow of visitors swelled, the residents of the parish increasingly embraced Our Lady's messages. It brought me great joy to see the effects of the apparitions in the people closest to me. My aunt, uncle and cousins prayed more fervently. My grandmother added even more decades of the rosary to her daily routine. And, like a true pilgrim, Marko regularly walked the 30 kilometers from Mostar to Međugorje in honor of Our Lady.

Podbrdo, later known as Apparition Hill, towers over the hamlet of Bijakovići in Međugorje.

CHAPTER 7

"For those who will live the word of my Son and who will love, death will be life."

— *From Our Lady's Message of August 2nd, 2015*

O N JUNE 29, the feast day of St. Peter and St. Paul, we were again summoned to the Čitluk police station for an interrogation.

One of the officers glared at me angrily. "Where's that little shit?" he said, referring to Jakov.

Knowing how horrible the police could be, we were happy that Jakov did not come with us this time. It seemed unthinkable to subject a child his age to so much hostility. The police were like artists when it came to cursing, as if they were competing to see who could be the most offensive.

"Jakov is only ten years old," I said. "Leave him alone. He's too little."

"You lying bitch," growled the policeman. "He's not little when he can climb that hill in two minutes."

I closed my eyes and asked God to give the policeman peace, but the interrogation went on like that for hours. Finally, unable to make us deny our claims, the police crammed us in a small ambulance car and took us to a clinic for an examination by Dr. Darinka Glamuzina, a local pediatrician.

A confident and intelligent woman with short, dark hair, Dr. Glamuzina indicated to us that she was an atheist. Certain there had to be a logical explanation for our story, she began spouting questions as fast as we could answer them: *What did you see? Where did it happen? How did you feel? Have you ever been hypnotized?*

Her last question seemed particularly outlandish, but we answered everything with patience and honesty. At the end of the meeting, Dr. Glamuzina said, "My colleague and I will come to Bijakovići later to observe you."

Observe us? I thought. *Does she think we're wild animals?*

Six days had passed since the first apparition and thousands of people were coming to Međugorje every afternoon from as far away as Sarajevo and Zagreb. Increasingly paranoid about losing their control after President Tito's death one year earlier, the communist authorities utilized their favorite weapons—fear and intimidation.

The police put us in the ambulance again. Packed together with nowhere to sit, every bump in the road was excruciating. After an hour, we finally arrived at Mostar Hospital.

"Get used to this place," said the driver. "It might be your new home when the doctors declare you insane."

The police first took us to a dark, windowless room and locked the door behind us. The air inside was damp and cold and foul. I saw what I thought was someone sleeping on a table, but as my vision adjusted, I realized the person was dead. Scanning the room, I saw more bodies.

"The morgue," I whispered.

We were horrified. How could they do this to children?

After they finally released us from the morgue, we were taken to be examined by a doctor. His questions were similar to Dr. Glamuzina's, but his demeanor was noticeably colder.

"You know," he said, "we have a special place for the insane."

Tricking us into thinking it was a waiting room, he locked us in a ward filled with mentally-ill patients. The people moved around aimlessly, shouting and making strange noises.

One patient approached us. "I'm a soldier," he said, and he started marching around the room.

We huddled together, terrified. Were they planning to lock us away in there forever? Thankfully, a nurse pulled us out.

"You don't belong in here," she said.

She led us through a dim corridor and into a room where other nurses had gathered.

"Tell us about seeing Our Lady," said the nurse. "Everyone is talking about it."

We told them what we had seen, and we answered countless questions. By the end of our testimony, some of the nurses were even crying. Their interest and reactions surprised me.

Next, the head of the neuropsychiatric department of Mostar Hospital, Dr. Mulija Džudža, examined us. We were told later that she found us to be healthy, balanced children, adding, "Whoever brought them here are the ones who should be declared insane!"

What struck me the most—and confirmed to me that I should never be afraid to speak about Our Lady to *anyone*—was that Dr. Džudža was a Muslim.

Even though the police released us that day, the experience of visiting the morgue and psychiatric ward left me traumatized. Disturbing images kept popping into my mind: a corpse on a stainless-steel table, the disturbed "soldier" marching around, the patients babbling and wandering. But I knew that if a time ever came when I had to choose between being locked away in an asylum or denying that I had seen Our Lady, I would choose the asylum without question. Nothing could make me forsake her—not incarceration, not even death.

That evening, we gathered for the apparition, still distressed about the day's experiences. When Our Lady appeared, all of us started crying. Her vast love seemed to bring out our emotions. But my fears and worries all disappeared as Our Lady showed me a series of vivid scenes from her earthly life. It was like watching a movie. The conditions in which Mary lived were nothing like the romanticized versions of her life that I had seen in religious art. From the time she was a little girl, I saw that she lived a humble and modest life—difficult but beautiful in its simplicity. I saw glimpses of her most important moments, like the angel approaching her and the birth of Jesus. I realized that Mary was once a girl who endured many of the same pains and joys that everyone does, but with one profound exception: she became the mother of God.

One of the other visionaries expressed her anguish about the day's events to the Virgin. "Will we be able to endure all of this?"

"You will, my angels," she said in the most motherly way. *"Do not fear."*

The heavenly blueness behind Our Lady dimmed as an unfamiliar form appeared above her right shoulder—the figure of a bloodied and bruised man with brown eyes, long hair and a beard. I could only see the man's shoulders and head, and his face was locked in an expression of intense suffering. Unlike Our Lady—who always appeared to us like a human being—the man looked more like the bust of a statue. I realized who it was when I saw the thorny crown on his head.

"Look at the one who gave everything for faith," said Our Lady, *"so that what you are going through might not seem like too much."*

The figure melded back into the blueness behind Our Lady. I was thankful to have seen a glimpse of Jesus but also a little ashamed that I ever thought of my suffering as too much. The experience made me careful to never give myself too much importance or think of myself as some kind of victim.

Dr. Glamuzina, the skeptical pediatrician who examined us that morning, came to observe the apparition—or, more precisely, to observe *us* during it. Witnesses said that her look of skepticism changed to fascination when she saw our faces. She asked Vicka to present a few questions to Our Lady and Vicka agreed to do so.

"Ask her who she is," Dr. Glamuzina said.

Vicka presented the question and Our Lady replied, *"I am the Queen of Peace."*

"How can we have peace when there are so many different religions?" asked the doctor.

Vicka relayed the question and Our Lady answered, *"There is but one faith and one God."*

Dr. Glamuzina asked why Our Lady chose to appear in Bijakovići of all places.

"I came here because people pray and have strong faith," she answered.

The doctor then asked if she could try to touch what we were looking at, and we presented the question.

"She may," said Our Lady.

We directed Dr. Glamuzina to Our Lady. The doctor reached out, but Our Lady suddenly ascended and disappeared. Dr. Glamuzina immediately turned to us with a look of distress on her face and said, "She's gone, hasn't she?"

"Yes," said Vicka. "She's gone."

"Did she say anything?"

"She said, *'There have always been doubting Judases,'* and then she left."

Dr. Glamuzina's face filled with sadness. She descended the hill with an astonished look on her face. She declared that she believed us, and, soon after, she returned to her Catholic roots and even started singing in the church choir.

"When I tried to touch Our Lady," she said, recounting her experience, "I had this incredible feeling. It was as if I knew that she was leaving and in what direction. I later confirmed it with the visionaries. At first, when they told me what Our Lady said about doubting Judases, I was offended. But then a clear and peaceful realization came over me: these children really see Our Lady! I was indeed like Judas: I wanted to unmask them. I did not believe them. But after my experience, I was ashamed and I felt a deep humility before the grandeur of Our Lady who read me and—like a good mother—gave me a warning."

That apparition was also memorable because a man brought his severely disabled three-year-old son to the hill. The boy's name was Danijel Šetka, and he had been paralyzed and unable to talk from the time he was a baby. His parents came hoping for a healing.

"Blessed Mother," we said, "will this child ever speak? Heal him so that everyone will believe us."

Our Lady turned towards Danijel and looked at him for a long time with an expression of compassion and love. Finally, she said, *"Let them believe strongly that he will get well."*

We were perhaps a little disappointed that there was no immediate change visible in Danijel's condition, but later his parents returned to the hill to give thanks to God. That night, Danijel had started walking and talking.

The next morning, Fr. Jozo interviewed me again. He seemed frustrated that although there had been seven days of apparitions, Our Lady had not been especially vocal. In apparitions of the past, he reasoned, she had given intense messages and prophecies for the world. How could this be Our Lady if she had so little to say?

"People have started to despise and reject you," he told me, "because you don't give them anything, no sign. And they keep coming, more and more, and what now?"

I kept silent because I did not have an answer for him. We had continued asking Our Lady for a sign every time we saw her but she still had not responded to our request.

Fr. Jozo continued, "How will you justify yourselves before the people? God severely punishes those who deceive, you know. Are you familiar with that?"

I nodded my head, but inside I was sad that he suspected us of doing something that required God's punishment. He went on to say that the bad behavior of some of the people in the crowds—like swearing and pushing—was perhaps a sign that it was not truly Our Lady appearing.

"Those who tricked the people or delivered false messages were chastised harshly," he continued. "Among the Israelites, or in the early Church, they were excluded from the community. God rebuked them severely. Are you afraid of anything like that?"

"I'm not," I said.

"What if God punishes the six of you tomorrow?"

"I don't think He will."

"Why do you think He won't?"

I looked him in the eyes. "Because we are not lying."

Fr. Jozo was silent for a moment. His gaze softened.

"Why does Our Lady appear to some people and not to others?" he said, this time with a much gentler tone. "Do you think you should be different from those who don't see her?"

"Yes," I said. "I should be even better, believe even more, and be an example."

He looked into my eyes. "And you truly believe, don't you?"

"I do. I believe."

Fr. Jozo nodded. "What does your faith make you do?"

"I simply want to do good deeds."

"And what would these good deeds consist of?"

"I'd like to help everyone I can and ask them to pray a little bit more."

"Do you feel sorry for the people when they don't see Our Lady and you do?"

"I do. I want everybody to see her. I watch the people, how they take the trouble to climb up the hill. Some even walk barefoot for six hours to be there. Wouldn't it be nice if she appeared to them, too?"

Our conversation turned to the place of the apparitions. Fr. Jozo was still troubled that so many people were going to what pilgrims were now calling "Apparition Hill" instead of praying in St. James Church. The increasing police presence also concerned him. The government prohibited large gatherings and the crowds grew every day. Fr. Jozo wanted us to come to the church at the time of the apparitions, and to invite the faithful there. It sounded safer and more comfortable than dealing with the crowds, police, and oppressive heat on the hill every afternoon, but would Our Lady appear to us in a different place?

The four girls of the group. From left: Marija, Ivanka, me and Vicka.

CHAPTER 8

"My poor children, look around you and look at the signs of the times... From the depth of your heart cry out for my Son. His Name disperses even the greatest darkness."

— *From Our Lady's Message of May 2nd, 2009*

SHORTLY AFTER MY meeting with Fr. Jozo, some of the other visionaries and I were approached by two women, Mica and Ljubica, who identified themselves as social workers. I had never seen Ljubica before, but I recognized Mica. She lived in Bijakovići at the base of the hill and had been present during at least one of the apparitions.

"The secret police are planning to come for you today," Mica said with urgency.

"They have orders from Belgrade," Ljubica added.

We told the women that we would lock ourselves in our rooms and not come out, but they shook their heads.

"Do you really think you can hide from the secret police in your rooms?" said Ljubica.

"What do you think of us going off somewhere together?" said Mica.

"We can go to Čapljina and get some ice cream," Ljubica added, which caused Jakov's eyes to widen.

Vicka knew and trusted Mica so I felt comfortable about her, but I was a little skeptical of Ljubica. Still, the thought of the Internal Secret Police coming for me sent chills through my body. They were like the gestapo of the Yugoslav government, notorious for violent interrogations, beatings and even executions. The crowds were growing exponentially so it was not far-fetched to think that they would soon intervene. After quickly discussing it amongst ourselves, the five of us piled into the back seat of Mica's car. Ivan was not with us that day.

As we were leaving Bijakovići, however, the local police commander, Zdravko, waved us down. We rolled to a stop and he came to our window. Peering into the back seat, he seemed both surprised and concerned to see us. "Mica," he said. "What's going on here?"

"We're in a hurry," said Mica.

Zdravko spoke in a hushed but stern tone. "I need to ask you something, Mica."

Mica looked out at all the people streaming into the village. Some of them had stopped to gawk at us in the car. "Crowds will form around the children if we stay here."

"Mica, wait just a minute."

"We can't wait."

More onlookers had stopped near the car. Zdravko looked at them, and then back at us. "Alright," he said, and he got into his car and followed us.

We soon came to a *milicija* car parked sideways to prevent anyone from driving into the village, or, in our case, out of it. Several policemen stood near the car. They stared at us, seemingly confused about what they should do.

"Move!" Mica yelled out the window. "We're in a hurry."

Her assertiveness surprised us, but the policemen stayed put—that is, until they saw Zdravko pull up behind us in his car. Thinking he was with us, they quickly moved their car out of the way. We waved at the confused policemen as we drove past the checkpoint, and Mica sped away fast enough to lose Zdravko. Soon we were zooming down the road, windows open, savoring the wind in our hair and laughing.

Our first stop was Počitelj, an ancient walled city with a historic mosque and the crumbling remnants of a medieval fortress. As we climbed the stone walls and explored the ruins, our worries disappeared. I gazed at the emerald-colored Neretva River that flowed through the valley below Počitelj. The moving water made me think of all the pilgrims streaming into Međugorje. Like the mighty Neretva, it seemed like nothing could stop them.

After Počitelj, we drove to Čapljina, one of the larger and more modern towns in the local area. Mica and Ljubica took us to a café. I had been to cafés before in Sarajevo, but it was a novelty for the others.

"Do they have juice in bottles?" asked Jakov.

Mica smiled. "Of course they do."

We all laughed. The women ordered us cake and ice cream, and juice in bottles, of course. We sat there eating and talking until a young man approached us.

"Are you from Međugorje?" he asked.

"Where's Međugorje?" said Mica.

The young man looked at Jakov. "But I recognize some of you. Aren't you the ones who see Our Lady? I was there on the hill last night."

"We don't know you," said Ljubica.

The young man looked at me, and then at my wrist. "Where's your watch? Don't you remember how I asked to see it?"

"Perhaps you did," I said. Many people had asked to see it, but the police had taken it from me after word spread about how it changed. They never gave it back, but later I heard that the police took it to a watchmaker who examined it and said it was impossible for the watch to have changed like that and still be working.

Other people in the café overheard the young man and soon everyone was watching us. An older woman came up and said, "Aren't you going to be up there on the hill today?"

The attention became too much and we had to leave. I realized then that my privacy was a thing of the past. Even people who lived outside of Međugorje were treating me differently and looking at me as if I were some kind of holy person, when, in truth, I was the same girl I had always been.

After leaving the café, we spotted a swing-set at a kindergarten. We asked the women if we could use the swings, and Ljubica reluctantly agreed. We took turns swinging. Ivanka went the highest, her smile a pleasing contrast to her black mourning clothes.

Our next destination was *Kravice*, a magnificent waterfall on the Trebižat River. On the way there, we expressed our worry that we would not make it back to Međugorje in time for the apparition, which had been taking place at around 6:40 pm every day. Mica and Ljubica assured us that we needn't worry. When we reached *Kravice*, we were so captivated by the torrent of water, lush foliage, and cool mist in the air that we stopped paying attention to the time altogether. I did not have my watch anyway.

It was not until the sun descended below the trees and shade filled the river valley that we suddenly realized how late it had gotten. We implored Mica and Ljubica to take us back to Međugorje. They finally agreed, although it seemed like they drove the car slower than they had all day. It was starting to appear like Mica and Ljubica had not exactly come to save us.

As the car got closer to Međugorje, we could see Apparition Hill in the distance, as well as the immense crowd of people waiting there. I felt a tinge of guilt. We should have been there among them, but reaching the hill in time seemed impossible. Just as I was about to cry, the intense anticipation I always felt before the apparition suddenly washed over me.

"Pull over," I said.

"Where?" said Mica.

"Anywhere!"

Mica pulled the car off the road, onto a rocky trail. We all hopped out and knelt in a barren wasteland of karst and briars. The tranquility of the surrounding wilderness was a nice change from the chaotic crowds to which we had become accustomed.

Mica and Ljubica stood by the car and watched as we began to pray.

"Ask the Virgin what she's going to do to me for stealing you this way," joked Ljubica.

Mica laughed, but then she suddenly pointed at Apparition Hill. "Do you see that?" she said.

"My God," said Ljubica, fear in her voice. "What is that?"

"Some kind of mist." Mica said, making the sign of the cross.

"Or like a light," said Ljubica.

I looked toward the hill and saw a glowing shape in the air above all the people.

"That's her," said Vicka.

Sadness gripped me. Our Lady and thousands of faithful pilgrims were waiting for us on the hill and we were stuck on the side of a road. How could we have let this happen?

But then the light began gliding towards us. As it approached, we could see Our Lady within it.

"She's coming!" shouted Ivanka.

Upon reaching us, Our Lady said *"Praised be Jesus,"* which had become her standard greeting. Thinking back on my conversation with Fr. Jozo, I realized that my question was now being answered—it *was* possible for Our Lady to appear somewhere other than the hillside. As always, her radiance and beauty rendered me momentarily speechless, but I wanted to make sure she was not disappointed.

"Are you upset that we were not on the hill?" I asked.

"It does not matter," she replied.

"Would you be upset if we did not return to the hill," I asked, "but instead waited for you in the church?"

She smiled in a gentle, motherly way. *"Always at the same time."*

We asked her if she would leave a sign, but as always she did not answer. She moved slowly away until her light was once again shining on all the people who had gathered on the hill.

"Go in the peace of God," we heard her say, and the light faded away.

Upon arriving back in Međugorje, Fr. Jozo asked all of us—including Mica and Ljubica—to come to the rectory and tell him everything. He was initially concerned that the people on the hill would feel deceived since we were not among them, but when we told him that Our Lady said she would appear in the church, he became joyful. He was also eager to know what Mica and Ljubica had experienced.

"What did you see?" he said to Ljubica.

"I saw something moving," she said.

"It was some kind of mistiness," Mica added.

"Or some kind of shade, or like a breeze," said Ljubica.

The women obviously had not seen everything that we saw, but they had seen something, and now they struggled to put it into words. I could relate.

"Were you scared, Mica?" said Fr. Jozo.

"Not really," said Mica. "I was shaking a bit, but more from excitement than fear."

"I was afraid," admitted Ljubica. "I got goosebumps, and then I took Mica by the hands."

Mica nodded. "I started shaking more and more. I wasn't scared, but just the thought of the Blessed Virgin Mary being in front of me—it can't leave a person unmoved."

We later found out that Ljubica and Mica had been following government orders to remove us from Međugorje that day. Some locals were angry, but I knew that the women were just doing their jobs, as everyone in the communist system had to do.

Although Ljubica was not a Catholic, the experience must have affected her—she returned to Sarajevo and informed her superiors that she no longer wanted to participate.

The six of us experience an apparition. From left:
Vicka, Jakov, me, Ivanka, Marija and Ivan.

CHAPTER 9

"You will be universally hated on account of my name; but anyone who stands firm to the end will be saved."

— *Jesus in The Gospel of Matthew, 10:22*

NEWS ABOUT THE apparitions spread all over Yugoslavia through television, radio and newspaper. The one commonality in all the reporting was skepticism, if not outright condemnation. Journalists ridiculed us and referred to the thousands of pilgrims coming to Međugorje as "religious fanatics," or worse.

State-run news outlets accused us and the local priests of being Croat nationalists who had fabricated the apparitions to foment a counter-revolution. The national television news labeled us "bitter enemies of the state," and newspaper headlines referring to Međugorje seemed like they had come from a tabloid:

RELIGIOUS HOAX DRAWS THOUSANDS OF ZEALOTS

FRIARS SUSPECTED OF NATIONALIST PLOT

SIX YOKELS INVENT VISIONS OF MARY

The authorities held a community meeting at the elementary school and summoned our parents and relatives to attend. They said that if the "nonsense" did not stop, then we would be expelled from school and locked away in a mental institution, and our parents would lose their jobs and passports. The police arrested Vicka's neighbor, Ivan, when he stood up at the meeting and defended us. He spent two months in prison.

Fr. Jozo was in anguish over the escalating tensions. The communists threatened him with imprisonment if he could not stop the "demonstrations" in his parish, and he still had not decided if he believed that we were seeing Our Lady. The fact that his two assistant priests believed us added to his stress. But a declaration by his superior, Bishop Pavao Žanić of Mostar, probably distressed him the most.

Upon hearing about our claims, the bishop called the six of us to a meeting. He asked us questions for over an hour and recorded our answers on tape. He then told us to put our hands on a cross and swear that we were telling the truth, which we all did without hesitation. After our meeting, he told Fr. Jozo that he was certain Our Lady was appearing to us. Fr. Jozo urged the bishop to be prudent, but eventually a newspaper article quoted Bishop Žanić as saying, "It is definite that the children were not incited by anyone, and especially not by the church, to lie."

Fr. Jozo became so troubled by everything one day that he simply wanted to be alone. He locked the doors of St. James Church, sat in a pew, and prayed for God to guide him through what had become the most difficult situation he'd ever encountered in his priesthood. He opened his bible and came across the passage where God performed miracles through Moses, such as parting the Red Sea.

On the same day, I met some of the other visionaries near Apparition Hill to pray. The government had recently positioned policemen on the hill to keep people out of the area. When the policemen saw us, they rushed towards us with their batons held high. We fled through the fields.

In the church, Fr. Jozo prayed, "My Lord, you know how much I love you. You talked to Moses, but it was easy for him. His people knew that it was you leading them, but here nobody knows."

At that moment, Fr. Jozo heard a voice within his heart. *Go out and protect the children.*

Astonished, he jumped to his feet and hurried to the church doors. Opening them, he found several of us waiting outside.

"The police!" said Vicka, pausing to catch her breath. "They're chasing us!"

Fr. Jozo opened his arms. "My dear angels," he said lovingly. "Come inside."

His demeanor had changed so drastically that I wondered if he was being sarcastic, but as he ushered us inside, I realized that his tenderness was genuine.

That evening, Our Lady visited us in a small room near the church's altar, just opposite the sacristy. In the days ahead, she continued to visit us there, and Fr. Jozo never doubted us again.

His support brought us momentary solace, but nothing could curb our fear and anxiety as what we thought might be Our Lady's final apparition approached. How would we go on without her?

When that day came, we were full of emotion. The crowd, esti-mated at tens of thousands of people, was the biggest we had ever seen, and it seemed that many expected some sort of miracle to accompany the apparition.

When Our Lady appeared, however, there was nothing out of the ordinary, and no special message for the world. We asked again if she would leave a sign, but she only smiled. After she departed, we addressed the crowd.

Many of them seemed disappointed that there had not been some magnificent conclusion to the events. Personally, more than anything, I was confused. I did not feel in my heart that the apparitions were over.

The next day, we all tried to go back to our normal routines. I was at my uncle's house when I felt something within—a familiar flutter of expectation that rapidly became a cacophony of excitement. I felt like I would explode if Our Lady did not come at that moment. As sudden as a breath of wind, she appeared in front of me. I fell to my knees, enrapt, wanting nothing but to look at her. I cried profusely after she departed.

The other visionaries saw her, too, and that's when we realized Međugorje was not exactly like Lourdes. Our Lady continued to appear to us every day.

Around the same time, the persecution rose to a dangerous new level when the Yugoslav government declared a state of emergency in Međugorje. The effects of the apparitions had reverberated all the way to Belgrade, the capitol of Yugoslavia, and the communists—incensed by our unwillingness to bow to their pressures and afraid that they were losing control—became intent on quashing the problem as quickly as possible.

Within days, the military pushed into the village. Soldiers with automatic rifles and snarling German Shephard dogs took positions on the hill and in front of our homes. Military vehicles patrolled the streets. Helicopters buzzed over pilgrims as they tried to pray. It felt like we had disturbed a gigantic nest of hornets.

The interrogations, now done by federal police instead of local ones, became lengthier and more intense. I was taken in one day and a foul-mouthed policeman became increasingly frustrated when I refused to deny the apparitions.

"Confess," he said.

"I only confess to my priest," I replied.

His face turned a reddish-purple color and the veins in his neck bulged. "Admit that you do not see Our Lady!"

"But I do."

At this, he pulled his handgun out of its holster and laid it on the table between us.

"Come clean," he said, glancing at the gun. "You didn't see *anything.*"

Help me, Gospa, I prayed silently.

Despite the deadly weapon on the table, I felt a strange sense of calm. After seeing Our Lady and experiencing Heaven, it was nearly impossible to be afraid of anything.

"Time's up," said the policeman. "Now give me the truth."

I looked him in the eyes. "The truth is that I see Our Lady, and I'm willing to die for her."

He slammed his fist on the table, holstered his gun, and stormed out of the room.

If we had been adults, the communists would have surely locked us away in the deepest, darkest prison cell they could find, or we simply would have vanished in the same way that my grandfather did. But as brutal as the government authorities could be, they knew they would face public outrage if they imprisoned children. In a way, our youth protected us, but nothing prevented them from trying to terrify us.

Aside from all the frightening experiences, there was excitement as well. Every morning brought the promise of a new surprise or adventure.

Sometimes we experienced multiple apparitions on the same evening. The police chased us and tried to disrupt our plans, so to evade them, we constantly changed the meeting place. In the woods behind one of our houses, in the middle of an unkempt field, beneath a grove of shade trees—it somehow felt appropriate to experience the apparition in the seclusion of nature, where the fresh air and starlight afforded a serenity befitting Our Lady. Years later, in one of her messages, she said, *"Today I invite you to observe nature because there you will meet God,"* and in another, *"I call you to give glory to God the Creator in the colors of nature. Through even the smallest flower, He speaks to you about His beauty and the depth of His love."*

During one of these extraordinary visitations, Our Lady interacted with the villagers in a surprisingly intimate way. On August 2, 1981, she appeared at the regular time and asked us to await her again that evening. My memories of this and other early apparitions are foggy, but Marija reported that Our Lady said, *"All of you together go to the meadow at Gumno. A great struggle is about to unfold—a struggle between my Son and Satan. Human souls are at stake."*

Later that evening, we went to the area known as Gumno, near my uncle's house. In our language, the word *gumno* means *threshing floor*—a large, circular area of hard ground where farmers separated grain by having cows or horses walk in circles over it. In the Bible, John the Baptist used the same word when he figuratively described Jesus' mission as a harvest of souls: "His winnowing fork is in his hand, and he will clear his threshing floor and gather his wheat into the barn, but the chaff he will burn with unquenchable fire."

About forty local people joined us at Gumno. Crickets chirped loudly and mosquitos flitted around our faces as we knelt in the red clay. We prayed and waited, and suddenly Our Lady appeared in front of us.

Some of the people had asked us if they could touch Our Lady, and when we presented their request, she said that whoever wanted to could approach her.

One by one, we took their hands and guided them to touch Our Lady's dress. The experience was strange for us visionaries—it was difficult to comprehend that only we could see Our Lady. From our perspective, guiding people to touch her was like leading the blind. Their reactions were lovely, especially the children. It seemed that most felt something. A few reported a sensation like "electricity" and others were overcome with emotion. But as more people touched Our Lady, I noticed black spots forming on her dress, and the spots congealed into a large, coal-colored stain. I cried at the sight of it.

"Her dress!" yelled Marija, also crying.

The stains, said Our Lady, represented sins that had never been confessed. She suddenly vanished. After praying for a while, we stood in the darkness and told the people what we saw. They were nearly as upset as we were. Someone suggested that everyone there should go to confession, and the next day repentant villagers inundated the priests.

My cousin, Vlado, just a little boy, was among those who touched

Our Lady's dress. When I told him about the stains, he exclaimed, "But I washed my hands, Mirjana! They were clean! I promise!"

Anytime I saw him after that, I smiled and said, "Have you washed your hands lately, Vlado?"

During these daily encounters, Our Lady emphasized things like prayer, fasting, confession, reading the Bible and going to Mass. Later, people identified these as Our Lady's "main messages"—or, as Fr. Jozo called them, her "five stones," an allusion to the story of David and Goliath. She was not asking us to pray or fast just for the sake of it. The fruit of living our faith, she said, was love. As she said in one of her messages, *"I come to you as a mother, who, above all, loves her children. My children, I want to teach you to love."*

Our Lady's ethereal beauty captivated us from the very beginning. One day during an apparition, we asked a childish question. "How is it possible that you are so beautiful?"

Our Lady gently smiled. *"I am beautiful because I love,"* she said. *"If you want to be beautiful, then love."*

After the apparition, Jakov, who was only ten years old, looked at us and said, "I don't think she was telling the truth."

I reproached him. "How can you say that the Blessed Mother didn't tell the truth?"

"Well, look at some of us," he replied. "Some of us can love our entire lives and we'd still never be beautiful like she said!"

We all laughed. Jakov did not understand the type of beauty that she was talking about. Hers is eternal and comes from within, and she wants that kind of beauty for each of us. If you are clean inside, and if you are full of love, then you will be beautiful on the outside as well.

Despite such lighthearted moments, the overall gravity of the apparitions was becoming clear to us.

Through our daily encounters with the Blessed Virgin, we realized that her plans with Međugorje were not merely for the village itself, nor were they limited to Yugoslavia. She had come to change the entire world.

She revealed to us that God's plan would ultimately be realized through a series of future events. She began to relate these events to us with instructions to keep them secret until just before they were to take place.

Since the early days of the apparitions, large numbers of pilgrims and locals have experienced confession outside St. James Church.

CHAPTER 10

"I am showing you the way to forgive yourselves, to forgive others, and, with sincere repentance of heart, to kneel before the Father."

— *From Our Lady's Message of January 2nd, 2010*

A FEW YEARS ago, a man came to my door. He looked vaguely familiar, but I did not recognize him at first. He seemed reluctant to speak and he avoided eye contact.

"Can I help you?" I said.

"Please forgive me."

"For what?"

"I'm one of the policemen who interrogated you back in 1981. I'm really sorry for what we put you through."

It was not the first time someone had apologized to me like that, but I could never remember the specific incidents they felt guilty about. I had long since forgiven and forgotten. I prayed for my persecutors during even the worst harassments, like when they raised their batons as if to strike me or called Our Lady terrible names.

"It's ok," I said to the man. "That was a long time ago."

He seemed relieved.

"I have something for you," he said, and he held up a cassette tape. "I've saved the recording of that interrogation for all these years. I thought you might like to hear it."

A tape recorder lay on the table during almost every interrogation. I recalled the distinct *click* of the record button that marked the beginning of each session. I never had the opportunity nor the desire to listen to any of the recordings. I worried that doing so now might resurrect some bad memories, but I was also curious.

"Come in," I said, and we sat in my living room.

He put the tape in a cassette player. "At first I thought you were lying. But after we questioned you, I just wanted to shake your hand. I couldn't then—not in front of my colleagues—but now I want to, and here's why."

He pressed *play* and a memory from the past crackled through the speakers.

Interrogator: *You're deceiving the people.*

Me: *I'm not deceiving anyone.*

Interrogator: *Don't you see that your story is absurd?*

Me: *I'm telling the truth. That's all I can do.*

Hearing my teenaged voice through the tape player was a surreal experience. I could hardly believe that the other voice on the tape—with all its gruffness and anger—belonged to the same meek man who was now sitting in front of me. The tape continued.

Interrogator: *I'll ask you one more time. What did you see on that hill?*

Me: *I saw Our Lady.*

Interrogator: *You saw shit!*

Me: *No. That's what I'm looking at right now.*

I was surprised to hear myself being so bold. It would have been different had I been interrogated *before* I started seeing Our Lady; fear would have overwhelmed me to the point of tears, and I never could have challenged a policeman—or any adult—in such a way. But from June 24, 1981 onwards, the timidity that had plagued me for most of my child-hood had all but vanished.

The man stopped the tape and said, "It was your lack of fear that con-vinced me that you were telling the truth."

I thanked him for bringing the recording and reassured him that I harbored no ill feelings from those days. "You were just doing your job," I said.

After he left, I sat down and tried to process all the memories that the recording had stirred up. I closed my eyes and my mind wandered back to the time when the interrogation had taken place.

By August 1981, the events in Međugorje seemed to be moving faster than ever. Considering the enormous *milicija* presence in the village, it was amazing that any pilgrims still came at all. But even the police and soldiers could not deter the faithful. News of the apparitions had spread throughout the world, drawing pilgrims from faraway places we had only heard about in school.

Many pilgrims were eager to meet the visionaries, and they often came to my aunt and uncle's house looking for me. At first, I talked to everyone who came. I'd spend hours listening to their saddest stories, crying with them, and consoling them. But I soon realized that there were simply too many people for me to help. I was taking so much of their pain on my shoulders, and losing so much sleep, that I often felt exhausted and ill.

Worried about my health, Uncle Šimun became increasingly protec-tive, and he began answering the door whenever pilgrims came looking for me.

"Is the visionary home?" they'd say. "We want to see her!"

My uncle always tried to send them away as nicely as possible. "I'm sorry, but Mirjana is tired."

He was too kind to shut the door on them, so if the pilgrims insisted, or if they told him a sad story, he'd ask Aunt Slava for help. She, too, had seen how difficult it was for me to deal with all the attention, so she guarded my privacy, especially when people were merely curious to see me. She only asked me to come out if someone truly needed help, and even then she pulled me inside if it got too late.

At first, I felt guilty that I could not talk to everyone, but I began to understand that pilgrims did not need to meet me to have a fruitful pilgrimage. I was simply called to be a messenger, and I relayed my experiences as best I could. Otherwise, Our Lady's messages were expressed through Međugorje itself—in the solitude of the fields, on the stony slopes of the hills, in the confessionals, and on the altar at St. James Church. As visionaries, we simply had to transmit her words, and once we did that, then Our Lady could speak to everyone.

I loved to watch Grandma Jela interact with pilgrims. She used to pray, "God, since you created all of us, why didn't you make it so that we could all speak the same language? I so desperately want to tell all the pilgrims about you, but they don't understand me."

But she *was* speaking to the pilgrims. Despite her declining health, she welcomed them with a smile. She fed them from what little she had and she housed them, all at no charge. She prayed with them, and they saw how her rosary was practically attached to her hand at all times. Even if she didn't realize it, she was telling them about God in the most powerful way possible—by her example.

Grandma Jela and most of the villagers even regarded the military presence with peace and kindness. On hot afternoons, they would bring cold drinks to the soldiers, and, sometimes in the evenings, home-cooked meals. It was a strange and beautiful sight to see a hunched-over old woman reach up to give a glass of milk or a fresh loaf of bread to a uniformed soldier. The mothers of Međugorje treated the soldiers as if they were their own children, and the affect was profound: the longer the soldiers stayed, the kinder they became to everyone, including the pilgrims.

This probably infuriated the communist leadership even more, and they intensified their propaganda campaign against Međugorje in hopes of stopping the flow of visitors. *Television Sarajevo* presented a special report claiming to have proof that it was all a hoax intended to stir up Croatian nationalism. They showed footage of stone tablets allegedly found on Apparition Hill, and etched upon the tablets were statements like *Our Lady bring back the Croatian state* and *Join Our Lady against communism.* No one had ever seen anything like that on the hill, so we all knew it was the communists who had made the tablets and planted them there for the news report.

The program also twisted one of Fr. Jozo's homilies by claiming he had said "forty years of suffering under the communists is enough."

What he really said in his July 11, 1981 homily did not even include the word "communists," but the government spies planted in the pews had long been waiting for any kind of pretext to accuse Fr. Jozo of anti-government behavior. They finally got what they were waiting for.

Fr. Jozo's sermon started out with a gentle welcome to all the people in the church. "Looking at the license plates of your cars, I could see that you've come from many different places. Many of you are coming to me and asking me what exactly is happening here. Yesterday and today many journalists arrived and they all asked how it was possible that our post office and telephone lines were burnt a week prior to these events, and yet despite that the whole country and even Europe found out about Međugorje in less than one day.

"Even if we had put some large notice in the sky, we couldn't have attracted so many people here. But when the Lord works, He doesn't need advertising. Without any noise or commotion, our God uses a simple human being—not mighty people, but little ones—for 'He casts the mighty from their thrones and raises the lowly.' He uses a simple person, one who has faith and trust, and through that servant, He can proclaim His most profound and greatest mysteries. Mary was one such humble servant of the Lord."

Fr. Jozo continued his sermon with a call for people to seek freedom from sin. "Jesus came amongst His lost sons and said: 'The Spirit of the Lord is on me, because He has anointed me to preach good news to the poor. He has sent me to proclaim freedom for prisoners and recovery of sight for the blind, to release the oppressed, to proclaim the year of the Lord's favor.' We understand that tonight! Hasn't He come to release me, the prisoner, you, the oppressed, who for forty years have been imprisoned, that tonight or tomorrow you may kneel down in front of Him and say: 'Open those chains, open those locks, open the chains that have been tightening my life, for I've been chained by sins for so many years.'?"

Fr. Jozo never imagined that his words would bring *actual* locks and chains to himself, but a secret recording of his homily was given to government officials. His references to "prisoners" and "oppression" seemed scandalous to a regime paranoid about losing its grip on its people. The communists finally had what they needed to indict the man they suspected of orchestrating the events at Međugorje.

Early on the morning of August 17, 1981, two undercover agents from Belgrade came to St. James Church. They searched the grounds and finally found Fr. Jozo in the parish house. "Are you Jozo?"

"I am. How can I help you?"

"You must come with us."

After making Fr. Jozo put on civilian clothes, the agents handcuffed him and escorted him outside. He looked at the people who had gathered near the church steps.

"Goodbye," said Fr. Jozo. "God be with you always. Don't be afraid. Our Lady is with us."

People watched in horror as the agents shoved Fr. Jozo into a car and sped away. Would they torture him? Kill him? Everyone feared the worst.

Right after Fr. Jozo was arrested, a huge squad of policemen surrounded the church and parish office. They barricaded the doors and searched both buildings for a long time, ultimately carting away all of the money from the Mass offerings and arresting several more priests.

I came to the church later that morning and was shocked to find it surrounded by fences and police. I felt like my life had stopped. My heart ached for Fr. Jozo and I prayed for God to give him strength.

Some of the policemen taunted us, saying, "Haha, Jozo is gone! You're done!" It was clear they expected everything to end that day.

Was this the "great struggle" that Our Lady had warned about on August 2? And was she preparing the villagers by allowing them to touch her dress in the field at Gumno?

With so many armed policemen around, it felt like we were in a war. I assumed that the six of us visionaries would be next. Would we even live to see the next day? Somehow I felt fear and peace within myself at the same time—fear because I knew how much my family would suffer if I died, and peace because I would finally be with Our Lady. I was not afraid of death because I knew that Heaven existed, but I felt sad for the people I would have to leave behind.

Amazingly, a priest from a nearby village was able to reopen the church and celebrate Mass that night, thereby continuing the evening prayer program that Fr. Jozo had established. The church was filled to capacity that night. People cried and prayed. The six of us visionaries led the congregation in the rosary, and when the time of the apparition drew near, we went into the room adjacent to the altar. As soon as Our Lady appeared, we asked her about our beloved priest.

"Do not be afraid," she told us. *"I wish for you to be filled with joy, and for joy to be seen on your face. I will protect Father Jozo. I am with him."*

When the apparition ended, we told the priest what she had said. The priest looked out at the worried faces in the congregation, and then he took little Jakov by the hand and led him to the front of the altar. Jakov was so small that no one could have seen him behind the altar.

"Please tell them, Jakov," said the priest.

Jakov looked at the crowd, took a deep breath, and then fearlessly told them what Our Lady had said. The mood in the church changed from despair to hope. We tried our best to smile as Jakov relayed the message. Our Lady had brought us some comfort, but it was impossible to ignore the absence of the priest who—despite his initial doubts—had become our staunch ally. We wondered where he was and what he was experiencing at that moment.

When the authorities tried to pressure another local priest to cancel all evening Masses by pointing out that such services were usually held in the morning, the priest responded by saying, "Mass is not a commemoration of the last *breakfast* of Jesus, but the last *supper!*"

Interestingly, Fr. Jozo had ended his controversial sermon with words that, in retrospect, almost seemed like a foretelling of the suffering he would have to endure.

"Christians in this world are like a light in the darkness," he said. "Our strength is on our knees, in our hands put together for prayer, in our carrying of the cross. Our strength comes from our Lord God. There is no other strength, no other wisdom, no other victory, but the victory over the absurdity of this world—through humbleness, love, and sacrifice."

The large cement cross on top of Križevac, also known as Cross Mountain.

CHAPTER 11

"I have chosen you, my apostles, because all of you carry something beautiful within you."

— *From Our Lady's Message of April 2, 2015*

DESPITE WHAT THE communists had envisioned, the apparitions continued after Fr. Jozo's arrest, and the flow of pilgrims persisted. I had become just as good at hiding from pilgrims as I was at hiding from police. I still woke early every day to pick and string tobacco, and I worked until it was time for the apparition.

On August 25, 1981, Our Lady responded to our constant requests for a sign, perhaps to help reassure the people of Međugorje and calm their fears. Vicka and I were at Ivan's house when we heard a commotion outside. We ran out to find people standing in the street and staring at Križevac. Some of them pointed. Others dropped to their knees.

Turning to look at the mountain, I saw a figure of Our Lady in the place where the 8.5-meter-tall cross usually was. She looked different from how we normally saw her—more like a statue than a real person. The figure slowly faded away and the cross reappeared. Moments later, strange shapes materialized in the sky over the mountain, forming huge, luminous letters that spelled out *mir*, which means *peace* in our language. *Mir* is also the first part of *Miriam*, the original Hebrew name for Mary.

No one could ignore what was happening in Međugorje. It was as if we lived in Biblical times.

We nervously followed the news reports about Fr. Jozo's trial. Every time someone mentioned his name, I felt empty inside. In the days before his trial, Our Lady asked us to fast on bread and water, and to pray for him. With no evidence that he had committed a crime, the government used lies and false accusations to prove their case. Fr. Jozo was ultimately convicted of sedition, a serious crime that could have carried the death penalty, but in the end he was sentenced to three years of imprisonment and hard labor.

Fr. Jozo had done nothing wrong, but the Yugoslav government distorted the truth to achieve its goals. It made me realize that the communists could do whatever they wanted to anyone.

At the end of August, I experienced their callousness firsthand.

The police instructed Uncle Šimun to bring me to Čitluk for yet another interrogation. The repeated questionings had practically become routine: time after time, they would put me in an empty room and make me wait for what seemed like an eternity, and then after grilling me with questions and not getting the answers they wanted, they would threaten me, curse at me, and finally let me go. What more did they want?

But when my uncle and I entered the police station this time, I knew this was not another interrogation. Two men in suits stood with a group of uniformed policemen. They shoved Uncle Šimun back outside and locked me in a holding cell. I sat there for a couple of hours and no one said anything to me. Finally, they put me in the backseat of a government car. The men in suits—agents from the secret police—sat in the front. I cried as the car sped away. "Where are you taking me?"

"Shut up," said the driver.

"Stupid girl," said the other man. "Your fraud ends today."

They shouted and cursed at me as we drove. I put my hands over my ears and curled up into a ball. I tried to pray, but my heart thumped with anxiety. More than anything, I was concerned about Uncle Šimun.

Distraught about not being able protect me, he stood outside the police station crying. How would he explain to my mother—his sister—that he lost me? For the first time in his life, my uncle walked into a nearby bar and ordered *rakija*—Croatian brandy.

After riding in the car for three hours, I began to recognize the surroundings and realized that we were entering Sarajevo. Were they taking me to prison? Or a place of execution? I thought of all the possible ways they might kill me and hoped it would be something quick like a firing squad.

But when the car finally stopped, I peeked through the window and saw my parents' apartment building. *Thank you, God,* I prayed. The officers escorted me to our unit. My mom opened the door and gasped when she saw me flanked by policemen, but she forced a smile and greeted the men with far more kindness than I thought they deserved.

"Good day, gentlemen," she said. "How kind of you to give my daughter a ride home."

"Mom!" I said. "If you only knew how they treated me!"

She looked at me, still smiling. "You just come in, dear. It doesn't matter." And then, turning to the policemen, she said, "Gentlemen, would you like to come in for a coffee?"

"But mom!"

My mom gave me a look as if to say "be quiet," so I took a deep breath and remained silent. The police explained to my mother that I was to stay in Sarajevo, and that I would need their permission if I wanted to go anywhere, just like any other "enemy of the state." Who were they to tell me where I could and could not go? Most of my personal belongings were still at my uncle's house, but more than anything, I worried that my apparitions would end if I was not in Međugorje.

As the policemen left, one of them glared at me. "We'll be watching you," he said.

As soon as they were gone, my mother's fake smile disappeared and she embraced me. "The only important thing is that you came back safe and sound," she said. "You're alive and nothing else matters."

With Fr. Jozo in prison and me alienated from Međugorje, the communists probably thought that everything would end quietly. Once again, however, they underestimated the power of God.

It was bittersweet to be back in Sarajevo. I had missed my parents and my brother, but home did not feel the same. What had once been my refuge was now like a prison. Although I was only away for two months, it seemed like I came back a different person. So much happened in such a short time that I grew up overnight. The things I used to care about did not seem important anymore.

During those first hours of being home, I felt a knot in my chest. Being so far from Međugorje and separated from the others, I was convinced that Our Lady would stop coming to me. But my worries were extinguished that afternoon as I sat in our apartment and suddenly felt her presence. I kneeled on the floor and experienced what would be the first of many apparitions in Sarajevo.

Because of constant surveillance and harassment by the police, my apparitions could only take place in the secrecy of our home, in the living room which was also my bedroom. Being with Our Lady in Sarajevo was a lovely and intimate experience. In fact, despite the intense persecution that I had to endure there, I look back at it as one of the most beautiful periods of my life. In Međugorje I had to "share" Our Lady with the others, but in Sarajevo, I had her all to myself. She visited me every day and helped me understand God's plan.

I set up a makeshift prayer altar in the room with a cross and a statue of the Blessed Mother. There could never be many people with me during the apparitions. My mother, father and brother were always present. And with them, when possible, a few nuns, priests or close friends would sometimes come, but we could not let too many people gather in the apartment. The police would find it suspicious. We even asked visitors to enter the apartment at different times.

One priest who often came was Dr. Fr. Ljudevit Rupčić, a well-known theologian at Sarajevo's *Franjevacka Teologija*—the Franciscan School of Theology. Born near Medugorje in 1920, Fr. Rupčić had been chronicling the apparitions from the first days. Whenever he visited me, he recorded our conversations and took notes, but he always left quickly if the police ever came near. He'd been imprisoned by the communists twice before.

If not for my afternoon visits with Our Lady, I don't know how I would have endured living in Sarajevo during that time. My parents and brother suffered as well. The police came to our home regularly and even our closest friends distanced themselves. Most people were afraid to be seen with us.

One day, the police summoned me to the station and an officer ordered me to relinquish my passport to ensure that I would not flee the country. I took it out of my pocket but hesitated to give it to him.

"I'm a human being," I said. "I have rights."

He glared at me from behind his desk. "Your rights don't exist here," he snarled.

"I'm beginning to see that."

He snatched the passport from my hand and screamed at me like I was a dog. "Now get out of here!"

Such was the environment. Communism had to be especially harsh in Sarajevo because all of Yugoslavia's ethnic groups were represented there. The authorities were experts at using fear as a means of control. How else would the government treat a girl who spoke about God when it taught everyone in schools that He was an invention?

I tried to go back to living like an ordinary teenager—ordinary with the exception of my daily apparitions. As the beginning of the school year approached, I looked forward to seeing my friends. I was also eager to continue my education, something that had always been important to me. I would be entering my junior year at one of the best high schools in Sarajevo, conveniently located just a few blocks from our apartment.

Taking a walk through the city one morning, I glanced in a corner shop and abruptly stopped when I read the day's newspaper headline:

MIRJANA DRAGIĆEVIĆ, GRANDDAUGHTER OF FASCIST, CLAIMS VISIONS

It did not even seem real. I scanned the first few lines of the article.

Mirjana Dragičević, a 16-year-old high school student from Sarajevo, says that she sees and speaks with an imaginary Virgin Mary. Her anti-government activity should come as no surprise, though. Her grandfather was a fascist.

It had been forty years since my grandfather disappeared. How far would they go to discredit me? I hardly even knew what a fascist was, but suddenly everybody thought I was one. Some even accused me of being an anti-government "subversive." On the contrary, I did not harbor any misgivings about the Yugoslav government—at least not before I became one of its targets. A month before the apparitions began, in fact, I had been chosen to represent the people of Sarajevo and recite a communist poem about President Tito on national television.

Now, as a visionary, I was suddenly an outcast. The local newspapers informed all of Sarajevo about my presence there. As the school year was about to begin, the police knocked on our door and gave my father devastating news: I had been expelled from high school.

According to the policemen, when the principal saw my name on the roster and realized that I was the girl from the newspapers, he shouted, "Who enrolled this crap here?"

Before the apparitions, I went to one of the best schools in Sarajevo. That's me on the bottom row, third from the right.

CHAPTER 12

"Love conquers death and makes life last."

— From Our Lady's Message of October 2, 2015

ASIDE FROM THE miracle of seeing Our Lady every day, my life seemed to be falling apart. I had always been a dedicated student, so my expulsion from school left me distraught and perplexed. Was God putting me through some kind of test? A penance for something I had done wrong?

Every evening as I knelt to wait for Our Lady, I hoped she would give me an answer, or at least some words of encouragement. *She'll know what to do*, I thought. *She can fix everything.* But when she appeared, she said nothing about my personal struggles.

Only through prayer did I finally understand that I was no different from anyone else who suffered. Our Lady remained silent about my situation out of respect for my free will and out of love for *all* her children—those who could see her and those who could not. Like any good mother, I realized, Our Lady did not choose favorites.

My parents tried to enroll me in other Sarajevo schools but none accepted me. Each rejection hurt more than the last. There were times when I wanted to give up. Before the apparitions, my goals even involved going to university, but now I was praying just for the chance to finish high school.

My parents were as insistent as my own heart. "We only ask you one thing," said my mother. "Finish school."

Newspapers labelled me and the other visionaries all sorts of derogatory names intended to cast doubt on our intelligence. *Six yokels still claim apparitions,* read one headline. After seeing it, my father looked at me with an uncharacteristic seriousness. "We will find you a school," he said, "and you will show the world that the six of you aren't yokels."

Despite my father's carefree nature, he took education seriously. In a country with few opportunities, he knew that living a life above the poverty line was difficult without at least a high school diploma. Still, he never pushed us, and he never yelled at us. If my mother ever got angry with me or Miro, he'd calmly tell her, "There's no need to raise your voice. Don't worry. The children are smart. They'll learn."

One time, Miro got terrible grades in school. My mother was upset and asked my father to punish him. My dad looked at Miro with the sternest expression I had ever seen on his face. "The two of us need to go into the room to talk."

What's going to happen to Miro? I thought.

Ten minutes later, my dad came out holding Miro in his arms. They were both crying. My mom put her hands on her hips and shook her head. "Jozo! Is *this* your idea of discipline?"

"Don't worry," said my dad. "He promised he'll study more."

With the same kind of love and patience, Dad endeavored to help me continue my education. When it seemed like I was doomed to be a high school dropout, my father enlisted the help of a friend and managed to enroll me in what could be described as a last resort. It was a school for delinquent children, meant to be a final chance for the "worst of the worst" expelled from all the other high schools in Sarajevo. I had to take a tram to school because it was located in

Skenderija, a central district known for its large sports center and the historic bridge where Gavrilo Princip assassinated Archduke Ferdinand in 1914, making Sarajevo the catalyst for World War I.

The student body was comprised of troubled youths who had problems with drugs, alcohol and crime—and now there was me, a girl who claimed to have apparitions of the Virgin Mary. I was nervous and even a little frightened the first time I entered the new school. Nearly all the other kids in the classroom were Serbs and Muslims. Most had a streetwise hardness about them, with stern faces and hair hanging down over their eyes. Some dressed like hippies from the 1960s, while a few girls wore tight skirts, high-heeled shoes and an excess of makeup. A boy with spiked hair and ripped jeans lounged at his desk smoking a cigarette.

As a diligent student coming from the city's most elite high school where everyone dressed accordingly, I was shocked that this place existed. If any of the students at my previous school smoked, they would never dare do it in the schoolyard, let alone in the classroom.

I sat at my desk and tried to hide my anxiety, but my incessant foot-tapping gave it away. The girl sitting next to me leaned over and held out a little pill. "Hey," she said, "if you're worried about something, take this *Valium* and drink a beer. You'll be so high that nothing will bother you."

I looked at her in shock.

Where am I? I thought. *God help me.*

The teacher entered the classroom and the girl shoved the pill in her pocket. I expected the teacher to be angry when she saw the boy with the cigarette, but instead she timidly said, "It would be better if you didn't smoke in the classroom."

Without saying anything, the boy took another drag, blew a smoke ring, and put the cigarette out on his desk. The teacher, with a look of relief, thanked him. What kind of school was this where the teachers feared the students?

The students did not pay much attention to me at first, aside from frequently asking for money. I thought they needed it to buy food, since most of them came from poor families. I gave them what little I had, but when I realized that they were using my money to buy drugs, I stopped being so generous.

My obscurity allowed me to focus on my studies and quietly observe this strange new world. As days went by, the apprehension I felt towards my classmates gradually turned into empathy. I guessed that most of them came from troubled families and were simply searching for love. Many found acceptance in groups involved with drugs, theft, and gambling, ultimately getting entangled in those vices themselves. I prayed for them every day.

Some things were more difficult to accept. Many of the girls in my school spoke about having abortions as if it was nothing. One might have assumed that they had simply gone to the dentist to have a tooth pulled. In the morning, for example, a girl would go to have an abortion, and then she would show up for afternoon classes and talk about whatever concert or party was happening that night. I suffered whenever I overheard someone talking about it so casually.

There were times when I wanted to confront the girls about it, to say something like, "Don't you know it's wrong to kill the child within you?"

But through my daily apparitions, and through prayer, Our Lady taught me that preaching to them and being judgmental would only drive them farther away. Instead, I learned to show them love, and I tried to live as an example of someone who knew God's love.

I once heard that souls of unbaptized infants and victims of abortion went to a place known as Limbo—a perpetual state of separation from God. But how could God, the Pure Love, exclude innocent babies from Heaven? During an apparition, I asked Our Lady, "Where do they go?"

"They are with me in Heaven," she replied.

As the school year progressed, the kids in my new school drew closer to me. They knew about my situation—the newspapers contin-ued to print articles about me, insinuating that the apparitions were a plot against the government. But the students never said anything rude to me, not even Azra, a Muslim girl with a reputation for being cold and mean. The other students avoided her and even the teachers kept their distance. One time, she came to school in the afternoon when there was only half an hour left in the school day. She barged into the classroom, interrupting the teacher's lesson, and slumped down at her desk.

The teacher glared at her. "Do you know what time it is, Azra? Where have you been?"

Azra stared coldly at the teacher and shrugged her shoulders. "A funeral?"

The teacher looked at her for a moment but did not respond. It was clear that Azra was lying, but the teacher must have been too scared of Azra to reprimand her.

After school, I was surprised when Azra came up to me with tears in her eyes. "Can I talk to you?" she asked.

I had never seen her crying and looking so vulnerable. "Of course," I said.

"You're the only one who will listen to me."

We sat together and I held her hand. "Tell me."

"I wasn't late because of a funeral."

"I know that," I said, and then I laughed. "*Everyone* knows that."

Azra smiled, and for the first time I saw how beautiful she was. I silently vowed to make her smile more.

"I live in a terrible situation at home," she continued. "My father abuses my mom, and I don't know what to do. I can't tell the police because he's the only one with a job. Without him, we'd be on the streets. But I can't stand up to him and tell him to stop because then he'd beat me too."

I squeezed her hand. "I'm so sorry, Azra."

"The only thing that gives me relief are the tablets the doctors prescribe to help me relax, but I don't want to feel like a zombie all the time. That's why everyone at school thinks I'm unfriendly. The medicine numbs my pain, but it numbs everything else in me, too."

Azra wiped her tears, and then she looked at me questioningly. "How do you stay so happy when the police are constantly bothering you? You're never angry. I don't get it."

"Well, it's an interesting story," I said, and I told her how prayer brought me peace in my darkest moments. I also spoke to her about the apparitions. From that day on, Azra continued to ask me about my faith.

Soon, other children began confiding in me as well. They'd tell me about their family problems and share their deepest wounds with me as if they were making a confession, even if none of them actually knew what that was. I tried to give them comfort, and then, if they asked, I told them about God's love.

I was always eager to know what was happening in Međugorje during my absence. News came sporadically. Sometimes Marko called to give me updates, and family members occasionally visited us in Sarajevo, so I was never completely cut off. Contrary to what the communists had hoped for, the other five visionaries were still experiencing daily apparitions. Imprisoning Fr. Jozo had not stopped it. Neither had exiling me. And despite the government's relentless coercion, the numbers of pilgrims continued to grow. Međugorje was thriving. I often thought about the other visionaries and wondered when I might see them again.

There was one bit of news, however, that confused me deeply—just after Fr. Jozo's arrest, Bishop Žanić reversed his position on Međugorje. How was this the same bishop quoted in newspapers just months before as saying that he believed us? And the same bishop who said he was "certain the children are not lying" during his homily for the feast of St. James in Međugorje? I began praying for him every day.

Fr. Ljudevit Rupčić and other clergy seemed equally confused about the bishop. "No one can close God's mouth," wrote Fr. Rupčić. "He has not finished His conversation nor His revelation to people. It goes on continuously in the Church and the world in different ways."

I became less vocal about my experiences after coming back to Sarajevo, mainly because few people there were interested to know about them, and my visions only took place in the privacy of my home. Yet it was in Sarajevo that I experienced the most intense persecution. Sarajevo was full of hardline communists, whereas most of the policemen in Medugorje were Catholics, many of whom had come to believe in the apparitions. It was also clear that the government looked at me as the root of the problem, and now they had me isolated in a place where I would be easier to break.

Nearly every morning, the police came to our apartment and took me in for questioning before school. These were not ordinary policemen. Wearing suits and ties, they were members of the state police, similar to the FBI in America or the KGB in the Soviet Union. When the interrogations made me late for school, I had to give my teacher an excuse note from the Secretariat as if I was some notorious criminal. Sometimes the police forced me to spend the entire day at the station.

To get what they wanted, the police played a game of good cop/ bad cop, where one acted kind and the other aggressive. One day they put me in an interrogation room all alone. The mean one entered first. With a scowl on his face, he assailed me with threats and accusing questions. "Do you want to spend your life in prison? Or how about a mental hospital? You *do* know that people want to have you shot, right?"

When he did not get the answers he wanted, he screamed and cursed. Then he stormed out and the "nice cop" entered.

"I'm so sorry," he said. "My colleague has no patience. You don't deserve to be treated like that."

Flashing a fake smile, he asked me if I wanted anything to eat or drink. I was very thin at that time—perhaps dangerously so—because

I rarely had time to eat. And although I was both hungry and thirsty, I refused his offer.

"You know," he said, "you're very beautiful. We should go out some time. I'll take you to a nice restaurant in the mountains and buy you dinner. You don't need all these hassles."

"Thank you, but no," I said.

Seeing he was not making progress, he switched tactics.

"Listen, I'm your friend. I want to help you. What do you want? I can make sure you get enrolled back in your last school. I can get you any university degree you want. How about your own apartment? And for your family to have a better home? No problem. I just need one thing from you. Admit that Fr. Jozo invented everything."

He put a document in front of me and held out a pen. "Just sign this and it will all be over."

When I explained to him with childlike naivety that I had not even known Fr. Jozo before the apparitions, and that I truly saw Our Lady, his fake smiled disappeared and he left the room. The "bad cop" came in again, screaming and yelling and threatening to beat me to death. Instead of asking, he demanded that I sign the document, and if I did not, he would make sure my family and I "suffered in ways we could not imagine."

Eventually I realized that the police were not actually interested in hearing the truth, and I remembered the words of the Little Prince: "Grown-ups never understand anything by themselves, and it is tiresome for children to always be explaining things to them."

From then on, when the police cursed, threatened, or made promises, I put my hands over my face and prayed in silence because I knew nothing good could come from talking to them.

What will happen will happen, I thought. *Imprison me, kill me, I don't care—just let this end.*

The most difficult part of the police interrogations was having to bear all their profanity. Our Lady was always in my thoughts, so it was difficult to hear such terrible things while thinking about her beauty. The communists prohibited me from holding my rosary during the questioning, so I figured out a way to pray the rosary on my hands—counting the fingers on my left hand for the five mysteries and the fingers on my right hand twice for the ten *Hail Mary* prayers.

Praying the rosary after seeing Our Lady was a profound experience. Every time I said a *Hail Mary*, I could envision her—her beautiful face, her expressions of pain and joy—and I could feel her in my heart. When I was a child, praying the rosary felt like it would never end, but now it was always over too soon. It was impossible to think of it as merely a repetitive prayer any more.

The police in Sarajevo also seemed to be preoccupied with my ethnicity. Most communists in Yugoslavia identified themselves as Serbian, and throughout recent history there had always been some level of animosity between Serbs and Croats. Growing up, though, I had never given it any thought. In a way, the policemen taught me who I was—I did not even think about the fact that I was a Croat until they kept telling me so.

They also called me a fascist, and I still did not know what that meant. I finally asked my mom and dad at home. "Am I a fascist? What does that mean?"

My parents explained that communists used the term *fascist* for Croats who wanted to separate Croatia from Yugoslavia. I was 16. I had never been concerned about Croatian nationalism, nor did my parents ever talk about it. We loved people of all ethnicities and religions.

Our mail was often opened before it reached our apartment, and we guessed that the police had also installed listening devices in our home, but that did not matter because we never spoke against the state. The frequent unannounced searches bothered us the most. Police would barge in and turn everything upside down without any consideration for our belongings. I did not know what they were looking for, but I was afraid they would plant some kind of "incriminating evidence" in our apartment and pretend to find it. We could only sit and wait for them to finish.

I recall looking at my family during one such intrusion, and I will never forget what I saw—my father's eyes filled with shame because he felt powerless to protect us; tears streaming down my mother's face as policemen defiled the home that she had worked so hard to clean; and my innocent little brother shivering and cowering in fear, and who, for many years after that, was afraid to sleep alone.

I felt responsible for the suffering that had entered their lives. I had the solace of seeing Our Lady every day, but my parents and brother did not. They suffered because of me, and although they never complained about it, I promised myself that I would carry as much of the burden as I could.

Arriving at the door to our apartment one night after a particularly harsh interrogation, I dried my tears, took a deep breath, and forced myself to smile before going in. My mother was in the kitchen and she immediately looked at me with concern. "Mirjana?"

"Hi Mom!" I said.

"Why were you gone so long? Are you ok?"

"No big deal. The police just asked me some questions."

"Are you sure?"

"Don't worry, Mom." I leaned over and kissed her on the cheek, trying to maintain my smile. "I have school tomorrow, so goodnight!"

I went into the bathroom, locked the door, and broke down sobbing. It was the one place where no one could see me cry. From that night onward, the bathroom became my sanctuary, and I often took refuge there so as not to burden anyone else with my pain.

One day, I came across Psalm 23, the psalm of David. The words haunted me and spoke to my heart. From then on, whenever I experienced hardship, the psalm soothed me.

The Lord is my shepherd, I shall not want. He makes me lie down in green pastures; he leads me beside still waters; he restores my soul. He leads me in right paths for his name's sake.

Even though I walk through the darkest valley, I fear no evil; for you are with me; your rod and your staff—they comfort me.

You prepare a table before me in the presence of my enemies; you anoint my head with oil; my cup overflows.

Surely goodness and mercy shall follow me all the days of my life; and I shall dwell in the house of the Lord forever.

*Christmas in Međugorje, 1981, when Our Lady
presented herself in an extraordinary way.*

CHAPTER 13

---

*"I know your pain and suffering because I lived through them.
I laugh with you in your joy and I cry with you in your pain. I
will never leave you."*

— *From Our Lady's Message of May 2, 2015*

DURING THOSE DAYS, I was ready to die at any moment. I
expected it was all leading to a point where they would kill me;
I would vanish overnight like Grandpa Mate. I wasn't afraid of
dying, though, because then I could be with the Blessed Mother forever.

I never relented. I was seeing Our Lady, and no one could persuade
me to deny such a miracle. I would never forsake my faith. Through
prayer, God gave me the strength to persist. He helped me grow up
and forget about the pampered little girl I had been.

My mother always told me that I should never oppose the inter-
rogators, and that I should always keep quiet no matter what they said.
Most of the time I followed her advice, but sometimes I had to stand
up for myself.

My mom and I had to meet with a government-appointed social
worker whose role, it seemed, was to persuade me to deny the apparitions. When we entered the office, we found him leaning back in his
chair with his feet on the desk, cleaning his fingernails.

"Sit down," he said without even glancing at us.

We sat across from him. He finally looked up at me and studied me for a moment. "You're prettier than I expected. Don't you think it's time to grow up and stop talking to this imaginary friend of yours? Who will ever want to marry you?"

"Is it important to get married? I can be a nun." That possibility, in fact, had been on my mind.

The man jumped out of his chair and looked down at me, his nostrils flaring. "What have *nuns* done for Yugoslavia!?"

I stood, too. "And what have *you* contributed? You sit in that chair picking at your nails. Is that a contribution?"

Stunned by my reaction, the social worker and my mom both stared at me, mouths agape. I had reached a point where I no longer cared anymore. If the police wanted me to stop having apparitions, they would have to kill me.

Even though I walk through the darkest valley, I thought, *I fear no evil.*

Nearly all of my old friends had abandoned me, and anytime I made a new friend, it did not take long for the communists to drive them away. One afternoon, I went to a café and had coffee with a Serbian boy from my school. We had a nice conversation and then went our separate ways.

That evening, he called me at home. "Who *are* you?" he said.

I was confused. "What do you mean?"

"Well, as soon as I got home, the police came for me."

I felt pain in my heart. "I'm so sorry. What did they say?"

"They took me to the state police station and interrogated me. They demanded to know what you and I had talked about. 'Nothing really,' I said. 'School and homework mainly.' And then they asked me, 'Did she speak about the destruction of Yugoslavia?' I was shocked. 'Of course not,' I told them. I had no idea what was going on."

I felt like it would be better for everybody if I just disappeared. I was tired of being the source of problems for people. It got so bad that when I walked down the sidewalk, people who knew me would go to the other side of the street so they would not have to greet me. They were afraid that the police would harass them as well. I got used to being alone.

One person who never avoided me, though, was our neighbor, Paasha. She had seen the police taking me with them and she could not imagine her "Little Blonde" doing anything against the law. One day she asked my mother what was going on.

"Mirjana sees the Virgin Mary," said my mother, not sure how Paasha would react.

"Ah," said Paasha, nodding and smiling. "Blessed Maryam."

My mother explained the entire situation, and Paasha listened with interest and respect. The Blessed Mother, it turned out, was the only woman mentioned by name in the Quran. Mary's Islamic titles included *Sa'imah* (she who fasts) and *Siddiqah* (she who confirms the truth). The Quran even describes angels as saying, "O Mary! God has chosen you and purified you—chosen you above all women of all nations of the world."

So, my story sounded plausible to Paasha and she accepted it with love. Instead of distancing herself from us as so many others had done, she drew closer. She was in our apartment one time when a priest came over to be present at an apparition. Paasha greeted him warmly and kissed his hand before politely excusing herself to leave. On another occasion, she stopped me in the hallway and looked in my eyes. "I pray for you every day," she said.

Her support was a ray of solace amidst the constant torment, but nothing helped me cope more than my daily apparitions. Sometimes I was still in police custody when the time of the apparition approached, but Our Lady always waited to appear until I returned home. My entire life revolved around those few moments I spent with her each afternoon. It was my escape from the persecution and even from my own thoughts—when I was with Our Lady, I was not *me*. I felt like a different person in another place and time.

Our Lady spoke of the importance of prayer and fasting, and she invited us to conversion—to abandon sin and put God first in our lives. Only then would we know real love, she said.

Fr. Ljudevit Rupčić, who continued to visit me in Sarajevo, wrote, "True conversion means the purifying or cleansing of the heart, because a corrupt or deteriorated heart is the basis of bad relations, which in turn brings social disorder, unjust laws, and base constitutions. Without a radical change of heart, there is no peace."

At other times during my daily apparitions, Our Lady spoke about the secrets. By then, they had become a source of intense curiosity and speculation for everyone who followed Međugorje. The six of us were together when she began to divulge the secrets to us one by one.

There is so little I can say about the secrets. They are, after all, *secrets*. When Our Lady entrusted me with the third secret, though, she allowed me to reveal a few details about it, perhaps because we had asked her so many times to leave a sign.

I can say this much—after the events contained in the first two secrets come to pass, Our Lady will leave a permanent sign on Apparition Hill where she first appeared. Everyone will be able to see that human hands could not have made it. People will be able to photograph and film the sign, but in order to truly comprehend it—to experience it with the heart—they will need to come to Međugorje. Seeing it live, with the eyes, will be far more beautiful.

The six of us visionaries do not speak to each other about the secrets. The only part of the secrets that we know we share in common is the permanent sign.

I cannot speak about the details of the other secrets before the time comes to reveal them to the world, except to say that they will be announced before they occur. After the events take place as predicted, it will be difficult for even the staunchest skeptics to doubt the existence of God and the authenticity of the apparitions.

All of the secrets are for the world; none are for me personally. Our Lady relayed most of the events of the secrets through words, but she also showed me some of them like scenes from a film. When I saw these glimpses of the future during apparitions, people near me often noted the intense expressions on my face and asked me about it later.

Each secret will happen exactly as it was relayed to me, with one exception. I was alone in our apartment when Our Lady entrusted me with the seventh secret. Its contents troubled me greatly.

"Is it possible for the secret to be lessened?" I begged her.

"Pray," she replied.

I rallied friends, family members, nuns and priests to pray and fast for the intention of changing the seventh secret, and we did so with intensity and conviction. We often met in Sarajevo as a group to pray about it. Eight months later, during an apparition, I asked Our Lady again about the seventh secret.

"By the grace of God, it has been softened," she said. *"But you must never ask such things again, because God's will must be done."*

Our Lady also taught me to accept God's will for my own life. As difficult as it was to live in Sarajevo, problems always seemed to get resolved somehow. Our Lady never specifically said that she would help me, but I know she was always near. I constantly noticed her intervention. If a situation seemed hopeless, a door would suddenly open. If I felt all alone, someone would come to help me. I began to see how God worked through different people.

My parents also began to sense this protection. Frustrated by my refusal to bow to their pressures, the communists directed their intimidation at my father. Party officials told him that if he could not silence his daughter, then he would lose his job at the hospital. Our family depended on his income, but my parents never suggested that I keep quiet about Our Lady. Instead, they suffered and endured.

The communists, of course, were not pleased with that.

Police inspectors came to the hospital and told the hospital director, who was both Serbian and communist, that my father had to leave his job immediately because of his daughter's religious activities.

"But Jozo is beloved here," said the director, "and an exemplary worker."

"There's no discussion about it," the inspectors said.

The director stood up. "If Jozo leaves the hospital, then I will leave as well, and the whole system will fall apart. Is that what you want?"

The director's support saved my father's job.

"It's surely a sign from Our Lady," said my father, "when a person with different beliefs stands by you."

Before the apparitions, I had never heard him speak like that. It was always beautiful to see anyone grow in faith, but nothing compared to watching my own father embrace Our Lady's messages. Still, I began to notice more gray hair on his head every day.

The police also brought my parents in to be interrogated. They threatened to throw my father in prison and evict us from our state-owned apartment if my "religious activities" did not cease. We knew they could do almost anything they wanted. In communism, we could not consider anything our own.

That night, my parents discussed what they should do. Instead of asking me to stop talking about the apparitions, they decided to get separated—or at least make people think they had. They agreed that since my father's wage was higher than my mother's, he would give the impression in public that he did not condone my claims and that he had separated from my mother because she believed me. That way, he could keep his job and we could all live on his salary even if Mom got fired. I did not like the idea of it, but they were my parents and I tried to respect their decision.

The police soon found a new way to hurt and embarrass me—they began coming to my school. In a way, it was a little funny. When police cars parked in front of the school building, some of the students from my class fled, thinking the officers were coming to arrest them. But the police were usually coming for me. I felt ashamed. I wanted to explain to everyone in my school that I was not a criminal.

After every harsh interrogation, I asked God to give me more love, and to help me understand. I came to believe that even the policemen were instruments. I was not sure why, but it seemed like they had to be as they were, even when they were shouting and cursing.

My Lord, I thought. *How hopeless these people must be. How much pain they must carry inside.*

Only a miserable man could swear at a child or threaten to kill her. I never hated them. On the contrary, I pitied them and I asked God to give them peace.

Calm their restless hearts, I prayed. *Lead them beside still waters.*

By praying for my persecutors, I found peace as well. Soon, anytime the police took me from school, I always came back cheerful. On one such morning, some of the students in my class turned and looked at me.

"Who *are* you?" said one boy. "The cops take you in, but you come back with a smile! What's wrong with you?"

I smiled. "Well, I wasn't really alone with them."

"Oh? And who was with you?"

Azra chimed in. "Tell him, Mirjana."

I looked in the boy's eyes. "God was with me. He always is."

The students continued asking questions. I spoke to them about Jesus, about Our Lady, and about God's mercy. Through that experience, I came to see the difference between preaching and evangelizing. They told me that I seemed different from other people—that I was patient and full of love—and although I did not necessarily feel unique, I was happy to tell them about my faith. When they asked me about God, a door was opened, giving me the chance to speak with people who normally would never be interested in faith.

But our bonds went even deeper than that. Everyone at that school had been pushed aside and shunned from society. We were all out-casts, and we all suffered, but we helped each other, sharing everything from study notes to *burek*—a Bosnian pastry filled with meat, cheese, spinach or potatoes. I was surprised that anyone would want to be my friend with such horrible things being written about me in the communist newspapers, but my classmates showed me more love than almost anyone else did.

We became so close that many of the students even pledged to protect me—but every time the police came, of course, they fled.

When the first semester ended, I was thrilled to get an opportunity to return to Međugorje for the first time since the government forced me to leave. My family planned to spend the holidays there with our relatives, and the parish priests had invited me and the other visionar-ies to lead the rosary in the church on Christmas Eve. Although the police in Sarajevo had forbidden me to return to Međugorje, I knew it was still technically legal for me to travel within my own country, so I took the risk.

Going back was a beautiful experience and I savored every moment—the familiar faces of the villagers, the smell of fresh country air mingling with smoke from wood-burning stoves, the symphony of prayers and hymns flowing through the streets. For the first time in several months, I could hold a rosary in public and not be afraid. I felt like I was home again.

Reconnecting with the other visionaries was wonderful. They had matured since I last saw them, yet their personalities were still the same. They seemed shocked when I told them about the terrible things the police had done to me in Sarajevo. I realized the persecution they were experiencing in Međugorje was mild in comparison.

I joined them behind the altar for the Midnight Mass service on Christmas Eve. St. James Church overflowed with parishioners and pil-grims. Christmas trees, a nativity crèche, and candles adorned the interior of the church. With no electricity at night, the only illumination besides candlelight came from two light bulbs powered by a small generator.

The main celebrant that night was Fr. Jozo Vasilj, a Franciscan priest who had been born in Medugorje—and who would later spend over a decade of his life helping the poor in Africa before his death in 2007. Bringing the six of us visionaries to the front of the altar before Mass, Fr. Vasilj asked us to share some of our experiences. As I listened to the other five repeat some of the messages they had received, I was surprised to discover that they were nearly identical to the ones Our Lady had given me on the same dates. My messages, however, were always somewhat longer.

For example, when Our Lady asked everyone to fast on bread and water on Wednesdays and Fridays, she included additional things when she said it to me, such as the importance of praying while fasting, and how pleasing it was to God when we made small sacrifices.

Why, I wondered, was Our Lady telling me extra details? By then she had also given me more secrets than she had given to the others.

Fr. Vasilj gave an impassioned homily that night. "Jesus was born at midnight and transformed night into day," he said. "He died during the day and transformed day into night. He resurrected at midnight and transformed night into day. But it does not stop there. Jesus remained to live among us. There will always be Christians on Earth, but it all depends on me and you, dear brother or dear sister, if there will be more or less."

Looking out at all the people who braved the midnight chill to attend Mass, I felt confident that Our Lady's appearances were already resulting in more believers. Praying in the dimness of St. James Church on Christmas Eve was a beautiful experience, but I could not suppress a nagging dread in my heart; I knew I had to depart Medugorje before school began again and the thought of returning to the unfriendly secular culture of Sarajevo—where faith was viewed as a mental illness and believers were shunned like lepers—made me shiver.

Dear Jesus, I prayed. *I don't want to go home. Let me dwell in the house of the Lord forever.*

I thought of His words from the Bible: *Do not worry about tomorrow; tomorrow will take care of itself.*

My prayer, coupled with the atmosphere in the church, filled me with a sense of calm. With Midnight Mass nearly over, tears filled my eyes as the choir sang *Narodi Nam Se Kralj Nebeski—Unto Us Was Born the Heavenly King*—one of the most popular Croatian Christmas carols. Composed in the 13th century, the lyrics were a testament to the enduring faith of the local people.

> *Of Mary, the Immaculate Virgin unto us was*
> *born the heavenly King. In this New Year*
> *we rejoice, to the young King, we pray.*

> *He is followed by Saint Stephen, the first*
> *martyr of the Lord God. In this New Year*
> *we rejoice, to the young King, we pray.*

> *God give us health and happiness with it, in this*
> *New Year abundance of everything! In this New*
> *Year we rejoice, to the young King, we pray.*

Waking up on Christmas morning in Međugorje brought back memories from the first days of the apparitions, and it was wonderful to be with my cousins and relatives again. With a house full of people, we had a typical Croatian Christmas celebration, and a much freer one than what I was used to in Sarajevo. It was unthinkable for anyone in Međugorje to work on Christmas.

My family in Međugorje lovingly kept the Christmas traditions of Herzegovina. St. Nicholas had come and gone weeks before. It was not on Christmas Eve but on the eve of his feast day, December 6, when the beloved saint came to fill the boots of good little girls and boys with treats and surprises. He did not travel alone, though. If the child had been naughty, or had not polished his or her boots well, a mischievous creature named Krampus would leave a twig behind. The naughtier the child, the longer the twig.

People celebrated various other feast days and Christmas customs throughout December, but the magic of Christmas Eve was reserved for baby Jesus Himself. He came in the wee hours of the night to bring gifts to all the little boys and girls. Although gifts were always a nice part of Christmas, God was the main focus of the holidays in Herzegovina, and families spent most of their time together praying and attending church services. Every tradition, in fact, was somehow rooted in religion.

One such custom—the burning of the *badnjak* log—brings families together for prayer every Christmas Eve. The ritual varies from region to region, but in Herzegovina, usually the entire family gathers around the fireplace in the *crna kuhinja*, an outdoor kitchen where meats like *pršut* (prosciutto) and *kulen* (sausage) are usually smoked and cured. Outside, the father of the family prepares three logs and gives each one to a different boy. One by one, the boys enter the kitchen carrying the logs while their family members throw grains of wheat on them.

"Happy Christmas Eve," says the first boy, and then he presents the log to the oldest member of the family—usually the grandfather—who then puts it on the fire.

Moments later, the second boy enters and says, "Happy Christmas Eve and the Holy Birth of Jesus." He, too, hands the log to the grand-father and it goes into the fire.

Finally, the third boy comes in. "Happy Christmas Eve, the Holy Birth of Jesus, and St. Stephen," he says.

When all three logs are in the fire, the grandfather prays aloud, "In the name of the Father and of the Son and of the Holy Spirit." And while saying those words, he sprinkles some wine on the fire three times. After that, everyone else says "Amen."

The *badnjak* log represents a traditional story in which the shep-herds of Bethlehem made a fire to warm Mary and the newborn baby Jesus in the stable. As a commemoration of that, family members take turns keeping solitary vigil through the night to ensure that the *badn-jak* stays lit.

Another important part of Christmas was the food. Christmas Eve was a day of fasting, but the next day the entire family gathered for a feast. Preparing the Christmas meal and dining together as a family was a beautiful experience. And it was simply not possible to have Christmas in Herzegovina without copious amounts of Christmas cookies.

As Christmas day wound down for everyone else, I prepared for my apparition, and I was more excited about it than usual. After all, it was Jesus' birthday, and what mother is not filled with joy on her child's birthday? I would get to experience the apparition with the others for the first time in months.

I joined Ivanka, Vicka, Marija, Ivan, and little Jakov in the church. After praying together, we all felt Our Lady's presence. She appeared before us in a gleaming, golden dress unlike anything I had ever seen—the style was identical to the grey one she usually wore, but the fabric looked like molten metal. It *radiated* gold, and Our Lady herself emitted the same lustrous hues.

Describing her dress as "golden" hardly defines it, though. There are no human words that can convey the beauty of such a color. Even the word "color" is inadequate, unless a color can be alive and infused with emotion. I can say that my couch, for example, is a beige color, and in earthly terms I would be correct. The "color" of her dress, however, is almost like light—but an ethereal sort of light that bends, flows, and undulates according to Our Lady's movements and the feelings she wishes to convey.

Our Lady's arms were folded across the front of her dress, which seemed peculiar until I realized she was holding an infant, just like the first time we saw her. She hadn't come again with an infant until now. I yearned for a closer look, but something prevented me from seeing the baby's face. *"Love one another, my children,"* Our Lady said with a warm smile. *"You are brothers and sisters."*

She then blessed us and departed. Regaining my senses, I was surprised to find myself in Međugorje with the others and not at our apartment in Sarajevo. The experience was so intense that I forgot where I was.

The next day, we celebrated the feast of St. Stephen—known as St. Stjepan in Croatian. The people of Međugorje celebrated his feast day on December 26 by spending time with friends and family. According to the Bible, Stephen was an early Christian who preached in Jerusalem. Temple authorities accused him of blasphemy and an angry crowd stoned him to death, making him the first Christian martyr after the crucifixion.

That afternoon, I said *Sretan Imendan*—or Happy Name Day—to Marko's brother, Stjepan. In Croatian tradition, a person's Name Day is celebrated on the feast of his or her namesake saint. People often get more attention on their Name Days than on their birthdays, and this was especially true for Stjepan because his Name Day was a popular Christmastime holiday. Four years younger than Marko, Stjepan was kind and joyful. People loved being around him—his good looks mirrored his personality. Stjepan had deep faith.

I continued to visit Međugorje occasionally, but I never again experienced an apparition with the other visionaries.

When the second semester of school started, I was surprisingly upbeat about going back and seeing my classmates. The teachers at the school were kind to me as well, even though they were all communists. Maybe it was refreshing for them to have a student in class who took academics a little more seriously. For whatever reason, they seemed to empathize with my situation.

My history teacher would often ask me to get up and address the class on certain topics. And my chemistry teacher, a Muslim woman, would always caress my hair when she passed by me in class. The girl who sat next to me leaned over and joked, "She loves you."

"Stop it," I whispered.

When the class got disruptive later, the teacher got upset. "You've all earned an F for today's grade," she said.

I decided to say something. "Please don't do that, Comrade Teacher. We'll be better."

She looked at me tenderly. "Oh, I wasn't talking about you, dear. You don't have to worry."

The girl next to me leaned over again. "See! I told you she loves you!"

One day authorities took me back to Međugorje to undergo a medical examination alongside the other visionaries. It lasted all weekend and left me with no time to prepare for a math test scheduled for Monday morning. I could not tell my math teacher that the apparitions had prevented me from studying, so I came to school unprepared. A boy named Željko Vasilj—who had the same test but at a different hour—gave me his notebook with all of his study notes.

"Use it during the test, but don't get caught," he said. "It's not your fault that you couldn't study."

When I sat down for the test and tried to conceal Luka's notebook on my desk, I was so nervous and uncomfortable that I began fidgeting. I simply could not do it. Out of 35 students, the teacher noticed my nervousness, so he walked over. He picked up the notebook and opened it to see pages scribbled with masculine handwriting and the name *Luka Vasilj* on top. I wanted to die.

"Tell me about this," he said.

My face went completely red. "I'm sorry."

Instead of punishing me like I expected, he placed the opened notebook on my desk in a way that was easier for me to read. "Listen," he said in a quiet voice. "I'll let you copy everything, and I'll grade your work on how well you copy it."

When he walked away, I took a deep breath and looked at the notebook. I still felt unpleasant about it. The answers were right in front of me and the teacher had given me permission to copy them, but it just felt wrong. I closed my test paper and ran out of the classroom.

The next day, I sat in the math class as the teacher called out the test scores, fully expecting to hear the "F" that I deserved.

"Mirjana Dragićević," he said. "B."

"Really?" I said, shocked. I had barely finished any of the test.

A girl jumped up from her desk. "That's not fair, Comrade Teacher! You gave me a C and I studied all night! How can Mirjana get a B when she didn't know anything?"

"Sit down," said the teacher. "It's me who grades the tests, not you."

Later, I tried to make peace with that girl and we became friends, but she would constantly try to persuade me to cut class during our mathematics lecture. I always told her no, but she kept insisting, and to please her, I finally relented.

Sitting with her in the café when we should have been at school, I felt too guilty to enjoy myself. She was laughing and telling a funny story when her eyes froze on the front door and she stopped talking.

"What's wrong?" I said.

"He's here," she whispered.

"Who's here?" Turning to look, a feeling of shame overcame me. Our mathematics teacher was coming through the door. I hid my face and looked at my friend. "Quick, let's get under the table!"

"Too late. He already saw us."

Moments later, I felt a hand on my shoulder. "What would you two like to drink?" said our teacher, sarcastically of course. Again, my face turned red.

The next day in school, I looked in the class attendance log and saw that the teacher had excused my absence but he had not excused the other girl's. It seemed unfair.

"Comrade Teacher, if she gets penalized, then I should, too," I said.

"You're not the type to skip class," he said. "I know your friend made you do it."

In truth, he knew my predicament. The police had taken me for so many interrogations that I had already missed an excessive number of classes that year. I even missed entire days because they sometimes took me in the morning and did not release me until the afternoon. I never knew what each day would bring, and that is exactly what the communists wanted—to keep me in a perpetual state of wondering. The police obviously hoped that I would flunk due to low attendance, but my teachers did not allow that to happen.

I was especially shy as a little girl, so when the apparitions began,
I had to quickly adjust to being the center of attention.

CHAPTER 14

"If you are not afraid and witness courageously, the truth will miraculously win."

— *From Our Lady's Message of June 2, 2015*

FOR THE FIRST 18 months, Our Lady came every day. When she spoke to me, it was as if the whole universe was speaking to me. I drew strength and love from those moments—strength to persevere in my daily struggles, and love to forgive the people who persecuted me. When you see Our Lady, it is impossible to hate anyone because you become aware that she loves even the person who mistreats you. That person is her child as much as you are, and her love for all of her children is indescribable. I have never seen that kind of love on Earth.

Initially the thought of not being in Međugorje with the other visionaries troubled me, but eventually I realized that I did not need to be with anybody. Perhaps it would have been nice to have the others to talk to since they were living the same experience, but I was alone in Sarajevo. Instead, I had God, and I shared everything with Him. Through my prayers after each apparition, I received the strength to continue and comprehend.

On December 23, 1982, Our Lady appeared to me as usual, and, like always, it was a beautiful experience that filled my soul with joy. But towards the end, she looked at me with tenderness and said, *"On Christmas Day, I will appear to you for the last time."*

The apparition ended and I was left stunned. I had clearly heard what she said, but I could not believe it. How could I live without apparitions? It seemed impossible and I prayed intensely for it not to be true.

The next day, on Christmas Eve, she again tried to prepare me, but I still could not comprehend it. I spent most of the night begging God to give me more time with her.

While my parents and brother celebrated Christmas day with singing, prayers and food, I was far too consumed with worry to join in. There I was, surrounded by my loving family, about to spend part of Christmas with the same woman who gave birth to Jesus two thousand years before, and I could not even smile.

My anticipation soared as the time of the apparition approached. My mother, father and brother, wearing their finest Christmas attire, kneeled beside me. We prayed the rosary in preparation for her coming. When Our Lady finally appeared, she smiled gently and greeted me in her usual motherly way. I was captivated; her dress radiated the same spectacular golden color it had the previous Christmas, and in that moment—with all of her grace and beauty shining down on me—it was impossible to be sad anymore.

My parents told me later that my final daily apparition lasted for an extraordinary 45 minutes. Our Lady and I talked about many things. We summarized our entire 18 months together—everything we had said to each other and everything she had revealed to me. She entrusted me with the tenth and final secret, and she explained that I will need to choose a priest for a special role. Ten days before the date of the event foretold in the first secret, I am to tell him what will happen and when. He and I are then supposed to pray and fast for seven days, and, three days before the event, the priest will reveal it to the world. All ten secrets will be revealed in this way.

Our Lady also gave me a precious gift. She told me that she would appear to me once a year, on March 18, for the rest of my life. March 18 is my birthday, but Our Lady did not choose that date for that reason. For her, my birthday is no different from anyone else's. Only when the things contained in the secrets start to happen will the world understand why she chose the 18th of March. The significance of the date will be clear. She also said that I would experience some additional apparitions.

She then held out something like a rolled-up scroll, explaining that all ten secrets were written on it, and that I should show it to the priest I choose when the time comes to reveal them. I took it from her hand without looking at it.

"Now you will have to turn to God in faith like any other person," she said. *"Mirjana, I have chosen you; I have confided in you everything that is essential. I have also shown you many terrible things. You must now bear it all with courage. Think of me and think of the tears I must shed for that. You must remain brave. You have quickly grasped the messages. You must also understand now that I have to go away. Be courageous."*

She promised to always be near me and to help me in my most difficult situations, but the pain I felt in my soul was nearly unbearable. Our Lady was aware of my torment and she asked me to pray. I recited the prayer that I often prayed when I was alone with her—the *Salve Regina*:

*Hail Holy Queen, Mother of Mercy, our
life, our sweetness and our hope.*

*To thee do we cry, poor banished children of Eve. To thee do we
send up our sighs, mourning and weeping in this valley of tears.*

*Turn, then, most gracious advocate,
thine eyes of mercy toward us, and after this, our
exile, show unto us the blessed fruit of thy womb,
Jesus. O clement, o loving, o sweet Virgin Mary.*

She smiled in the most motherly way, and then she was gone. I collapsed on the floor and sobbed. I could never have imagined a more sorrowful Christmas.

How? I thought. *How can it be that I will no longer see Our Lady every day?*

I realized that I was still holding the scroll she had given me. Having always seen Our Lady as a physical being, it seemed natural at that time to take the object from her hand, just as I would from anyone. But now that the apparition was over, I was awestruck to see the scroll still with me. *How did that happen?* I wondered. *How am I holding an object from Heaven?* Like so many occurrences over the previous 18 months, I could only explain it as a mystery of God.

Beige in color, the scroll was made of a material akin to parchment—not quite paper and not quite fabric, but perhaps something in between. I carefully unrolled it and found all ten secrets written in a simple and elegant cursive handwriting. There were no decorations or illustrations on the parchment; each secret was described in simple, clear words, similar to how Our Lady originally explained them to me. The secrets were not numbered, but they appeared in order, one after another, with the first secret at the top and the tenth at the bottom, and included the dates of the future events.

At that moment, however, I was too miserable to think about the future.

I lay in bed that night unable to sleep. I convinced myself that it was all some sort of trial—that Our Lady was testing me for some greater reason—because living without her daily visits seemed impossible. It could not be.

The next day, I knelt down and prayed at the time Our Lady had always appeared. When the usual time of her appearance passed and I was still alone, sorrow overcame me and I cried profusely. My mother and father came in and tried to console me.

"Please don't do this to yourself, Mirjana," said my dad.

My mom embraced me. "I'm so sorry, dear."

For the next several hours, I knelt there praying and sobbing, begging Our Lady to come. But she did not appear. I wanted to die. Even the worst of my suffering at the hands of the communists was nothing compared to how I felt in that moment. The words of the *Salve Regina* suddenly spoke to me in a way they never had before—there I was, a poor banished child of Eve, mourning and weeping in a valley of tears, crying out to the Mother of Mercy from my exile.

I continued doing the same thing every afternoon for the next ten days—I knelt and prayed and waited, and then, when she did not come, I collapsed in misery and tears. The other five visionaries were still seeing Our Lady, so why was I the only one who had to live without her? Now I knew why she gave me more detailed messages, and why she entrusted me with the secrets faster. She knew that our time together was limited.

My mother constantly pleaded with me to calm down and pray with her. She was full of love and patience, and she wanted to help me understand. "Just as you accepted the daily apparitions," she said, "now you have to accept that there won't be any more."

Her words gave me comfort, but I still fell into deep states of depression anytime I thought about Our Lady's absence for too long. Aside from yearning for the apparitions, the stress of receiving all the secrets in such a short time also weighed on my heart. The teachers and students at my school were baffled; the girl they all knew as sunny and optimistic was suddenly miserable. Even Azra was now trying to cheer *me* up.

I felt guilty for being so sad, which just made me sadder. How could I claim to be a believer if I refused to accept God's plan? I knew I had to trust, but the pain seemed insurmountable. Our Lady's promise of a yearly apparition was a tiny sparkle of hope and I counted the days until March 18, but sometimes I feared that I might never see her again.

What if she only told me I'd see her again to calm me down? I thought, but then I reassured myself. *No, Our Lady only speaks truth.*

My desire to see Our Lady was so strong that I finally decided to attempt drawing her. Every artist has a focus and by chance mine had always been portraits of girls and women. If I could capture just a little of her beauty on paper, then at least I would have something to gaze at in her absence. I took out my drawing supplies and sketched her outline, her dress, her outstretched arms, and even the locks of long, dark hair that peek out from behind her veil. But when I tried to draw her face, it looked nothing like her. I tried repeatedly but my disappointment grew with each unsuccessful attempt. Why couldn't I do it?

Eventually I understood that hers is another kind of beauty altogether. Just as words cannot describe how she looks, neither can art. Great artists have attempted likenesses of Our Lady according to our descriptions, but none came close. Even the world's finest paintings, icons, and sculptures of the Blessed Mother are only shadows of her splendor.

When word reached Međugorje that my daily apparitions had ceased, everyone was shocked. Speculation about the secrets became rampant, but I was careful not to say anything that might even hint at their hour and contents. I wondered if we visionaries should have even mentioned that we had received secrets; it often seemed like people were focusing more on those than on the messages.

When Our Lady first entrusted the secrets to me, they caused me a great amount of stress and anxiety. In time, however, God helped me comprehend and accept everything. People have always asked me about the secrets, and I cannot fault them for being curious. Many have a natural fascination with the unknown. Some have said that I am privileged to know what will happen in the future, but I do not see it that way. It would be far easier for me if I could reveal everything now. But the secrets are God's will. I am aware of my human weaknesses and I can say with certainty that it is not me who keeps the secrets; it is only with God's help that I am able to do it.

Jakov was at an age when most children do not know how to keep secrets. Policemen, family members and even priests tried to get him to reveal what he knew, but nobody succeeded. I often joke that even now, as adults, if I tell Jakov anything private, the entire village knows the next day—and yet he keeps Our Lady's secrets.

I unrolled the parchment and kept it with my important documents, but I constantly worried that someone might find it and read it. One day, when my cousin and a friend were in our apartment, it was as if something told me to show it to them. I resisted at first, but the feeling was overwhelming. I removed the parchment from its hiding place. My cousin held it in her hands and said that she saw some sort of prayer or poem. My friend, however, said she saw a letter in which a person was asking for help. Neither of them saw the same thing. I realized then that only I could read what was actually written on it. Most likely, it had to happen that way for me to have peace, and I never thought about it or worried about it after that. Our Lady never mentioned the incident.

Many people wondered why Our Lady gave me the parchment. Some assumed it was so I would not forget the secrets, but that's not accurate. If I forgot any details, God is almighty and He could give me the gift of remembering them at the right moment. I interpreted the parchment differently—its existence means that I do not necessarily have to be alive to reveal the secrets. Otherwise I would be too privileged. If they were not written, it would mean that I could not die today, and that I'm guaranteed to be alive when the time comes to reveal them. No human being lives forever, and no one is invincible.

There are things that I am not supposed to think about. Our Lady will take care of it all. Through God's will, she knows how I am supposed to fulfill everything. My task is to be obedient, and nothing else, because I cannot change anything.

If I was not capable of keeping the secrets, then Our Lady wouldn't have entrusted them to me. I've always felt that God has been leading me, and that I'm only an instrument. Who am I without Him, anyway? I rely on prayer and fasting to help me live according to His will, and to help me fulfill my role as a messenger.

Contrary to what many people think, the secrets are hardly on my mind. If I was not always asked about them, days and months could pass without me thinking of the secrets. Perhaps it is a gift of God, or a result of my prayers.

When people ask me gloomy questions about Biblical catastrophes and the end of the world, I feel sorry for them. Some seem to think that all the secrets are negative. Maybe they have a guilty conscience; maybe they are afraid of how they've lived their life and so they fear God's punishment. Perhaps when we do not have enough good inside, we expect bad things. But nothing can be changed by worrying about the secrets. Instead, people should only worry about how to change themselves.

People have asked me how I cope with the burden of the secrets, but I often think that the secrets burden others more than they do me. The people who are concerned about the secrets have not seen Our Lady and do not know about God's complete project—why Our Lady comes here at all, or what she's preparing us for. But if your life is in her hands, and God is in your heart, what can harm you?

If everyone knew me and could see how much I laugh and joke, no one would be afraid of the secrets. Those who truly know God's love should be full of joy. It does not make sense to talk about the future when any of us might die tomorrow. Our Lady constantly reminds us about that in her messages, like when she said, *"My children, your life is only a blink in contrast to eternal life."*

I cannot divulge much more about the secrets, but I can say this—Our Lady is planning to change the world. She did not come to announce our destruction; she came to save us, and with her Son, she will triumph over evil.

If our Mother has promised to defeat evil, then what do we have to fear?

The three visionaries of Fátima, Portugal, in 1917.

CHAPTER 15

"My beloved children, may the words of my Son and His love be the first and the last thought of your day."
— *From Our Lady's Message of January 2, 2016*

"*WHAT I STARTED in Fátima, I will complete in Međugorje. My heart will triumph.*"

When Our Lady said these words, all I knew about Fátima was that it was vaguely similar to Međugorje—the Blessed Mother had appeared to three children there. But after this message, I became curious about it, and the more I learned, the more I began to see deeper connections between Fátima and Međugorje.

On May 13, 1981, exactly 64 years after the first apparition in Fátima—and just six weeks *before* the Blessed Mother first appeared in Međugorje—Pope John Paul II was shot in St. Peter's Square by a gunman. I remember being horrified when I heard about it on the news. Why would anyone want to kill the pope?

Four bullets hit the Holy Father and his injuries were nearly fatal, but he miraculously recovered and attributed his survival to the intercession of Our Lady. "It was a mother's hand that guided the bullet's path," he said.

Many people suspected that the assassination attempt was a Soviet plot. The pope's message of faith and courage was a clear threat to communism, especially when he brought that message to his own people in Poland.

Reading about Lourdes taught me that the Blessed Virgin Mary had appeared in other places, but I was surprised to discover that we were not the first to receive secrets, either. On May 13, 1917, ten-year-old Lucia, eight-year-old Francisco and seven-year-old Jacinta were tending their sheep on the outskirts of Fátima, Portugal when they saw what they thought was a flash of lightning. Thinking a storm was brewing, they began to herd their sheep together. But when another flash caught their attention, they turned and saw a beautiful lady suspended in the air above an oak tree. She was dressed in white and "shining more brilliantly than the sun."

"Be not afraid," she said. *"I shall do you no harm."*

Lucia, the oldest of the children, asked her, "Where have you come from?"

"I come from Heaven."

The lady asked the children to come back to see her on the thirteenth of every month. The sixth and final apparition took place on October 13, 1917 when over 70,000 people witnessed the Miracle of the Sun when the sun seemed to "dance" in the sky.

Just like in Fátima, the first words Our Lady said to us in Međugorje were "Be not afraid," and John Paul II said the same thing when he addressed the crowd in St. Peter's Square for the first time as the new pope. We were certainly frightened on June 25, 1981 when we stood in front of Our Lady for the first time, but I've come to understand that every word she says to us has a deeper meaning. When she speaks to me, she speaks to the entire world. As the Queen of Peace, and as our Mother, she comes to tell all her children "Be not afraid" because she will never abandon us.

When the apparitions began in Fátima, Europe was engulfed in the First World War. I remember seeing the plaque on the *Latin Bridge* near my school in Sarajevo indicating the spot where Archduke Ferdinand, heir to the throne of Austria-Hungary, was assassinated in 1914. That spark of violence lit a wildfire of unprecedented carnage across Europe, and 17 million people died in just a few years. By the spring of 1917, Pope Benedict XV had failed in every attempt at diplomacy and was dismayed by the bleak outlook. He realized there was only one person left to turn to.

On May 5, 1917, he sent out a pastoral letter imploring every person of faith to ask the Blessed Mother to intercede.

Excerpt from Pastoral Letter from Pope Benedict XV - *To Mary, who is the Mother of Mercy and omnipotent by grace, let loving and devout appeal go up from every corner of the earth—from noble temples and tiniest chapels, from royal palaces and mansions of the rich as from the poorest hut—from blood-drenched plains and seas. Let it bear to her the anguished cry of mothers and wives, the wailing of innocent little ones, the sighs of every generous heart: that Her most tender and benign solicitude may be moved and the peace we ask for be obtained for our agitated world.* - **May 5, 1917**

The pope also mandated that the invocation "Queen of Peace, pray for us" be added to the *Litany of Loreto*—a series of Marian prayers often recited during processions.

The Blessed Mother appeared in Fátima just days after the pope's letter went out. During her first apparition, she asked Lucia, Jacinta and Francisco if they were willing to do acts of penance and make personal sacrifices to save sinners, to which they all said yes.

"Pray the Rosary every day," Our Lady said, *"to obtain peace for the world and the end of the war."* Then, she rose towards the sky and disappeared.

The children continued to see her once a month. During the apparition of July 13, 1917, she entrusted them with three secrets, two of which concerned the future.

When Lucia announced that she had been given secrets, she probably faced the same kind of fearful speculation that we've had to endure all these years. But the Blessed Mother did not entrust me with secrets for the purpose of causing fear. When you come to know Heaven, you learn to accept the will of God with all your heart.

Why be afraid of what might happen tomorrow if we don't even know what will happen in an hour? The only thing we need to fear is sin, which distances us from God. Fear of the future, and fear of the secrets, wastes our limited time on Earth. Your future could end today. We should cherish life while it lasts.

So, when Our Lady told us that Međugorje would be the fulfillment of Fátima and that her heart would triumph, it was a message of hope, not gloom. She was reminding us that when we walk with her we have nothing to worry about. But even now, people often ask me how they should prepare for the time of the secrets. Should they stock their basements with food? Move to the countryside and live off the land? Buy a weapon to protect themselves?

I tell them, "Yes, you should get a weapon, and you should use it often." I show them my rosary. "This is the only weapon you'll ever need. But it only works if you use it."

In one of her earliest messages, Our Lady told us, *"Prayer and fasting can stop wars and change the laws of nature."* She was not speaking figuratively; prayer is more effective at creating change than anything we can do alone. The rosary is an especially powerful prayer.

So, should you prepare for the future? Yes. Prepare by making sure your soul is always ready to stand in front of God—not by building bunkers and stockpiling supplies. No one can live in this world forever. We should focus on what comes next. I have experienced Paradise, and I can attest that there's no place on Earth—no mountain range, tropical island or seventh wonder—that compares to what awaits those who choose light over darkness.

"God gave you free will to choose life or death," Our Lady said on

March 18, 2003 during my annual apparition. *"My children, without God you can do nothing; do not forget this even for a moment."*

Our Lady's message is clear: we are all destined for eternity, but our actions on Earth dictate what it will be like for us. Our Lady showed me just a hint of what awaits those who reject God's love, and even the little I know is enough for me to feel immense sadness for every wayward soul.

In Fátima, Our Lady showed the seers a vision of Hell. According to Lucia, the Blessed Mother showed them "a vast sea of fire. Plunged in this fire, we saw demons and souls. The latter were like transparent burning embers, all blackened or burnished bronze, having human forms."

According to eyewitnesses at the apparition, it was during this vision that Lucia cried out with fright. The lost souls, said Lucia, were being thrown about in the chaos "like sparks in huge fires," and she could hear them groaning with despair. She described the demons mixed in amongst the souls as having a "terrifying and repellent likeness to frightful and unknown animals, black and transparent like burning coals."

Lucia said that the vision of Hell lasted only a moment. When it was over, Our Lady dictated a special prayer to the children.

"When you pray the Rosary," the Virgin told her, *"after each mystery, say:* O my Jesus, forgive us our sins, save us from the fires of hell. Lead all souls to heaven, especially those most in need of your mercy."

The so-called "Fátima prayer" is now recited throughout the world whenever people pray the rosary. I was taught from an early age to include it in my own prayers, although I did not know its origin until years later. I must admit that I wasn't as fond of it then as I am now. The concept of Hell was always difficult for me to comprehend, and I struggled with it even after the apparitions began.

If a man commits a crime and goes to prison, I thought, he's usually released and forgiven after he does his time. Sentencing a soul to an eternity of suffering seemed contrary to the merciful and loving God I had come to know.

So, one day during an apparition I asked Our Lady, "How can God be so unmerciful as to condemn people to Hell for eternity?"

"Souls who go to Hell have ceased thinking favorably of God," Our Lady told me. In life they cursed Him, she explained, and in death they will continue to do the same. In essence, they've already become part of Hell. God does not send people to Hell. They choose to be there.

"But even if people go to Hell, can't they pray for salvation?" I asked. Surely God could still deliver them, I thought.

"People in Hell do not pray at all," said Our Lady, explaining that they blame God for everything instead. They become one with Hell and they get used to it. They rage against God, and they suffer, but they always refuse to pray. In Hell, they hate God even more than they hated Him on Earth.

Of course, the line between salvation and exile is not as black-and-white as some people seem to think. Everything in the hereafter is governed by love. The Church teaches of a place between Heaven and Hell, and Our Lady has confirmed its existence. I asked her once where most people go when they die. She said that most go to Purgatory before ultimately passing through to Heaven. The next greatest number go to Hell, and few go directly to Heaven.

Our Lady once showed me a brief glimpse of Purgatory. In something similar to a movie projection, I saw a vast, gloomy mist in which obscure human forms shivered and writhed. The vision only lasted a few seconds and it troubled me deeply, but Our Lady assured me that Purgatory was more of a mercy than a penalty. *"Since nothing can live in the sight of God but pure love,"* she said, *"God's justice cleanses."*

There are different levels to Purgatory, she explained—levels closer to Hell and levels closer to Heaven. Every soul there is already saved, which is why I envision Purgatory to be more like an outer rim of Heaven instead of a separate place altogether. Even the word "place" is inadequate to describe something that exists beyond the temporal world.

John Paul II described Purgatory as "the process of purification for those who die in the love of God but who are not completely imbued with that love."

He also said, "The term does not indicate a place, but a condition of existence."

Our Lady told me that our prayers on Earth can help the souls there. Occasionally a person will ask me to pray for a loved one who they believe is in Purgatory, but only God knows where our deceased ones are. The most beautiful thing we can do is pray and fast for our deceased, and participate in Masses while keeping them in our hearts and minds.

John Paul II said that every attachment to evil and imperfection in our soul must be eliminated before we can enter God's Kingdom, adding, "Those who live in this state of purification after death are not separated from God but are immersed in the love of Christ."

In the early days, whenever I tried to explain what Our Lady was asking of us, Uncle Šimun always used to joke and say, "Don't tell me everything! The less I know, the better for me. If I can just grab on to the edge of Purgatory with my little finger, then I can pull myself up and I'll be fine."

The Bible speaks of different levels in God's Kingdom. In *2 Corinthians 12*, Paul wrote about his own "visions and revelations" after he was taken up to "the third heaven," where he "heard privileged things which no one may utter."

Similar to how I feel during the apparitions, Paul was confused about how he experienced his vision, writing "whether in the body or out of the body I do not know; God knows."

Vicka and Jakov told me that on All Souls' Day in November, 1981, Our Lady appeared unexpectedly and said that she would take them to Heaven.

Jakov panicked. He thought she meant forever. "Don't take me!" he shrieked. "Take Vicka! She has seven brothers and sisters, and I'm my mother's only child!"

Our Lady smiled, told them not to be afraid, and took them by their hands. They found themselves in an expansive place filled with a beautiful light and indescribable joy. They also saw Purgatory and Hell. Even today Jakov does not like to speak about Hell, but Vicka's description was strikingly similar to Lucia's—an ocean of raging flames filled with souls and grotesque beings.

"Do not be afraid," Our Lady said to them. *"I have shown you Hell so that you may know the state of those who are there."*

I've never seen Hell. I've never wanted to. But Our Lady showed me a glimpse of Heaven in the same way she showed me Purgatory—like a scene from a film. The people there were youthful, joyful, and dressed in pastel robes, but they looked different from people on Earth, radiating light from within. They dwelt in an endless space surrounded by the most beautiful trees and meadows, all of which emanated the same light. There was something like a sky overhead which seemed to be *made* of that light, and the light itself was imbued with joy—the kind of joy that makes you want to sing or cry.

I cannot speak for God, but I believe that if a person lives with peace, honesty, and love, then he or she can go to Heaven. Faith and prayer help us achieve that. One does not have to do miracles. Certainly, we are called to strive for holiness—or at least something better than just getting into Purgatory with our little finger—but, in the end, I think it all comes down to love. Did we love God? Did we love our neighbor? Did we love ourselves? More importantly, how did we express that love?

With a terrible war smoldering across Europe in 1917, the world must have seemed totally devoid of love before the Blessed Mother came to Fátima. But her apparitions brought countless people together to pray for peace and the war ended the following year. That was no surprise to Lucia, because while the first secret was a vision of the spiritual realm, the second one was a detailed prediction about the world's future.

"You have seen Hell where the souls of poor sinners go," Our Lady told the three visionaries. *"To save them, God wishes to establish in the world devotion to my Immaculate Heart."*

She went on to say that WWI would end, but a worse one would break out if people continued to offend God. Russia, she warned, would spread "her errors" throughout the world, "causing wars and persecutions of the Church." But the Blessed Mother also revealed a remedy—a period of peace would be granted to the world, she promised, if the pope consecrated Russia to her Immaculate Heart.

Here, again, we see an example of the immeasurable power of prayer. As Jesus said, "Therefore I tell you, whatever you ask for in prayer, believe that you have received it, and it will be yours." (Matthew 11:24)

It was also in 1917—the same year this secret was given—that Vladimir Lenin led the Bolshevik Revolution in Russia, and the Soviet Union formed soon after. Two decades later, an estimated 50 million people died during the Second World War, and then, just as predicted, communism spread rapidly throughout the world, infiltrating China, Poland, Cuba, and, of course, Yugoslavia. Decades of suffering ensued. By the early 1980s, the Cold War had brought the world to the brink of nuclear catastrophe.

After almost being assassinated, Pope John Paul II noted the "mysterious coincidence with the anniversary of the first apparition at Fátima." The date connection inspired him to study the Fátima apparitions as he lay in his hospital bed. With communism threatening world peace, he became determined to fulfill Our Lady's request by consecrating Russia to the Immaculate Heart of Mary. He knew it would take time to gather the bishops and cardinals for the consecration, so, as a sort of preemptor, he composed a prayer for what he called an *Act of Entrustment*, which was celebrated on June 7, 1981 in the Basilica of St. Mary Major.

Excerpt from the Act of Entrustment by Pope John Paul II -
"Mother of all individuals and peoples, you know all their sufferings and hopes," he prayed. "In your motherly heart you feel all the struggles between good and evil, between light and darkness that convulse the world. Take under your motherly protection the whole human family, which with affectionate love we entrust to you, O Mother. May there

dawn for everyone the time of peace and freedom, the time of truth, of justice and of hope." – **June 7, 1981**

I was not aware of his prayer then, but just a few weeks later, Our Lady appeared for the first time in Međugorje.

Pope John Paul II made a pilgrimage to Fátima on May 13, 1982 and placed one of the bullets that almost killed him in the crown of Our Lady's statue. In his homily that day, the pope spoke about "places in which a special presence of the Mother is felt," adding, "These places sometimes radiate their light over a great distance and draw people from afar. Their radiance may extend over a diocese, a whole nation, or at times over several countries and even continents. These places are the Marian sanctuaries or shrines."

The pope completed the consecration on March 25, 1984. As if on cue, the USSR suffered a series of military disasters, the worst of which took place on May 13, 1984, the anniversary of Fátima. After the election of moderate Mikhail Gorbachev, the dominos continued to fall. The Berlin Wall came down in 1989, and the first Christian Mass since the Communist Revolution was held at the iconic *Cathedral of the Intercession of the Most Holy Virgin* in Moscow's Red Square on October 13, 1990—which happened to be the anniversary of Fátima's Miracle of the Sun. A year later, the USSR was officially dissolved.

It seems that the second secret of Fátima came true, but what about the third secret? Years earlier, Lucia had put it in a sealed envelope and entrusted it to the Church. With speculation about its contents running rampant, the Vatican finally released the third secret in the year 2000.

Lucia claimed she was shown a vision of an angel about to strike the earth with a flaming sword. But "the splendor" emanating from Our Lady's right hand extinguished the flames. Next, Lucia saw a pope passing through a "city half in ruins," and then climbing a mountain with a large cross on it. When he reached the top of the mountain, he and other priests, nuns and lay people were killed by soldiers. Two angels appeared beneath the cross to gather the blood of the martyrs.

Some speculated that the third secret predicted the assassination attempt on John Paul II, while others—citing the fact that he survived—believed it represented something that had not yet happened.

I'm not personally called to interpret the secrets of Fátima, but Our Lady affirmed in Međugorje that both apparitions are connected to the triumph of her heart.

Third Secret of Fátima as written by Sr. Lucia - *After the two parts which I have already explained, at the left of Our Lady and a little above, we saw an Angel with a flaming sword in his left hand; flashing, it gave out flames that looked as though they would set the world on fire; but they died out in contact with the splendor that Our Lady radiated towards him from her right hand: pointing to the earth with his right hand, the Angel cried out in a loud voice: 'Penance, Penance, Penance!'. And we saw in an immense light that is God: 'something similar to how people appear in a mirror when they pass in front of it' a Bishop dressed in White 'we had the impression that it was the Holy Father'. Other Bishops, Priests, men and women Religious going up a steep mountain, at the top of which there was a big Cross of rough-hewn trunks as of a cork-tree with the bark; before reaching there the Holy Father passed through a big city half in ruins and half trembling with halting step, afflicted with pain and sorrow, he prayed for the souls of the corpses he met on his way; having reached the top of the mountain, on his knees at the foot of the big Cross he was killed by a group of soldiers who fired bullets and arrows at him, and in the same way there died one after another the other Bishops, Priests, men and women Religious, and various lay people of different ranks and positions. Beneath the two arms of the Cross there were two Angels each with a crystal aspersorium in his hand, in which they gathered up the blood of the Martyrs and with it sprinkled the souls that were making their way to God.*

I often prayed for Fr. Jozo Zovko in the years after he was arrested.

CHAPTER 16

"Much will be required of the person entrusted with much, and still more will be demanded of the person entrusted with more."

— *Jesus in the Gospel of Luke (12:48)*

IN THE BEGINNING of 1983, I finally came to accept that my daily apparitions were over. Through persistent prayer and fasting, I understood that I was the same as everyone else to Our Lady. In her eyes, there were no privileged ones. If I had a cross to carry, I could no longer rely on my daily apparitions to bring me comfort. I had to pray like everyone else.

I looked forward to March 18, 1983 like an impatient child waiting for her birthday. March 18 *was* my birthday, but I did not care about receiving gifts or turning a year older. I just wanted to see her again.

On February 18—exactly one month before my birthday—I received news that was both unexpected and fantastic: Fr. Jozo was out of prison. The government had reduced his three-year sentence to 18 months. Another priest had already filled his position at St. James Church, so he was sent to work in the parish of Bukovica and then later at St. Elijah Church in Tihaljina, not far from Međugorje. When I visited him, he did not speak about prison. If his experiences there traumatized him, he hid it well, although the scars on his face hinted at a more violent experience than his smile implied.

I had prayed for Fr. Jozo every day, and the stories I heard about his incarceration seemed to confirm that Our Lady protected him just as she promised.

He was imprisoned with murderers, thieves, and the types of major criminals one only hears about in the news. The guards beat him and tormented him, forced him to do hard labor, and intentionally spread terrible rumors about him through the prison population. But Fr. Jozo held tight to his faith and never denied what he believed to be true about Međugorje.

The prisoners, many of whom were atheists, Muslims and Orthodox, started to see something special about him, so they began asking him about God. He told them about Our Lady, about Međugorje, and about the mercy of Jesus.

Fr. Jozo later said that he was happy and at peace in prison because he had the opportunity to lead troubled men to Jesus. The greatest suffering was not having his Bible, his rosary, or permission to celebrate Mass.

Before long, some of the prison guards became frightened of him; they claimed to see strange lights in his cell at night, and, on many mornings, they found his cell door inexplicably unlocked. Fr. Jozo later revealed that Our Lady had appeared to him in prison, although he never expanded on the encounters. Those had been private meetings, he inferred, ones which gave him great comfort. Even after his release, the communists continued to harass him, but he remained a steadfast advocate of Međugorje.

Despite my joy about Fr. Jozo's release, I was preoccupied with the promised apparition, and somewhat nervous as well. What if she did not come? That possibility was too awful to ponder.

In the nights leading up to my 18th birthday, I could hardly sleep. I woke early that day and prepared by praying. My family gathered around and joined me in the rosary. My anticipation was stronger than ever before, and when that familiar feeling began to build within me—stealing my breath as it intensified—I was almost surprised. Suddenly it felt like my heart was about to burst inside my chest and I saw Our Lady in front of me. It was like a rebirth.

As I gazed at her beauty and savored the love that radiated from her, my only desire was for her to take me with her. Life on Earth seemed meaningless and bleak in comparison to that moment in her presence. I longed to be with her forever. But it was over all too soon, and after she left, I was crushed with the realization that I would not see her again for another 365 days.

Wrought with emotion, I knelt there sobbing for a long time. People who see me when an apparition ends say I have a tough time "coming back to reality," but I think of it differently: nothing is *closer* to reality than being with Our Lady. Heaven is the ultimate reality, and the Blessed Mother is more real than any person on this planet. The pain of leaving such indescribable bliss is immense. Still, her return filled me with peace because it confirmed that she'd visit me at least once a year for as long as I live.

When I gathered enough strength to lift my head, I saw that my parents and brother looked worried. They had never seen me so emotional during an apparition, they said. But they also seemed nearly as thankful as I was that Our Lady had returned, even if just for one day of the year. It reminded all of us how blessed we were to have had her company for 18 months.

At that point, I would have liked to have remained in continuous prayer, replaying the apparition over and over in my thoughts, but the so-called "real world" required my urgent attention. My final year of high school was drawing to a close and I was no longer the excellent student I used to be. The stress of being constantly harassed by the police—coupled with the depression I experienced after my daily apparitions ceased—had taken a toll on my grades.

But I was determined to graduate. All I had to do was pass the final exam. I studied hard, knowing that my four years of high school would all be in vain if I failed.

The night before the final exam, the headmistress of my school called our apartment. When I answered the phone, she asked to speak with my dad. I found it strange because no one from the school had ever called our home. I wondered if I had done something wrong.

"Why do you need my dad, Comrade Headmistress?" I asked.

"I have to ask him a favor," she said.

I gave the phone to my dad. He listened intently, barely saying anything. All sorts of thoughts ran through my head. What could she be saying when I had done nothing wrong? I knew she was Serbian and a member of the Communist Party, but she had always been kind to me.

Moments later, my dad hung up the phone and immediately left the apartment. Where could he be going at such a late hour? It all seemed so peculiar, but I could not let anything distract me from preparing for the exam.

I was still studying when I heard him come home. I went to wish my mom and dad goodnight, and I was troubled to find them both crying in the kitchen.

"What happened?" I said.

My mother wouldn't look at me. "Your dad's cousin died," she said.

It was a distant cousin, my mom added, and one I had never met before. I found it strange that they were crying for a cousin who I did not even know. Still, I was too focused on studying to ask them any questions.

The next morning, confident that I would pass, I was eager to take the exam. But just as I was about to leave for school, my dad stopped me.

"Listen, Mirjana," he said. "If you pass, you pass. But if you don't, it doesn't matter. You know that you will always have us, and you will always have your home. Just come back to me safe and sound."

It seemed like a strange thing for him to say, and the seriousness on his face was even more unusual. "Do you doubt me?" I said. "What's going on with you?"

"Just don't forget what I told you," he said. "Come back home."

It was not exactly the kind of thing one wants to hear before a big test, but by the time I got to class, I had dismissed my father's cryptic pep talk as nothing more than a misguided attempt to show his love. He *was* a man, after all.

When I began taking the exam, however, things got even weirder. The final exam was divided into multiple parts, with a separate test for each subject. Normally students would have a break after finishing each part, but the headmistress kept calling on me first for each subject. Exhausted, I finally spoke up.

"Comrade Headmistress," I said. "Can I at least take a breath between exams?"

"No," she snapped.

Her terse response disturbed me. Why was she so insistent about giving me the exams back to back? Was she trying to overwhelm me so that I would fail? I took a deep breath and prayed for help from above. No one was going to stop me from graduating, not after all the hardships I had endured. I set about completing the tests with determination, however fast they came.

When I was done, the headmistress graded my exam with uncharacteristic speed. "You passed," she said. "Now you can go home."

I was thrilled. Despite all the difficulties, I would graduate! But I wanted to stay and see how my fellow students fared. They'd probably want to celebrate at a café after school. "I'd like to wait here until everyone finishes," I said, not thinking it would be a problem.

The headmistress leaned forward and looked at me. "Go home," she said sternly and with such conviction that I immediately turned and left.

My feelings were a little hurt, but I told myself that I wouldn't let her brusqueness bother me. Perhaps she was just having a bad day.

I prayed for her, just as Our Lady had taught me to do. You do not know what crosses people might be carrying, she had said. By the time I reached our apartment, I felt much better. In fact, I was joyful.

"I passed!" I exclaimed as I walked through the door. "I'm graduating!"

My parents looked at me with surprise, neither of them saying a word, and then they looked at each other. It was not quite the congratulatory praise I had been expecting. They then asked me to sit down. Their faces seemed to be marred by a day of stress and worry.

"Is this about the cousin who died?" I asked. "I'm fine, really. I didn't even know him."

"No, dear," said my mom. "It's about school."

I suddenly felt worried. Had the headmistress missed something while grading my exam? Did I not truly pass?

"Yesterday the state police went to your school," said my dad.

He went on to explain that the police told the headmistress that she must not allow me to pass the final exam. They then asked her when I was supposed to take it so that they could come to the school at that time.

"I can't remember at the moment," she said to the police. "There are so many children."

"Inform us as soon as you find out," said one of the policemen, and then they left.

The headmistress had agonized over how to handle the situation. It didn't seem fair to her that I should fail through no fault of my own, but she knew that defying the police meant putting her career at risk and tarnishing her standing in the Communist Party. In the political vocabulary of that time, she would have been labeled a "subversive factor" and ostracized by her peers. She finally spoke with her daughter, who also worked as an educator, and explained the situation.

"Mirjana is a good and honest child who has done everything as she should have," said the headmistress. "She has never been problematic. It would pain me to stifle her future, but what choice do I have?"

Her daughter thought about it for a moment and said, "Mother, you should act according to your conscience. You are first and foremost a teacher, and a teacher is called to educate children, not work against them."

After speaking with her daughter, she decided it was worth the risk to try to protect me. That's when she called and asked my father to meet with her.

"If Mirjana does not pass," she told him, "it's not because of her but because of them. I will do my best to help her."

She had told the state police that the students would complete their exams at the end of the day. So, by pressuring me to complete mine and go home before everyone else, she was able to grade it and record it as passed before the police even showed up. At that point, it would have been too late for them to interfere.

This was one of many instances in which I noticed Our Lady's intervention. After all, why would a Serbian—a communist no less—risk everything by going against the state police just for me? The only explanation that made sense was divine intervention.

When I finally held my high school diploma in my hands, all I could think of were the words that the angel said to Mary at the Annunciation: *Nothing is impossible with God.*

And, after all these years, I still don't know if my dad's cousin really died, or if he even existed at all. Some things are better left as mysteries.

CHAPTER 17

"Dear children, today I call you to a complete union with God. Your body is on Earth, but I ask you for your soul to be all the more often in God's nearness."

— *From Our Lady's Message of November 2nd, 2008*

A S THE LAST wisps of Sarajevo's notorious springtime fog dispersed and the warmth of summer descended, I finally had time to ponder a question that had hardly crossed my mind since the apparitions began:

What should I do with my life?

I had been so focused on just graduating from high school that I had not given it much thought, but now that I had accomplished my goal, I was faced with uncertainty about my future. Should I get a job as a cook like my mother? If only I could cook, I thought to myself. Besides, the hours were arduous; she was always so exhausted after work.

On the other hand, my father loved his job in the medical field. A subject that had always interested me was psychology, and at one time I dreamed of being a psychologist. I loved speaking with people and helping them with their problems, and I empathized with anyone who suffered. My experiences with the troubled children in high school showed me that people felt comfortable sharing even their darkest struggles with me, and I found it was possible to alleviate suffering by talking with them. But being a psychologist was an impossible dream; to be a doctor in Yugoslavia, you had to be a member of the Communist Party, something I would never consider. Besides, it required far more education than a mere high school diploma and I doubted that any university would accept me given my bad reputation with the government.

But there was another option that I had been considering—one in which, like my mother's job, I would be able to serve people, and like my father's job, I would have the opportunity to make a difference in lives.

I could be a nun.

After the apparitions began, more than a few people asked me if I planned to enter the religious life like other visionaries had. I was told that Lucia of Fátima, for example, became a Carmelite nun, and Bernadette, the visionary of Lourdes, joined the Sisters of Charity after learning to read and write at the hospice school run by the sisters.

This knowledge consoled me as much as it concerned me. Was I now required to enter the religious life because I had seen Our Lady? And would people be disappointed if I chose a different path? I was not the only one wondering about it. Not long after the apparitions began, the six of us visionaries were together in Međugorje and we asked Our Lady what she desired from us later in our lives.

"Follow your hearts," she said. *"It is up to you to decide. If you enter the religious life, then I wish for it to be visible that I was with you. And if you decide to have families, then I wish for your family to be an example to other families."*

This was one of the rare moments when Our Lady gave us advice of a personal nature, but it's clear in her words that she was careful to respect our free will, which is one of God's most wonderful gifts. Our Lady reminds us that prayer and fasting can help us make the best decisions.

Although she told us to follow our hearts, my heart was probably too confused with all the emotions surrounding the apparitions to give me a clear signal. I would have done anything for Our Lady, and early in the apparitions I took whatever people said to me very seriously. If they said that a visionary had to become a nun, then it was simple—I would be a nun.

I was having dinner with my family when my father asked if I knew what kind of job I wanted to get after high school, or if I still wanted to enroll in the university. He was probably concerned that I had not spoken about my future at all since the apparitions began, whereas before I always seemed to have a new career aspiration every week.

"I'm going to be a nun," I said.

Dad choked on his food and Mom dropped her fork.

"*You?*" said Miro, giggling. "A nun?"

"Well, I'm a visionary," I said.

"But are you sure about this, honey?" said my mom.

"Yes, I think so," I said.

"My sister, Sister Mirjana!" said Miro, now laughing hysterically. "*Sister* Sister!"

Dad gave my brother "the look" and Miro shut his mouth, but that was not much better—his uncontrollable laughter now came out in little snorts. Dad glared at Miro and waited for him to stop, and then he turned and looked at me.

"Mirjana," he said, and then he paused for a long time as if to carefully select his words. "How about you go slowly? A lifelong decision like that shouldn't be rushed. Maybe you should finish school first and then see if religious life is truly your calling. Pray about it, and don't say it's your final decision until you know for sure what you want. You're still young, and it's alright to be undecided."

I knew in my heart that he was right, especially when he told me to pray about it. Up until that moment, I had just been repeating the words "I'm going to be a nun" in my head without thinking about what I was really saying. It was as if I was trying to accommodate what other people wanted me to say, and not what I necessarily felt in my heart. My father helped me realize that I had skipped the most important part: prayerful discernment.

So, I decided to pray for that intention—for God to show me the way and for Our Lady to tell me what she wanted from me. Through prayer, I thought I would get some kind of confirmation about my plans, but I did not feel the call to be a nun. On the contrary, my desire to have a family only seemed to grow. As a little girl, I dreamed of being a wife and mother. If being a visionary meant that I had to enter a convent, why had God put family in my heart?

Although I was torn about what to do, I finally decided to at least submit an application to the University of Sarajevo. Thumbing through the university's list of majors, I looked for one that might allow me to interact with people without sacrificing my beliefs. The course of study titled *Economics of Tourism* intrigued me immediately. Under communism, we did not have much opportunity to communicate with people from other countries. The government carefully shielded us from the outside world, especially from countries where people lived in freedom.

When the apparitions began and the first foreign pilgrims came to Međugorje, I wanted to know everything about them—how they spoke, the foods they ate, and anything unique to their culture. Learning about different nationalities also seemed to fit perfectly with Our Lady's role as the mother of all people. Even if I never got a job in tourism, at least I could expand my worldview by choosing it as a course of study. Plus, maybe it would help me in my role as a visionary.

When I researched the tourism program further, I was disappointed to learn that I could not immediately apply to it. Sarajevo had been chosen to host the 1984 Winter Olympics—making Yugoslavia the first communist country to ever be given that honor—and with the event less than a year away, every study course related to tourism had a waiting list. Officials expected enormous crowds from all over the world to visit Sarajevo for the games, and preparations were already underway. New construction transformed the city at a rapid pace.

All was not lost, though. I discovered that I could choose a different program and then transfer to my preferred subject later. I learned that the Faculty of Agriculture had the most lenient acceptance requirements, which made sense. Much of Yugoslavia's economy relied on farming, so the government wanted as many agriculture experts as possible. Perhaps they would even let a "religious fanatic" like me into the program.

I applied to the program and said a prayer. *Heavenly Father, if I get accepted, then I'll know it's your will.* And then I tried to forget about it. I did not want to get excited about something that would probably be a disappointment. I was fairly certain that I wouldn't be accepted, and my thoughts turned again to religious life. Every time I visualized myself as a nun, though, my mind wandered to images of motherhood and family life.

By the end of the summer, with my life at a hazy crossroads, I was more confused than ever. Expectations for me to enter a convent made me continually question my discernment. I finally decided to put Our Lady's messages into action in hopes of making sure that Heaven heard me. I closed myself off in our apartment for five days of prayer and fasting. I was desperate for a solution, and such a drastic move, I hoped, would result in one. For those five days, I only ate bread and water and I begged God to reveal what He wanted from me. In the end, my desire to have a family was stronger than ever, and I felt that I had been given a clear answer.

When I came to this realization, peace returned to me. I finally understood that God was not calling me to a religious vocation. If He wanted me to be a nun, all He had to do was put it in my heart. Back then, I had no particular desires or dreams, so I would have embraced whatever God asked of me or tried to inspire me to do.

Still, the decision not to become a nun only eliminated one

Marko calling from Herzegovina.

possibility for my life. I continued to ask God to lead me according to His will, not mine.

"Mirjana!" my mom called out a few days later. "You have a phone call!"

It was Marko calling from Herzegovina. "I'm coming to the city!" he said. "I'll be attending the University of Sarajevo. I start in the fall."

Marko had previously talked about going to college in Sarajevo so I was not entirely surprised. He had actually enrolled at the university in 1982 after graduating from high school but then decided to complete his obligatory conscription in the Yugoslav Army first. The government required a year of military service from every able-bodied young man in the country.

Now that he had fulfilled his duty, Marko was eager to continue his education. He'd been accepted into the Faculty of Agriculture in Sarajevo—the same one I had applied to—and would be living with his brother Željko in Sarajevo. Was he coming to Sarajevo to be closer to me? I did not give it much thought, even though I knew he was quite fond of me—that was a fact the entire village of Međugorje knew. I simply viewed Marko as a close friend.

I learned from Marko that a few other young people from the Međugorje region were planning to attend the University of Sarajevo. It would be nice to have some Catholic friends around, but I never even allowed myself to dream about attending classes with them. The police had almost certainly intercepted my application, and I imagined them laughing with delight as they tossed it in a trashcan.

A few days later, I received a letter from the University of Sarajevo. I opened it reluctantly, expecting to read that my application had been rejected, but the word *Accepted* immediately caught my eye. I could hardly believe it. I was going to college!

The famous Sebilj fountain in Baščaršija, Sarajevo's historic old town.

CHAPTER 18

"Blessed are you when they insult you and persecute you and utter every kind of evil against you because of me."

— *Jesus in the Gospel of Matthew (5:11)*

CLASSES BEGAN AT the university in September of 1983. I recall seeing the pride in my father's eyes—and perhaps even a few tears—as I left our apartment for my first day of studies. Neither of us had thought that moment would ever come.

"I love you," he said, hugging me for an unusually long time.

"I have to go, Dad," I said, squirming out of his arms. "I'll be late."

He stood in the doorway of our apartment as I waited in the hallway for the elevator to come.

"Do you want me to walk you to class?" he asked.

I smiled at him. "Dad, I'm not a little girl anymore!"

"I know you're not," he said sadly. At that moment, I wanted to run back and kiss him, but the elevator suddenly opened. Still, I did not want to leave him there frowning. "Besides," I said, stepping into the elevator, "you're still in your bathrobe."

He looked down at himself and chuckled. "So I am," he said.

"Bye, Dad! I lo—" The elevator closed in my face.

"I love you," I said softly, but by then I was already a floor below him.

The University of Sarajevo was divided into multiple faculties, or divisions, spread throughout the city. Walking into the large, imposing Faculty of Agriculture building for the first time was both exhilarating and intimidating. I took a deep breath. Despite many obstacles, I had made it—I had fulfilled one of my biggest dreams. Still, I was careful not to give myself all the credit; being accepted was a miracle, and by now God was probably tired of me constantly thanking Him.

As I sat down in the lecture hall, I wondered if the professors and students had read about me in the newspapers, or if the police had come to tell them. I finally convinced myself not to worry. This was a place of higher learning. Even if the students and faculty knew who I was, hopefully they were open-minded enough to welcome me regardless of their personal convictions.

I was partially right. The students at the university were wonderful. Everyone seemed happy to be there and eager to learn, which was a stark contrast to my previous school where many of the students treated their schoolwork like an infectious disease. I often thought about my classmates from high school and wondered where they were and what they were doing. I hoped I would see some of them at the university, but I never did.

The class sizes at the university were much larger than in high school, and the professors spoke with authority and confidence. Initially I felt comfortable with them and I paid close attention to every lecture. Being in such a lively academic environment inspired me to work my way back to being the excellent student I had once been.

Unfortunately my confidence did not last.

One day I overheard some professors talking about their plans to visit the Međugorje region, but they were not going on a pilgrimage. They were going to buy wine. The rich soils, abundant sunshine and ancient viticulture techniques of the Herzegovina highlands produced some of the finest wines in Yugoslavia. Sampling local produce was essential for professors of agriculture, but they always seemed to be more interested in wine than other crops.

I felt a pang of worry. If they did not already know who I was, then they would find out from the people who sold them wine. Everyone in and around Međugorje knew that I was attending the University of Sarajevo, and they would be eager to share that news with a visitor from the city. Still, school was going well, and I tried not to think about it.

The students at the university were from all over Yugoslavia but I mostly socialized with the ones from Međugorje—people like Marko and his brother, Željko, their cousin Mario, and a cheerful young man named Rajko who liked to sing and joke. Rajko had been courting Ivanka since before the apparitions began and he often surprised us, and anyone around, by declaring his love for her in a spontaneous song. We were full of joy and laughter, and it was a nice change to have friends who were not afraid to be seen with me. We rejoiced together, prayed together, and met for Mass at the Church of St. Anthony, where I had previously attended catechism class.

It was around this time that my family and I received sad news from Međugorje: Jakov's mother, Jaka, had passed away. Uncle Filip, my dad's brother, immediately took Jakov in. Our family made sure that Jakov knew we were there for him and that he could come to us if he needed anything.

I felt a strange sense of peace about it all. I was sad for Jakov, but, at the same time, I knew he still had Our Lady and that he was seeing her every day. I could relate to Jakov more than anyone in our family. Living on Earth, one is usually attached to earthly things—which is completely normal—but when you come to know heaven, you look at the world in a different way. You understand that life on Earth is only temporary and death is not an end.

On March 2, 2016, Our Lady said, *"Free yourselves from everything*

that binds you to only what is earthly and permit what is of God to form
your life by your prayer and sacrifice…"

Jakov knew that his mother had passed on to the next world and
that he would see her again one day, because no one stays on this
planet forever. Aware of these things, he was eventually able to accept
her passing. If nothing else, he still had his heavenly Mother visiting
every day.

In my first year at the university, the police persecuted me a little
less frequently, likely because my daily apparitions had ceased. But
they made sure I knew they were always watching. My family and I
still got hassled at home, and the interrogations were still just as horrible as they had always been, but, in a way, I had gotten used to it all.
Whenever they took me in for questioning, I followed my routine of
silently praying and saying as little as possible.

One day, the police notified me that I had to relinquish my passport again. I was frustrated because I had only just gotten in back.
Marko offered to accompany me to the police station to be my support. I was reluctant to get him involved in my problems with the
government, but he insisted. So, the two of us walked into the station
and approached the front desk.

"I was told that I have to bring you my passport," I said. "I'm
Mirjana Dra—"

"I know who you are," the policeman interrupted. "Hand it over."

As I took it out of my pocketbook, Marko said, "Comrade Officer,
is this really necessary?"

I froze in fear. The policeman glared at Marko and said, "Who the
hell are you?"

"I'm her boyfriend," said Marko.

"Are you crazy?" I whispered to Marko, and then I quickly gave the
policeman my passport.

"I'm sorry. He's just a friend from out of town." I grabbed Marko
by the arm and dragged him out.

"What's wrong?" said Marko.

We stopped in front of the police station. "Number one," I said, "you can't talk to the police like that. You don't know what they can do to you. And number two, you're not my boyfriend!"

Marko smiled. "OK," he said. "I'm sorry."

Marko and his brother came to our apartment often. My mom and dad welcomed the boys and cooked meals for them since they were so far from home. Marko would also come to study with me since we were both studying agriculture. My dad was always impressed with Marko. "He's well-educated, good-looking," my dad would say after Marko left. "What a great guy."

"Maybe you should marry him," I joked.

Through the course of that year, though, I found myself always making plans with Marko. He joined my family at Mass every Sunday at the Church of the Holy Trinity near our apartment. In our free time, we would talk for hours in one of the downtown cafés, and on warmer days, we'd stroll along the river or picnic in a park. I enjoyed Marko's company, and I started missing him when we had not seen each other for a while. Before I knew it, it felt natural to hold Marko's hand whenever we walked together. And that's when I realized—he really *was* my boyfriend.

There was never any singular moment when I knew that Marko was the one. It all happened gradually. He was persistent—he had been for many years. But more than anything, he was always there for me. In the worst of my suffering, he comforted me. After the police took me back to Sarajevo, he often called me on the phone just to check on me. When I contemplated becoming a nun, he never tried to sway me in a different direction. And when he moved to the city, he watched out for me. I realized that he truly cared, and my heart began opening to him little by little. A boy with less patience might have given up on me years before. From the moment I first saw Our Lady, I was consumed with the apparitions and overwhelmed with countless emotions. Between the complexities of my mystical experiences and the stress from constant interrogations, I never had time to fall in love. And yet, somehow, I did.

Marko, I realized, was exactly the kind of young man I had always envisioned meeting—and he had been right in front of me the whole time. Ever since I had known him, he was wonderful and kind, and, most importantly, he was a believer. I never had to teach him about faith and prayer; it was already the center of his life. After the apparitions began, he fasted regularly and made numerous pilgrimage walks from Mostar to Međugorje, and from the moment he moved to Sarajevo, he went to Mass every evening. Not long after we began dating, Marko came over one evening to have dinner with me and my family. I had already told my mom about our relationship, but I had not yet told my father. Throughout the night, Marko and my father talked and joked like they always did. At one point, however, Marko put his hand on mine, and my father looked at it suspiciously. He did not say anything until Marko left.

"What was that about?" said Dad.

"What was what about?" I said.

"The *hand*."

My mother smiled. "Mirjana and Marko are dating now, dear."

Miro's eyes got big. "Mirjana's got a boyfriend!" he teased.

"Dating?" said my father, his brow furrowing.

"Well—" I stammered.

"I thought you were going to be a nun!" said Miro.

"But, Marko?" my father continued. "Oh, he's no good at all."

"Dad," I said. "I thought you loved Marko."

Miro started making kissing noises but my father stopped him with one look.

"Well, of course," said my father. "But, *dating?* No, he's not good enough for my Mirjana."

My father immediately identified all kinds of flaws in Marko, but

I knew that he did not really mean any of it. His reaction was even a little endearing; it showed me how deeply he loved me. I was growing up, and, like any adoring father, he was struggling to accept it. His apprehension did not last long, though; he eventually gave us his blessing and began treating Marko like his own son.

By February of 1984, with the Winter Olympics about to start, Sarajevo emerged from a metamorphosis. The government had spent months strategically replacing the city's sterile communist gloom with a façade modeled after the free metropolises of the West. The authorities were desperate to present Sarajevo as a modern European city, and the only way to do that was through disguise and illusion. Suddenly, looking at my city was like seeing a monster wearing a mask—I knew how horrible the face beneath the mask looked, but I was in no hurry to see it again.

We all enjoyed the sense of freedom while it lasted, however artificial it might have been. For example, under communism, we only had one kind of chocolate in our shops, and it was made in Yugoslavia. But the day before the opening ceremony of the Olympics, the shelves were suddenly stocked with all kinds of European and American products, including more types of chocolate than I ever knew existed. We suddenly had access to things that the Iron Curtain never allowed through. There were bananas, foreign soft drinks, new candies and all sorts of other sweet and savory snacks. Every day on his way home from work, my father purchased as many of the exotic treats as he could carry, and our apartment was soon full of food. He and Miro gorged themselves nightly.

We knew that the products were not really brought to the city for us. They were for the visitors, and not even necessarily for the visitors to consume—they were simply part of the mask.

But as much as the local authorities wanted to present Sarajevo as a modern city, not everything went smoothly. In what could have been described as symbolic of the regime's backwards ideologies, the Olympic flag was accidentally raised upside down during the opening ceremonies at the stadium. Not only was the embarrassing blunder seen by the people of Sarajevo, but it was broadcast around the world and talked about in the news media for days to come. It was not the kind of media attention that the communists hoped for.

Preparations and security overwhelmed the police during the Olympics, which gave me a temporary reprieve from their scrutiny and presented the opportunity to earn my first wage. Many of my fellow students at the university picked up short-term work related to the games, so I applied for a job and got hired to guide a small group of Italian tourists visiting the city for the Olympics. Another girl and I welcomed them on their arrival, showed them to their accommodation, and took them on a walking tour of *Baščaršija*. The snow was so thick that my boots were constantly wet, and I could not ask them all the questions I wanted to because I had to act professional, but I was thrilled to earn my first paycheck. The experience even inspired me to start learning Italian.

I was too busy with my studies and my new job to watch any of the Olympic Games, but everyone in the city talked about them. The excitement all around was invigorating. When Jure Franko earned a silver in slalom skiing—Yugoslavia's first winter Olympic medal—cheering echoed throughout Sarajevo. Franko became a national hero.

In a way, the Sarajevo Olympics were perceived as a triumph for the Yugoslav government and its closest allies because communist countries won the most medals. The USSR took home 25 medals and East Germany took 24. In contrast, the USA only won eight and the usually victorious Austria collected just one. By the end of the games, the authorities had forgotten all about the upside down flag; they felt that they had shown the world that communism was there to stay.

But the people of Sarajevo had not only tasted foreign chocolate for the first time—they had also tasted freedom, and they were hungry for more.

Fr. Slavko Barbarić became one of the most beloved figures in Međugorje. (PHOTO BY JOE MIXAN)

CHAPTER 19

"My children, do not forget that you are not in this world only for yourselves, and that I am not calling you here only for your sake."

— *From Our Lady's Message of November 2, 2011*

FTER THE OLYMPICS, my college experience began to deteriorate.

As I feared, my professors at the Faculty of Agriculture had learned about my apparitions, whether from their wine-buying excursions in Herzegovina or from the police. To be a professor at the university, one had to be a member of the Communist Party, and many of them were active in politics. When they discovered there was a "subversive factor" in their midst, they sought to inflate their standing in the Communist Party by making my life miserable.

The Lord is my shepherd, I silently prayed in class.

Their tactics were subtle. I first noticed a few of my professors standing together in the hallway, eyeing me coldly and whispering to each other as I passed. In the classroom, they spoke rudely to me, whereas they treated the other students with respect, and although I studied hard for every exam, the professors seemed to grade mine harshly. My grades started to slide and I soon lost hope of ever overcoming their prejudice.

He makes me lie down in green pastures. He leads me beside quiet waters.

As soon as I could, I followed my original plan and switched my course of studies to the Economics of Tourism. I hoped the change would give me a fresh start, with new professors who would perhaps be kinder to me. But they were even worse. During school, I tried to ignore their constant underhanded taunts and instead just focus on my studies, but at home I cried in the bathroom almost every night.

He refreshes my soul. He guides me along the right paths for His name's sake.

As my 19th birthday approached, I was eager to see Our Lady again. On March 18, 1984, my closest friends and family members gathered in our apartment. We prayed together until she came. As always, I forgot all about my earthly troubles during that beautiful encounter, and I cried profusely when she departed.

"What did she say?" my mother asked me after I regained my senses.

"She gave us all her motherly blessing," I said. "And she told me that she would come again this year to give me more details about the secrets."

The promise of not having to wait an entire year to see her again filled me with joy. Indeed, for the next two years, she came again on several occasions aside from my annual apparition, often in a way that I had not expected—I could hear her voice within my heart but not see her. I later learned that these were called locutions. Those experiences were no less remarkable and poignant than my regular apparitions. Her lyrical voice resonated within me, and it felt as if she was embracing my soul. During the locutions, she sometimes led me in prayer, gave me messages, or expanded upon the secrets. My knowledge of the future continued to trouble me, especially because I still had so many questions.

Also in 1984, Our Lady began giving weekly messages to the parish of Međugorje, through the visionary Marija. The first of these occurred on March 1, 1984, and started with the words, *"Dear children! I have chosen this parish in a special way and I wish to lead it."*

Once a week, Our Lady urged the people of the parish to embrace prayer, fasting, confession and the other main tenets of her messages. Her simple and straightforward words allowed people to comprehend the messages without the help of theologians and Biblical scholars. It was as if Our Lady was a teacher and the parishioners were her pupils—a "school of love," as a local priest called it. She was preparing the people of Međugorje, it seemed, for something greater. *"My Son and I have a special plan for this parish,"* she said in one of the messages.

But Our Lady also continually warned the parish that the devil was angry, saying in one of the weekly messages, *"these days Satan wants to frustrate my plans."* Likewise, she once told me that Jesus struggles for each of us, but the devil tries to interfere. The devil, she warned, prowls around us and sets traps. He tries to divide and confuse us so that we will detest ourselves and abandon ourselves to him. An invisible spiritual war rages all around us, but Our Lady is here to help us win.

In one of her messages, Our Lady said, *"I desire to take you by the hand and to walk with you in the battle against the impure spirit."*

Although I rarely speak about the devil, I can tell you with certainty that he exists. I saw him once. All I will say is that it was the most terrifying experience of my life, but love drove him away. In that moment, I learned that nothing in this world compares to his ugliness and his hatred for God—but unlike God's power, his is limited.

According to exorcists, Satan is not some kind of evil god who fights against the God of the good. Instead, he's a being that God created as good, but he became evil by refusing God. Whereas pride is his hallmark, humble people who trust in God are stronger than every evil. As Our Lady said in one of her messages, *"With the love that comes forth from humility you will bring light to where darkness and blindness rule."*

My awful encounter with evil taught me something about his

tactics, too. The devil will try to convince you that following God only leads to suffering, and that living according to the teachings of Jesus will rob you of your freedom. In a way, becoming a believer *does* require you to give up certain freedoms—the freedom to destroy yourself, for example, or the freedom to lie and steal. There's a big difference between free will and God's will. One is a gift while the other is a choice. When we put our trust in God, then we become free in Him, and that's the only type of freedom that leads to eternal life.

I do not want to give the devil any importance. He has always been below Our Lady's feet, and I believe we should leave him there.

He only has as much power as we give him, and we can only give it to him through our free will. I think this is true on a personal level as well as collectively for mankind. But if Jesus and the Blessed Mother are at the center of our lives, then the devil cannot do anything to harm us. Love always triumphs.

"Whenever I come to you, my Son comes with me, but so does Satan," Our Lady once said.

Međugorje was a target of his attacks from the beginning. He could not watch so many people praying, going to Mass, confessing and converting without trying to do something. But unlike in the movies, he doesn't come as some grotesque creature lurking in the shadows—he attacks through people who have allowed him to reign in their hearts. People unknowingly accept his influence through their choices in life. Most do not realize how easy it is to get under his control, and that's one reason Our Lady always stresses the importance of prayer. If God reigns in your heart, then there is no room for anything bad.

As my first year at the University of Sarajevo ended, I, too, felt like I was under attack. I had passed all ten of the required exams that year despite the growing harassment by the faculty. Whenever I sat for a test, for example, I would see the professors discussing something amongst themselves and then they would all turn and stare at me as if intentionally trying to unnerve me.

I was consumed with worry for most of that summer. I dreaded going back for my second year at the university, and my knowledge of the future continued to haunt my thoughts. I did not feel qualified to handle such a huge responsibility and I worried that I might have a nervous breakdown. In one of my most difficult moments, I prayed, "My Lord, how could you entrust me with such a task? What was it that you saw in me? Don't you see that I can't do this?" But then, realizing that I was questioning God's plan, I said, "Forgive me, you know that deep in my heart I don't mean what I say. But I need your help."

On August 15, 1984, the Feast of the Assumption, I was deep in prayer when I heard Our Lady's familiar voice in my heart. She told me that she would appear on August 25, 1984, so I prepared myself with fasting and prayer. On that day, she came to me and stayed for 18 minutes. Seeing her just six months after the annual apparition was almost like having two birthdays in one year. She spoke about the secrets, clarifying the details of how everything would unfold and preparing me for my role. Then, on September 13, 1984, she appeared again and told me the date on which I must give the details of the first secrets to the priest. This new knowledge eased my distress and gave me strength to go on.

When I thought about which priest I should choose to reveal the secrets, there was one in particular who always came to mind. Fr. Petar Ljubičić, a tall Franciscan with thick glasses and a welcoming smile, ministered to the poor. If he met people in need, he would give them food and accommodation. If he saw any orphans, he would find them a home. His heart was open to those who suffered, and he always wanted to give people hope. I respected him and identified with his compassion, and he was there for me anytime I needed to speak to a priest, so naturally I felt like he should be the one.

When the time comes, however, it all depends on God's will and not mine. Although I've always wanted Fr. Petar to reveal the secrets, it doesn't necessarily have to be that way. What if the pope asks for them? He's also a priest, and I could never say no to the Holy Father.

I was finally at peace about the secrets, but when classes commenced again in the fall of 1984, the minor annoyances of the previous year quickly snowballed into a concerted effort to crush me. With their constant barbs and insults, some of the professors seemed intent on forcing me to drop out. Their pettiness seemed so pointless in contrast to everything Our Lady had revealed to me about the world beyond. I was like a tiny country being attacked by an alliance of superpowers, and I finally decided to quit.

I felt both sad and relieved. When I explained the situation to my parents, they accepted it with love and understanding, and Marko gave me his full support and a shoulder to cry on.

But leaving the university did not mean I had to stop learning. Even when I was still there, I always felt like it was for my own personal education anyway; a bastion of atheism like Yugoslavia, after all, wouldn't have many career opportunities for a visionary, college degree or not. I decided to just be my own professor. I read for hours every day in our apartment—historical novels like *Gordana* by Croatian author Marija Jurić Zagorka, books of Eastern European poetry, academic books I still had from the university, and whatever else I could find.

I also prayed a lot. Through prayer, I realized that a university degree would not have made me a happier or better person. Our Lady showed me that joy and goodness only come from God, and that nothing in this world is more valuable than a pure heart.

Perhaps life would have taken me down a different path if I had finished university, but I've never been concerned with that. I can't imagine being somewhere different than I am today.

And, of course, I still had Our Lady. My life revolved around Medugorje, which likely made leaving university easier than it might have been for someone else. One positive result of quitting college was that the pressures of the police finally abated. I was even able to retrieve my passport. Perhaps they thought they had won, or that I was no longer a threat. Even so, I knew they were always watching.

The other advantage of not being in school was that I could go to Medugorje more frequently, and I began making regular and lengthier visits. I even started spending the summers there again. Marko also went home in the summer to see his family. His uncle, Slavko Barbarić, a Franciscan priest, was now stationed in Međugorje.

Fr. Slavko was an interesting and enigmatic man. A doctor of religious pedagogy, with the title of psychotherapist, he first came to Međugorje to examine us visionaries. When he concluded that we showed no signs of hallucination or deception, Fr. Slavko's skepticism quickly changed to belief. The first time I met him, I was not impressed—it seemed like he had a somewhat cold personality when he spoke to pilgrims. But Međugorje transformed him, and he began transforming the parish. He cared for the pilgrims and organized the prayer program at the church. He climbed Cross Mountain or Apparition Hill every day, praying the rosary and picking up pieces of garbage left behind by careless tourists. He even played the organ in church sometimes. He dedicated himself to Our Lady and I began to love him.

Međugorje needed a priest like Fr. Slavko. By 1985, the village had become a major pilgrimage destination. It seemed like every week a different TV crew or team of scientific researchers came to document and study us, and the village was constantly filled with visitors from all over the world. Most of them stayed in the homes of local families who often did not even charge anything.

Where most people saw kindness, the communists saw opportunity. Unable to stop the apparitions or prevent people from coming, they took a surprising new approach—they began building hotels and gifts shops around the church, and they imposed a higher tax in the village. If they could not destroy Međugorje, they figured, then at least they could profit from it.

Back in Sarajevo, my family, Marko, and some of my friends gathered in our apartment to be present at my annual apparition on March 18, 1985. It was my twentieth birthday. Our Lady appeared just after 4 pm and stayed with me for 15 minutes. Speaking about non-believers—whom she called *"those who have yet to experience God's love"*—she said, *"They are my children too and I suffer for them because they do not know what awaits them if they are not converted to God."*

She then asked me to join her in prayer for them, and she led me in reciting both the *Our Father* and the *Glory Be* prayers twice. When we finished praying, she deplored the greed that had been building in the world and in Međugorje and said, *"Woe to those who seek to take everything from those who come, and blessed are those who give."*

We prayed about this, too. Then she gave me new details about the secrets. I also told her that I had many questions for her; in fact, people had given me nearly 30 questions to ask. She smiled and told me not to worry, because she would give me the gift of knowing the answers when the time came to answer them.

It seemed strange to me at the time, but I later found a similar directive in *The Gospel of Matthew* (10:19-20), when Jesus says, "...Do not worry about how to speak or what to say; what you are to say will be given to you when the time comes, because it is not you who will be speaking; the Spirit of your Father will be speaking in you."

After she blessed all the religious objects in the room, Our Lady pointed at the rosary in my hand and said, *"One should not leave the rosary about the home like an ornament as many people do."*

She then guided me on how to properly pray the rosary, which she asked me to share with everyone. And, just before the apparition ended, everyone in the room joined me in reciting the *Salve Regina* prayer. After she left—and after I composed myself—I relayed what Our Lady said about answering questions, first to the few people in the room and later to those who had not been present. I surprised myself by the wisdom of my answers, although I was well aware that I could not take credit.

This apparition was unique in that she promised to appear again the following day, March 19. There were four people with me that day—my father, mother, Miro and Marko—and the apparition lasted for seven minutes. Our Lady spoke to me about the secrets and, again, we prayed together.

Less than two months later, I received somewhat surprising news from Međugorje. Ivanka had experienced her last daily apparition on

May 7, 1985. The news quickly spread around the world and reignited fear and speculation that the secrets were imminent, but I was careful not to say anything that might fuel the flames. The time of the secrets was still many years away.

After giving Ivanka the tenth secret, Our Lady promised to appear to her on June 25th of every year, the anniversary of our first apparition. She urged Ivanka not to feel like she had done something wrong, and consoled her by saying, "*The plan which my Son and I have, you accepted with all your heart and completed your part. Be happy because I am your mother and I love you with all my heart.*"

And then, just before she departed, Our Lady said, "*Ivanka, the grace which you and the others received, nobody on this Earth has received up until now.*"

Ivanka and I had been the first visionaries to see Our Lady and now we were also the first to have our daily apparitions end. I felt sorry for Ivanka because I understood the pain and sadness she was going through. My daily apparitions had ceased two and a half years earlier and I still felt the void in my heart because of that. I knew there was nothing I could do or say to help Ivanka; only through prayer and fasting would she be able to accept it.

My locutions continued throughout 1985. Each one prepared me a little more for my role in the future. That year, I again heard Our Lady's voice on the Feast of the Assumption. She asked me to share an important message with the world. "*I have been calling you to conversion for the last four years,*" she said. "*Be converted before it may be too late.*"

Some people were alarmed by her words "*too late,*" like they were when she urged people not to wait for the sign. When the sign came, she warned, it would be too late for many to convert. But now, looking at it through the scope of history, think about how many people have died since that time. If those who have passed on were waiting for the sign to appear before converting, it would have been too late for them.

"But what does 'near' mean for prophets?" Fr. Slavko once said. "As Peter wrote, 'with the Lord a day is like a thousand years, and a thousand years are like a day.' We must be careful and not think of dates, of days. Conversion is always urgent. It is dangerous to wait."

I experienced several more of these extraordinary apparitions and locutions until June 4, 1986, when Our Lady appeared to me for several minutes. She told me that it would be the last of the special apparitions concerning the secrets because she had explained every-thing necessary. I understood that I wouldn't see her again until the following year, on March 18. Although I was sad, I also felt thankful for the extra time I got to spend with the Blessed Mother.

Fr. Slavko was with me that day, and he asked me later why I had cried so much during the apparition. I explained to him that Our Lady sometimes showed me scenes of what is to come.

"The warnings to mankind are very serious and at times they're hard to bear," I said. "But in spite of the difficulties, and the severity of what I've seen, I feel strong with Our Lady. A powerful life-giving force comes from her."

The following year, 1986, Ivanka again shared news that quickly spread around the world—she and Rajko were getting married. I was thrilled for them. The wedding took place in Međugorje on December 28, 1986, the Feast of the Holy Family, when Catholics celebrate the sacrament of marriage and the sanctity of parenthood by honoring Jesus, Mary and Joseph together.

Marko and I went to the wedding, and the other visionaries went as well. The day began with a beautiful ceremony at St. James Church, followed by a lively party that lasted late into the night—into the next morning, to be exact. Croatians have always loved weddings, which is especially apparent in our traditions. For example, all the guests parade through town in a motorcade and honk their horns as they make their way from the ceremony to the reception. When someone gets married in Međugorje, the entire village knows about it.

I had never seen Ivanka so beautiful, nor so happy, than she was on her wedding day. I smiled at her from across the party and she smiled back. Even before the apparitions, she and I had shared a special friendship, and now, as visionaries, our bonds went even deeper. I silently prayed for God to bless her marriage with many years of joy—and some babies as well. I laughed at the thought of Ivanka chasing around a tiny version of herself.

At the same moment, I noticed Marko looking at me.

"What?" I said.

Marko smiled. "Oh, nothing," he said. The wedding band suddenly broke into song and the guests gathered in a circle for the Croatian folk dance known as *kolo*. Marko could not resist. He winked at me and raced to the dance floor.

Meeting Pope John Paul II was like encountering a living saint. (PHOTO BY ARTURO MARI/L'OSSERVATORE ROMANO)

CHAPTER 20

"For if this endeavor or this activity is of human origin, it will destroy itself. But if it comes from God, you will not be able to destroy them; you may even find yourselves fighting against God."

— *Acts 5:38-39*

YOU MIGHT NOT think it's possible for someone who sees the Blessed Mother to be impressed by meeting anyone else, but in July, 1987, I met a living saint. The encounter had a lasting effect.

I went to Rome at the invitation of an Italian priest. Italy was itself a wonder. The history was fascinating—it was easy to envision gladiators sparring in the Coliseum and emperors addressing their subjects in the Roman Forum. But the countless holy sites in the "eternal city" affected me most. Exploring the ancient Christian catacombs gave me an appreciation for the resilience and courage of the earliest members of my religion. Gazing up at the Sistine Chapel and the soaring ceilings of basilicas like St. Mary Major showed me the amazing feats that could be accomplished by men of faith. Praying at the tombs of saints and martyrs—and being in a place where so many people before me had lived and died—made me ponder Our Lady's constant reminders about the brevity of life on Earth.

Being a pilgrim in a foreign land also gave me a new perspective on the experiences of pilgrims coming to Međugorje. And just when I thought my trip could not get better, we accompanied a Croatian youth group to see Pope John Paul II at the Vatican on Wednesday, July 22.

The first bands of sunlight had just struck the massive dome of St. Peter's Basilica when we arrived that morning. Coming early helped us get right up front for the papal audience about to take place in St. Peter's Square. Soon, thousands of other pilgrims arrived.

The crowd was ecstatic as the pope came out. He walked among the people, giving blessings. As he passed our group, he put his hand over my head and blessed me. It was over before I knew it. I stood there smiling, elated to have gotten my first papal blessing. But as the pope continued on, the Italian priest accompanying me said loudly, "Holy Father, this is Mirjana from Međugorje!" The pope stopped, came back, and reached out to bless me again. I was frozen. His vivid blue eyes seemed to pierce my soul. Unable to think of any words to say, I bowed my head and felt the warmth of his blessing. When he left again, I turned to the Italian priest and joked, "He just thought I needed a double blessing." We both laughed.

Later that afternoon, when I returned to my accommodation—still giddy from the whole experience—I was shocked to receive a personal invitation from the pope. He was requesting that I come to meet with him privately the next morning at Castel Gandolfo. I was so excited that I barely slept that night. What would our meeting be like? What would I say? Questions raced through my mind. For a moment I would calm down but then suddenly remember: *tomorrow I will be with the pope!* And so it went through the whole night.

The next day, I arrived at Castel Gandolfo just before our scheduled meeting time of 8 am. Located about 15 miles southeast of Rome, the fortified village had been the summer residence of popes for centuries. Perched on an airy hill, surrounded by gardens and olive groves, the Papal Palace overlooked Lake Albano, its waters nearly as blue and striking as John Paul II's eyes.

A man in a suit escorted me to the castle garden. When I saw the

Holy Father waiting there for me, I immediately started crying. He looked at me and smiled. His gaze was full of warmth and love, and I felt I was in the presence of a holy man—a true son of the Blessed Mother. By then I had come to recognize something special in the eyes of people who loved Our Lady, a tenderness that only the Mother could convey. I saw it in Pope John Paul II stronger than I had ever seen it in anyone else.

The pope motioned for me to sit with him. I had to convince myself I was not dreaming. I had always thought a meeting with the pope was unattainable for an insignificant person like me, and yet here I was in his midst. I wanted to greet him but I was far too nervous to even try forming a sentence.

The pope gently shook my hand. "Dzień dobry," he said.

I could not understand him. Was I so excited that my ears were playing tricks on me? Had my brain short-circuited?

"Dziękuję za przybycie," he said.

I was mortified—here I was with my once-in-a-lifetime chance to meet the pope and I had no idea what he was saying. His words sounded similar to Croatian yet I could not decipher them. I soon realized he was speaking Polish. Slavic languages like Croatian and Polish share a lot of common words, so he wanted to see if we might be able to communicate in our native tongues. Unfortunately it was not working, but I remembered there was one language we both knew.

"Santo Padre," I said. "Possiamo parlare in Italiano?"

He smiled and nodded. "Sì. Bene, Mirjana, bene."

We talked about many things—some I can share, some I cannot—and soon I felt completely at ease in his presence. He spoke with such love that I could have talked with him for hours.

"Please ask the pilgrims in Međugorje to pray for my intentions," he said.

"I will, Holy Father," I assured him.

"I know all about Međugorje. I've followed the messages from the beginning. Please, tell me what it's like for you when Our Lady appears."

The pope listened intently as I described what I experienced during apparitions. At times, he smiled and gently nodded his head.

"And when she departs," I concluded, "I feel so much pain, and all I can think of in that moment is when I will see her again."

The pope leaned towards me and said, "Take good care of Međugorje, Mirjana. Međugorje is the hope for the entire world."

The pope's words seemed like a confirmation of the importance of the apparitions and of my great responsibility as a visionary. I was surprised by the conviction in his voice, and by how his eyes sparkled every time he said the word Međugorje—not to mention how well he pronounced the name of the village, which had always been so amusingly difficult for outsiders to say.

"Holy Father," I said. "I wish you could see all the people who go there and pray."

The pope turned his head and gazed towards the east, releasing a pensive sigh.

"If I were not the pope," he said, "I would have gone to Međugorje a long time ago."

I will never forget the love that radiated from the Holy Father. What I felt with him is similar to what I feel when I am with Our Lady, and looking into his eyes was just like looking into hers. Later, a priest told me that the pope had been interested in Međugorje from the very beginning, because right before our apparitions started, he had been praying for Our Lady to appear again on Earth.

"I cannot do it all alone, Mother," he prayed. "In Yugoslavia, Czechoslovakia, Poland and so many other communist countries, people cannot freely practice their faith. I need your help, dear Mother."

According to this priest, when the pope heard that Our Lady had appeared in a tiny village in a communist country, he immediately thought Međugorje had to be an answer to his prayers.

The Holy Father's deep love for the Blessed Mother originated in his childhood. Karol Wojtyla was just 9 years old when his mother died. Karol's father took him to a Marian shrine near their home in Poland. Standing before a statue of the Virgin, his father said, "The Blessed Mother will look after you until you're reunited with your mother in Heaven."

Karol's faith carried him through times of suffering and persecution. When the Nazis invaded Poland, he decided to enter an underground seminary, knowing he'd be imprisoned or killed if he got caught. The war ended, and he was ordained a priest on All Saints Day, November 1, 1946.

Living as a priest in Krakow after the war was difficult and dangerous; Poland had been taken over by the communists. I could relate to it as a person of faith living under an atheistic regime.

Fr. Wojtyla was especially attentive to young adults and he often took them on hiking trips in the mountains where they prayed together, celebrated Mass and discussed their faith, far away from the watchful eye of the government. To protect him from the communists, his students called him "uncle." Under the Turkish occupation, Croatians called their priests "uncles" for the same reason.

Fr. Wojtyla's devotion to the Blessed Mother continued to blossom while he was a priest.

"I was already convinced that Mary leads us to Christ," he said, "but at that time I began to realize also that Christ leads us to his Mother. One can even say that just as Christ on Calvary indicated his mother to the disciple John, so he points her out to anyone who strives to know and love him."

One of the pope's closest friends later revealed that Fr. Wojtyla visited Padre Pio in 1947. The famed stigmatic and mystic heard the young priest's confession and told him, "One day, you will ascend to the highest post in the Church."

When Fr. Wojtyla became a Cardinal, he believed that Padre Pio's prediction had been fulfilled. But God had even greater plans for him.

He was elected pope in 1978—the first non-Italian to hold the throne of Peter in 455 years. Addressing the crowd from the balcony above St. Peter's Square for the first time, Pope John Paul II said that although he was afraid to accept the responsibility of the papacy, he would do so "in a spirit of obedience to the Lord and total faithfulness to Mary, our most Holy Mother."

He chose the papal motto *Totus Tuus*—Latin for "totally yours" and a reference to his complete dedication to the Blessed Mother. And, just one month before I met him, John Paul II formally designated 1987-88 as a Marian Year, saying, "O Mary, we want you to shine on the horizon of our age as we prepare for the third millennium of the Christian age."

"But shouldn't the focus be on Jesus?" a pilgrim once asked me.

"Absolutely," I answered. "And that's exactly why Our Lady comes."

In her messages, Our Lady has never said, "Come to me and I will give you…" On the contrary, she has only said, "Come to me and I will lead you to my Son and he will give you…"

The Blessed Mother, like everyone else, must pray to God to attain what she desires. That's why we call her an intercessor—she intercedes before God on our behalf. Even the *Hail Mary* prayer, which is rooted in the Bible, implores her intercession with the words *Pray for us sinners, now and at the hour of our death.*

Believers have venerated the Virgin Mary from the beginning of Christianity. One of her earliest titles, *Theotokos*, means "God-bearer" in Greek. And throughout the ages, saints have extolled their love for the Blessed Mother. Some of them were accused of putting too much attention on her instead of on Jesus, but they had come to see Mary's important role in human history. They knew that her divine mission was to lead people to her Son, just as it had been when she lived on Earth.

"Mary is the most important woman in history," said Dr. Fr. Tomislav Pervan, a parish priest in Međugorje. "By her Fiat—her 'Yes' to the Angel—she entered into human history and changed the course of the world. From the beginning, she was and is involved in the most important events of history and salvation. Therefore, whenever and wherever she was or she is appearing, it has been for a special reason."

"Never be afraid of loving the Blessed Virgin too much," said St. Maximilian Kolbe, a Franciscan priest who volunteered to die in place of a stranger at the Auschwitz concentration camp. "You can never love her more than Jesus did."

St. Augustine, a notorious sinner who experienced a profound conversion, spoke of Mary as something like a new Eve. "By the fall," he said, "a poison was handed to mankind through a woman, and by the Redemption, man was given salvation also through a woman."

St. Mother Teresa of Calcutta explained her love for Mary in simple terms. "If you ever feel distressed during your day," she said, "call upon Our Lady. Just say this simple prayer: *Mary, Mother of Jesus, please be a mother to me now.* I must admit—this prayer has never failed me."

Other saints used humor to describe her. "Only after the Last Judgment will Mary get any rest," said St. John Vianney. "From now until then, she is much too busy with her children."

And using an odd but effective fishing metaphor, St. Catherine of Siena said, "Mary is the sweetest bait—chosen, prepared, and ordained by God—to catch the hearts of men."

Pope John Paul II defined the Blessed Mother's role in salvation. "Mary, the first of the redeemed," he said, "shines before us like a lamp that guides the way of all humanity, reminding us of the last end to which the person is called: sanctity and eternal life."

Of course, the people who said these things were all members of the Catholic Church. But even the forefather of Protestantism, Martin Luther, voiced his respect for Our Lady. In one of his sermons, he said, "The veneration of Mary is inscribed in the very depths of the human heart."

Luther also called her the "highest woman and the noblest gem in Christianity after Christ" and described her as "nobility, wisdom, and holiness personified."

Even members of Protestant denominations that focus almost exclusively on the Bible might be surprised to know that the Bible actually says quite a lot about the Blessed Mother. In fact, it clearly explains who she was—and who she *is*.

Pope John Paull II summed up the Biblical account of the Blessed Mother by saying, "From Mary we learn to surrender to God's Will in all things. From Mary we learn to trust even when all hope seems gone. From Mary we learn to love Christ her Son and the Son of God!"

The beginning of the Bible, Genesis 3:15, speaks about a woman whose offspring would crush the head of the serpent. And in Isaiah 7:14, the Virgin Birth was clearly predicted: "Therefore the Lord himself shall give you a sign; Behold, a virgin shall conceive, and bear a son, and shall call his name Immanuel."

After my apparitions began, reading the Bible became a new experience. Coming to know someone who was actually mentioned in the Gospels brought the events to life for me. Personally, I preferred to read the New Testament over the Old. I had trouble reconciling the image of God as angry and jealous—as He is sometimes portrayed in the earlier books—with the God of mercy that I had come to know through my apparitions.

When I was a little girl, catechism class depicted God as an angry judge. The Blessed Mother taught me differently—that God is our father who loves us very much, and who, through love, is always trying to help us change. In fact, that's why He sent the Blessed Mother to us. Everything happening in Međugorje is a result of God's love.

The New Testament often speaks of this love, especially in the passages related to Mary.

In the Gospel according to Luke (1:26-28), I saw that Mary was described as "full of grace" even before the Incarnation: "In the sixth month the angel Gabriel was sent from God to a city of Galilee named Nazareth, to a virgin betrothed to a man whose name was Joseph, of the house of David; and the virgin's name was Mary. And he came to her and said, 'Hail, full of grace, the Lord is with you!'"

It may sound strange, but perhaps Mary could be described as a visionary herself—she saw an angel from Heaven and even communicated with him. The angel's greeting became the first line of the *Hail Mary*, and the prayer's next line came from Luke 1:41, where Elizabeth, the mother of John the Baptist, sees Mary and feels her own baby leap in her womb. "Blessed are you among women," exclaims Elizabeth, "and blessed is the fruit of your womb!"

As Jesus said, each tree is known by its fruit. If Jesus was the fruit of Mary's womb, then what can be said about the tree from which He came? Perhaps the answer is made clearest in the Gospel according to Luke (1:46-49), where we find the source of another beloved prayer known as the *Magnificat*. Here, Mary expresses her gratitude to God and seems to acknowledge her greater role in mankind's future. "My soul magnifies the Lord and my spirit rejoices in God my Savior," she says, "because He has regarded the lowliness of His handmaid. For behold, henceforth all generations shall call me blessed. Because He who is mighty has done great things for me, and holy is His name."

In reference to the Wedding Feast at Cana—where Jesus performed his first miracle at the request of his mother—Pope John Paul II once said, "Mary places herself between her Son and mankind in the reality of their wants, needs, and sufferings." When Pope John Paul II introduced the Luminous Mysteries of the Rosary in 2002, The Miracle at Cana was one of them. The Blessed Mother's instructions to the servants just before Jesus turned water into wine—"Do whatever he tells you"—are still just as meaningful today.

And in Luke 2:34, Simeon foretold how Mary's sufferings would be united with Jesus' sufferings, when he said, "Behold, this child is set for the fall and rising of many in Israel, and for a sign that is spoken against, and a sword will pierce through your own soul also, that thoughts out of many hearts may be revealed."

Simeon's prediction came true when Mary's Son was arrested, tortured and crucified. John 19:26 recounts the heartbreaking moment when Jesus, knowing he was about to die, entrusted Mary to his disciple John: "When Jesus saw his mother, and the disciple whom he loved standing near, he said to his mother, 'Woman, behold, your son!' Then he said to the disciple, 'Behold, your mother!' And from that hour the disciple took her to his own home."

And finally, the book of Revelation—written by St. John at Patmos after he experienced a vision—appears to confirm Mary's role as the Queen of Heaven. "A great sign appeared in heaven," he wrote. "A woman clothed with the sun, and the moon under her feet, and on her head a crown of twelve stars."

The woman, writes John, was about to give birth to a male child "who was to rule all nations."

The "great red dragon" waited for the woman's son to be born so that he might devour him, but "her son was taken up to God, and to his throne."

John then writes that the woman in his vision fled into the wilderness to a place prepared by God, but the great red dragon—"the ancient serpent, who is called the Devil and Satan, who deceived the whole world"—continued to pursue her. The dragon is described as being angry because he knows that his time on Earth is short.

Interestingly, the final book of the Bible seems to confirm what the first book predicted—the woman is still at enmity with the serpent. This part of St. John's vision concludes with what could also be seen as a depiction of Christian persecution: "Then the dragon became angry with the woman and went off to wage war against the rest of her offspring, those who keep God's commandments and bear witness to Jesus."

As St. John Paul II famously said, "Be not afraid!" The Bible clearly tells us that God will triumph, so instead of worrying about the future, there's really only one question we need to ask ourselves: *Whose side am I on?*

*Fr. Milan Mikulić presides over our wedding (top). Me
with my father, mother and brother (bottom).*

CHAPTER 21

"What good is it, my brothers, if someone says he has faith but does not have works? You believe that God is one. You do well. Even the demons believe that and tremble."

— *The Book of James (2:14, 19)*

THE YEAR 1987 turned out to be a "Marian" one for me as well, and not just because I met the pope.

My family rushed to Međugorje when we learned that Grandma Jela was dying. She'd been suffering through a prolonged disease. We were with her for the last week of her life and she endured all the pain without complaint. In her final hours, she lay in bed clutching her rosary, saying "Oh, my Mother…Oh, my Mother" repeatedly, and then she quietly passed away.

Seeing a loved one die for the first time struck me deeply, but it was clear that Grandma Jela's soul was no longer inside the body that lay before me. Through the rosary, she'd spent her life asking Our Lady to pray for her at the hour of her death, so I was certain that my grandmother was now looking at the same beautiful face that I longed to see every day.

After we returned to Sarajevo, a strange but familiar feeling began building in my heart, and during the final days of July, I wanted to be alone. It seemed as if my spirituality was heightened; merely reflecting on God brought me a great amount of peace, and when I prayed, I felt like I was practically in Heaven. It reminded me of how I felt in the days leading up to the first apparition.

But why? What was about to happen?

My answer came on August 2, 1987. My parents were at work that day and my brother was at school, so I was home alone in our apartment. At around 4 pm, I suddenly felt Our Lady's presence. I knelt in my room and she immediately appeared to me. Seeing her was a most welcome surprise.

She told me that my mission was *"to pray for those who do not believe—those have not yet come to know the love of God."*

When I asked her who these "unbelievers" were, she said, *"All those who do not feel the Church as their home and God as their Father."* She added, *"Do not call them unbelievers, because even by saying that, you judge them. You should think of them as your brothers and sisters."*

Our Lady said that she would come on the second day of every month to pray with me for my mission. Everything was suddenly clear—even the worst of my suffering was part of a greater plan. Growing up among unbelievers in Sarajevo, attending communist-run schools, having to hide my faith, being persecuted by police—it seemed like everything had been a kind of preparation. Even getting expelled and sent to a school for delinquent children was a blessing; it helped me understand the mission Our Lady would later ask of me.

I suddenly regretted ever complaining about my hardships, because it was only through them that I came to see "those who do not know the love of God" as my brothers and sisters.

"You cannot consider yourself a true believer," Our Lady said, *"if you do not see Jesus Christ in every person you meet."*

Earlier that year, in January, 1987, Our Lady stopped giving weekly messages to Marija and instead only gave them on the 25th of each month. When she started coming to me on the second of every month, she only gave messages occasionally, but eventually they became a regular part of her visits. I noticed that Our Lady ended the messages to Marija with the words *"Thank you for having responded to my call."* Sometimes she ended her messages on March 18 with the same or a similar phrase, but she concluded her second of the month messages with only *"Thank you."* Perhaps it was like a message within the message, one for the people she most desired to reach. She could not thank us for responding to her call if all had not responded. We cannot merely pray and fast and then think, *I've responded to her call.* The prayer and fasting she asks from us should fill us with love.

During the earliest 2nd of the month apparitions in 1987, Our Lady taught me a special prayer, which she and I still pray together today. It's a prayer for those who do not know God's love. I cannot yet reveal many details about this prayer because it is connected to the secrets, but I can say that it's a continuous prayer like the rosary. Otherwise, it's different from the rosary. In fact, I never pray the rosary with Our Lady because she doesn't pray to herself. Instead, this special prayer is directed at Jesus, and the words are addressed to Him. One day, the world can know the entire prayer, but only when Our Lady allows me to reveal it.

Unlike my annual apparitions—which will last as long as I live—I do not know how long the 2nd of the month apparitions will continue. After nearly 30 years, however, she still comes. During the 2nd of the month apparitions, I sometimes see tears on Our Lady's face. She loves her children more than we can ever imagine and she cries for each one who goes astray. If you saw her tears just once, I'm certain you would dedicate your life to praying for her intentions.

When Our Lady asks us to help her, she is not just asking me or the other visionaries. She is asking everyone. She says that our words alone cannot change those who do not believe. We can only make a difference with our prayers and example, and only if we have love in our hearts.

"Dear children," she said, *"When you pray for them, you pray for yourselves and for your future."*

All of the horrible things happening in our world today come from those who do not know the love of God. But she's not necessarily speaking about atheists. Unfortunately, many people who think of themselves as religious do not know His love yet, either.

"An unbeliever is not just someone who calls himself godless or says that he does not know whether God exists," said Fr. Slavko. "According to this intention, an unbeliever is also someone who says that he 'believes' and knows the Word of God but does not live according to it and does not do what is good. Such a 'faith' is actually knowledge that is not imbued with love."

And the Bible agrees. The apostle Paul wrote, "If I speak in human and angelic tongues but do not have love, I am a resounding gong or a clashing cymbal. And if I have the gift of prophecy and comprehend all mysteries and all knowledge; if I have all faith so as to move mountains but do not have love, I am nothing." (1 Corinthians 13:1-2)

In the same way, Our Lady does not want us to go around preaching to others. She wants us to talk, but with our lives, not our mouths. She asks believers to live as examples of people who know God's love. That way, those who do not believe can see the effect of that love in us.

"The only true peace," Our Lady said, *"is the one which my Son gives."*

Everyone hungers for peace, but most look in the wrong places. Only God gives peace. You can have millions of dollars, but without Him, you are destitute. You can live in a mansion, but without Him, you are homeless. No matter how much you acquire, you'll never be satisfied because you'll always think that peace is just around the corner. Many people think, "If only I can make more money, then I'll be happy." But peace is never around the corner. It's right in front of you, and to find it, you simply have to get on your knees and ask.

That's why the Queen of Peace has been coming. If you live her messages, then you'll be walking with Jesus. She basically repeats what's written in the Gospels, but in a simpler way.

"Extra-biblical revelations, in general, do not bring any new truths," wrote Dr. Fr. Ljudevit Rupčić, "but perhaps just a better recognition of the biblically revealed truths."

Let her lead you to love. Eventually, others will see in you what they're looking for, even if they didn't know they were looking for it, and your peace will spread to the people around you.

According to Our Lady, we who call ourselves believers must remember that we have a great responsibility.

At Mass in Međugorje one evening, I was having terrible back pain, something I've suffered with through the years. The church was crowded as usual, but I noticed a small space open on one of the benches, amidst a group of Italian pilgrims. Hoping to rest my back, I sat down, but one of the Italians started yelling at me.

"Stand up!" she said. "That's our bench! We were the first ones here!"

"I'm so sorry," I said. I quickly got up and stood in the aisle.

Later, one of their friends came to join them and she recognized me as one of the visionaries. When she told the others, they stood up and offered me the entire bench. I smiled and thanked them but remained standing.

I always laugh when I think about their reaction, but, at the same time, it serves as a cautionary tale. Imagine if I were someone who did not believe, and who, for the first time, entered a church to see what it was all about. After being "welcomed" in such a way, would I ever enter a church again? And whose responsibility would that be?

In a way, I think we are all unbelievers. No one can truthfully say, "I'm a good believer and I'm doing everything that God wants." Everyone makes mistakes. But it's important that we try, and if you desire to be an example—if you desire to show that you have faith and love—then you have to smile. You have to laugh and joke. If you are always nervous, fearful, or serious, then an unbeliever will say, "He's no different from anyone else. Why would I want to change and be like him?"

"Peace begins with a smile," said one of the great believers of our time—Mother Teresa—who was actually born in Yugoslavia and was said to have followed the messages of Međugorje.

Most importantly, we should never judge or criticize. When Our Lady asks us to pray for those who do not believe, she wants us to emulate her. First, we should feel love for them, to see them as our own brothers and sisters who were not as fortunate as we were to come to know the love of God. Only then will we be able to pray for them; otherwise our prayer will be ineffective and even hypocritical.

"The first and the last intention of our prayers needs to be for the grace to love God and our neighbor with our heart," said Fr. Slavko. "If our heart is not steeped in and completely permeated with divine love, nothing we do will have any value, nor will we be happy. The one who prays for the grace to love prays for happiness and peace for himself, for his family and for all mankind."

And if we follow Our Lady's example, then our peace will be evident to everyone around us, and they will want to know its source. Once, a cardinal from the Vatican came to Međugorje and said to me, "Do you know why I'm here?"

"Because Our Lady called you here," I said, and I meant it. She has said that no one learns about Međugorje by accident.

The cardinal smiled. "Perhaps you're right. But I had no desire to visit Međugorje until recently. You see, there's a church near the Vatican where I always see a few hundred Italians gathered once a month. They pray for hours. I simply could not understand what kept them there for so long. So, one day, I asked them. They said they were fruits of Međugorje, and they met there to replicate Međugorje's evening prayer program. That interested me enough to come and see what's happening here, and I'm happy I did."

So, their wordless example encouraged the cardinal to visit Međugorje.

"When you go home," I tell pilgrims, "resist the urge to tell everyone what you've experienced. Instead, focus on living the messages of

Our Lady, and when people see the changes in you, they will ask you about it."

Our Lady once said that she wishes to present all of us like a beautiful bouquet of flowers to her Son. She will continue to cry as long as there is even one person in the world who does not believe. That is why we need to pray. When we do, however, we do not need to pray for what we desire; God knows everything that is in our hearts, and He knows what is best for us in the long term—eternally speaking, of course. We should pray instead for our brothers and sisters. Every time we pray for someone who does not believe, we essentially wipe a tear from Our Lady's face.

Our Lady also gave prayer missions to the other visionaries. She asked Vicka and Jakov to pray for the sick, Ivanka for families, Marija for nuns and the souls in Purgatory, and Ivan for priests and young people.

When my friend's uncle became ill, she called Jakov and asked, "I know you pray for the sick. Will you pray for my uncle?"

"No problem," said Jakov, and he prayed for him that night.

The next morning, my friend called Jakov again.

"Thank you for praying for my uncle," she said.

"Is he feeling better?" Jakov asked hopefully.

"Well, he died last night."

Several months later, I came down with a mild cold. When Jakov saw me sneezing, he said, "Don't worry, Mirjana. I'll pray for you."

I shook my head. "Forget that I even exist. I know what happens to the people you pray for."

We've always joked about it, but clearly the prayer of a visionary is no more "special" than anyone else's. God hears the six of us at the same "volume" He hears everyone. The fact that we see Our Lady doesn't mean that our prayers get priority.

I believe that every person on the planet has a special mission.

Through prayer, we can discover God's plan for our lives. Just as I was prepared for my mission, think about your own trials, experiences, and dreams, and then ask yourself: *What mission is God preparing me for?*

At around the same time I received my prayer mission, my earthly mission was taking shape. Marko and I had been dating for several years, and I knew I wanted to spend the rest of my life with him. He felt the same way—he had since he was five years old. His persistence reminded me of *The Little Prince* and his flower: "It's the time you spent on your rose that makes your rose so important."

Now in his twenties, Marko was handsome and kind, but what really attracted me to him was his faith. He was always next to me during the apparitions with a rosary in his hand, and God had been the center of our relationship from the beginning.

By 1988, we were eager to get married, but neither of us had a steady income. I was 23 years old. Starting a life together seemed impossible, so we agreed to wait until one of us got a job. We prayed about it throughout the following year.

One day, a businessman asked me if I wanted to work as an office administrator at his travel agency in Medugorje. I said yes without even thinking about it or asking about the salary. I was too excited to care about details. I called Marko and said, "Now we can get married!"

That day marked the beginning of our engagement. When people ask how Marko proposed to me, I always laugh and say, "He didn't. I proposed to him!"

Reactions to our engagement were mixed. Friends and family in Sarajevo urged me not to get married too young, but people in Medugorje—where couples married earlier—saw things differently. They told me I had "caught that last train."

Mom and Dad were proud of me for getting a job. They had not expected me to find one in Sarajevo due to my "anti-government" reputation. I left home in the spring of 1989 and moved into a small house they had built in Bijakovići for their retirement. I began working right away. My main duties included paperwork, invoicing, and greeting visitors. Every time pilgrims came in, I played a game in my head—*will they recognize me or not?* I was happiest when they did not.

It was wonderful to be among so many believers, back where it all began eight years earlier. I reconnected with Uncle Šimun, Aunt Slava, my cousins, friends, and the other visionaries. The village had gone through significant changes since 1981—gift shops lined the main road, the field around St. James Church was now a paved promenade, and small hotels had replaced most of the tobacco fields.

Marko and I began planning our wedding for September 16th of that year. We intended to have a traditional wedding; if we were going to be residents of Međugorje, we knew it was important to do everything according to the local customs. I paid attention to what the other girls in the village did when they got married and tried to do the same.

Naturally, I was a little nervous on the evening before my wedding, but my father was an emotional mess. He and my mom had been in town for a week to help with preparations. Dad started crying every time he talked to me, and he could not even look at Marko.

"If he's not good to you," he said right in front of Marko, "then just come back to your dad, ok?"

Later that night, I was sitting with my mom when a knock at the door startled us. We opened the door to find some Italian pilgrims. One woman presented a beautiful bouquet of flowers.

"It would be our honor if you'll carry this bouquet tomorrow," she said.

I suddenly realized that Marko and I had worked so hard planning the wedding that I overlooked an important detail—I forgot to order my bouquet. In a small village like Međugorje, flower arrangements had to be ordered far in advance, and there were no flower shops nearby to buy one at the last minute. I would have been distraught to realize my mistake the next day.

"Thank you, thank you!" I said, crying. I hugged the Italians tightly. "You don't know what this means to me!"

The Italians were surprised and delighted by my reaction. They must have thought that I *really* liked flowers, but I was just awestruck to witness yet another example of how God always knows what we need—often before we ourselves even know we need it.

A typical Herzegovinian wedding begins with a lunch party hosted by the bride's parents at their house, but our house was too small for all the guests so my parents held the event at a hunting club in nearby Čitluk. The day had finally come. The scent of rosemary filled the air—according to custom, a branch of rosemary was given to every guest and worn as a corsage. Nearly every member of my family attended, including people I had not seen in years. The other visionaries came as well and wished me happiness and blessings.

After lunch, I arrived in front of St. James Church in my wedding gown. With the cool air of autumn finally providing some respite from the summer heat, Međugorje was crowded with pilgrims. As I ascended the church steps, I noticed dozens of people snapping photographs and hurrying towards me. Anywhere else in the world, a bride in a wedding dress is a lovely sight, but for some of the pilgrims in Međugorje that day, seeing a *visionary* in a wedding gown was impossible to resist. I was suddenly surrounded and unable to move. They touched me, kissed me, hugged me—and some of them started cutting off pieces of my wedding gown.

"It's for luck," said an Italian woman as she sliced off a lace.

I started crying. "Please don't," I said.

Luckily some of our guests saw what was happening and they quickly escorted me into the church. I took a deep breath, and when I saw Marko in his tuxedo, I was instantly at peace and excited about the new life that awaited us.

Fr. Milan Mikulić came all the way from the USA to officiate the ceremony. Originally from Proložac, a small village near Međugorje, Fr. Milan had been ministering in Portland, Oregon for many years.

When Marko and I met him a few years earlier during one of his visits to Međugorje, we both felt an immediate connection. Fr. Milan told us, "When you get married, you'll have to come visit me in America."

At the time, traveling across the world seemed so far-fetched that he might as well have been inviting us to the moon, but we were thrilled to now have Fr. Milan at our wedding.

Marko and I kneeled before the altar during the Mass. In his sermon, Fr. Milan described how Our Lady had left us free to choose our state in life. "Mirjana is giving her affirmative response that she intends to serve God in marriage," he said. "She has chosen Marko Soldo as her companion for life, to live the messages of Our Lady with him."

Per Herzegovinian tradition, Fr. Milan presented us with a blessed crucifix. As Marko and I exchanged vows, we put our hands on the cross, one on top of the other, and then we each kissed it before kissing each other. Mirjana Dragićević was now Mirjana Soldo.

After the wedding, we had a big reception at a hotel in Čitluk. My dad, with tears in his eyes, shook Marko's hand and said, "Finally, someone else can drive her around."

They both laughed and hugged each other, and then my father turned to me and said, "Take good care of my son."

"Well, now I'm obligated to," I said, smiling.

Marko, of course, spent half the night singing and dancing. As I watched him sing with the other men of the village, I felt grateful to have him in my life. His outgoing personality was the perfect complement to my introversion, and I knew that we were going to make a great team.

Marko makes a palačinka, the Croatian word for pancake.

CHAPTER 22

"I desire for the darkness, and the shadow of death which wants to encompass and mislead you, to be driven away."
— *From Our Lady's Message of March 18, 2014*

AFTER MARKO AND I got married, we lived with his parents at their home in Ograđenik, a small village near Međugorje on the road to Široki Brijeg. With seven family members sharing two bedrooms, living with Marko's family was challenging. But it was our only option at that time, and the excitement of being newly married helped us turn every inconvenience into fun and laughter.

A few months earlier, Marko's brother, Željko, had also gotten married, so he and his new wife were with us in the house. Marko's younger brother, Stjepan, also lived there. Stjepan had grown into a handsome, cheerful young man. He was now even a little taller than Marko, and he had a humility and gentleness that seemed unusual for a person of his age. He constantly asked me to tell him about the apparitions, and I was happy to do so.

Eventually Marko and I decided to move to my parents' house in Bijakovići. The house was tiny, but we enjoyed the solitude and finally felt like we had a place to call home. We put our wedding crucifix on the wall as a constant reminder of our Sacramental vows, and we prayed together every evening and had coffee together every morning.

Strange how there were some things I was not allowed to share with him—but I never let my knowledge of the future dictate our decisions.

"Every woman has at least one secret that she never tells her husband," Marko joked, "but my wife has an additional ten."

One of our dreams was to have children. My parents' house was too small for raising a family, and we knew we could not stay there forever, so we took a loan and started building a slightly larger house next door to my parents' house.

Marko and I settled into our new life together. He oversaw the construction of our home, and I continued working at the travel agency. I also shared my testimony with the pilgrims who were coming to Međugorje in ever-increasing numbers. I would usually speak to them from the steps of our house and sometimes hundreds of pilgrims stood in our front yard, crowding the street.

After I spoke, they always had numerous questions for me, ranging from simple ones—*What does Our Lady ask from us?*—to those I was not allowed to answer—*When will the secrets be revealed?* Some of my favorite questions, though, were the ones I could answer with a joke and a smile.

One day, a woman from Ireland raised her hand. "I know you see Mary, but have you ever seen an angel?"

"Yes, of course," I said, trying to seem serious. "I see one every morning when I wash my face in front of the mirror."

Everyone laughed, and I saw the love of God reflected back at me in hundreds of smiles. Many pilgrims came with somber faces, perhaps expecting me to have an entirely serious or apocalyptic message, but I was determined to show them what I had learned from Our Lady—that God is love. And love should make you happy.

During another talk, an American raised his hand and said, "Our Lady asks us to fast on bread and water every Wednesday and Friday.

But I'm used to drinking a cup of coffee in the morning. Is it ok to still have coffee?"

"Yes," I said, and I paused to look at the hopeful eyes of all the Americans. Then, I smiled and said, "As long as you drink it before Our Lady wakes up to see you."

A few questions, however, were strange or even judgmental. Dealing with those pilgrims helped me become more patient, and it showed me that even some people who called themselves believers still had not yet truly come to know the love of God.

"If the secrets are coming, why did you get married?" asked one man, an accusatory tone in his voice. "If you see Our Lady, don't you think you should have been a nun?"

I felt sorry for him, as I do for any person who complains or criticizes. How can we judge those we hardly know? And who among us can say we *truly* know anyone? Only God has the right to judge. When someone criticizes me, I keep in mind that there must be some other reason for their behavior. I think of how unhappy that person must be in wanting to hurt others, and I always try to respond to criticism with a joke and a smile.

"Well, there is value in suffering," I told the man, with a smile on my face. "What better way to come to know suffering than to have a husband?"

Everyone laughed—especially all the wives in the crowd—and the man who had asked the question could not help but smile.

"But to answer your question in a more serious way," I added, "perhaps the fact that we didn't become nuns and priests, and that none of us are perfect after seeing Our Lady, says less about us than it does about God's love for all of His children. He loves us in spite of our imperfections."

Some people forget that marriage is a sacrament, too. Nurturing the love between a husband and wife, and taking part in creation by welcoming new life into the world, is a beautiful and holy thing. In some cases, however, marriage is the more difficult path; no marriage is devoid of arguments, and anyone who says otherwise is not being truthful. Arguments happen, but the important thing is to refrain from words that offend.

Like every married couple, Marko and I occasionally had silly little squabbles, but we were determined to keep hurtful words out of our relationship. We respected each other's differences and we put God in the first place. Our faith helped us overlook the worldly challenges that often come between people. Plus, anytime Marko and I disagreed, I always joked that I would go to confession with his uncle, Fr. Slavko. When Marko and I laughed, it was impossible to be angry.

In the middle of building our house, we were deeply in debt, but we felt rich because we had love and peace. We constantly thanked God for what we had, and we never asked for more. I had just been handed my monthly salary at the travel agency when a man walked into the office and told me a sad story. He, his wife, and their three children had been evicted from their home. They had no food to eat and nowhere to go. I cried as I listened to him, and I envisioned myself in his situation.

"I will pray for you and your family," I said, and then I handed him the envelope with my entire month of pay inside. "This will help."

The man put his hands together in gratitude. "Thank you," he said.

"No, please don't thank me. Thank God."

But after he left, a feeling of panic suddenly hit me and I thought: *What did I just do?*

It felt nice to help him, but I realized that I wouldn't get paid again for another month. Perhaps my compassion had gone too far this time. I worried that I had done something irresponsible by giving the man everything, especially at a time when Marko and I were struggling financially. How would we pay our bills that month? And how was I going to tell Marko?

Now what will happen to us? I prayed.

Jesus' words in the Bible came to my mind: "You of little faith, why are you so afraid?"

The words rung true; I *was* afraid. By worldly standards, I was crazy and reckless to make such an outsized charitable contribution on a whim. But I had also begun to see that the very nature of Christian faith calls for actions which defy the status quo. If we truly believe, then we should never be afraid to be too "Christian," especially when it involves helping others. Although our brains might scream against being overly selfless, we are called to listen to our hearts.

I thought about *Mark's Gospel (12:41)*, which tells how a widow gave two little coins to the temple treasury while other people gave much larger amounts. Jesus gathered his disciples and said, "Truly I tell you, this poor widow has put more into the treasury than all the others. They all gave out of their wealth; but she, out of her poverty, put in everything—all she had to live on."

To change the world, lukewarm faith and tepid love will never be enough—in these trying times, our faith must be radical, and our love, limitless. We should endeavor to have our feet on the ground but our hearts in Heaven. It's not always easy to do. As Jesus said to the good young man who asked about eternal life, "If you wish to be perfect, go sell what you have and give to the poor, and you will have treasure in Heaven. Then come, follow me."

But the young man, who had many possessions, went away sad. Jesus had told the young man how to be *perfect*, and perfection is nearly unattainable for any human being. But as long as we continue striving for holiness, then we are on the right path. Even small acts of kindness can be beautiful to God, and every person on this planet can become a saint if they so desire.

Still, as I headed home after giving away my month's salary, I worried that Marko would be disappointed when I told him. We had not been married long, and I did not want him to suffer due to my unbridled empathy. At the dinner table that night, I sat there tapping my fork on my plate, too nervous to eat.

"What's wrong?" said Marko.

"I gave my monthly pay to a homeless man," I said, unable to even look at him. "I'm really sorry. He looked so sad and—"

"It's okay," said Marko.

I looked up. "It is?"

"God willed it so. Don't worry. We'll survive again this month, just like we did last month. And let's look on the bright side—fasting won't be difficult if we can't afford much food."

We both laughed, and we spent the rest of the evening thinking of creative ways to subsist for the next month. People in Herzegovina helped each other; the tradition of sharing homemade food and good harvests had been a part of life in the region for eons, and their generosity was amplified after the apparitions began. Although people here did not have much, they gave from the heart. When the first pilgrims started coming, my uncle set a table in front of his house, upon which he placed grapes, dried figs, water, and wine, as well as a handwritten sign that said: *If you are tired, hungry or thirsty, please take!*

The month passed with nothing but laughter, joy, and plenty of local produce. How fortunate I was to have married a man whose thoughts and feelings were so similar to my own. Our compatibility was clearly a fruit of trying to live Our Lady's messages. Prayer and fasting opened our hearts to be more compassionate and allowed us to see the value in giving. Jesus knew the value; he gave his life for us. But there are many other ways to give. We can spend time with a lonely person, cook a meal for a hungry family, teach a child how to pray, or help someone financially. It's most important to give for the right reasons—not because someone says you should or so you can deduct it from your taxes. In God's eyes, the only reason to give which has real worth is *love*.

By the end of 1989, Međugorje was thriving as a place of pilgrimage. At times one could see hundreds of priests hearing confessions out in the open around the church, so 25 new confessionals were added to help with the demand. The crowds had also outgrown the "oversized" St. James Church, so the parish constructed an outside altar fanning out from the back of the church and an open-air prayer area with roughly

5,000 seats. God's plan for the parish was coming to fruition. Fr. Slavko, inspired by Our Lady's messages, organized a youth fest in the first week of August. Hundreds of young people came from all over the world to celebrate their faith together.

It also became clear that Međugorje had an ideal geographic layout as a shrine. The main points of what had become the pilgrimage experience—Apparition Hill, Cross Mountain, and St. James Church—formed an almost perfect equilateral triangle on a map. Everything was in walking distance. A famous Italian artist named Carmelo Puzzolo crafted fifteen bronze reliefs depicting the Joyful, Sorrowful and Glorious mysteries of the rosary and the parish placed them on Apparition Hill. He also made fourteen bronze reliefs depicting the Stations of the Cross, and those were placed along the steep trail leading up Cross Mountain.

In the early days of the apparitions, Our Lady said *"the cross was also in God's plan when it was built,"* referring to the construction of the cement cross on top of the mountain in 1934. God clearly had a plan for Međugorje long before Our Lady first appeared. Within a decade, the small village had transformed into a sanctuary of prayer where those who opened their hearts could encounter the divine.

Pilgrims climbed Apparition Hill to pray the rosary and kneel at the metal cross marking the place of the first apparition. There they met their Mother.

On Cross Mountain, they recalled Christ's sufferings by praying the Stations of the Cross and enduring the physical pain of climbing the steep, rugged path. There they met Jesus.

And at St. James Church, with their hearts and minds beginning to open, they purified their souls in confession and took part in the Evening Prayer Program. There they met their Father.

Living in such an oasis of peace, one might never have known that the rest of Yugoslavia was simmering with unrest. The communist regime threatened to lash out at any moment like a cornered animal. I prayed for peace every day.

Just after the beginning of the next decade, Fr. Milan Mikulić repeated his invitation for Marko and me to visit his parish in Portland, Oregon—to spread the message of Međugorje in the USA, and to have something like a honeymoon. Our flights and expenses would be covered. Marko and I prayed about it, and on January 30, 1990, we soared over the Atlantic Ocean on a jumbo jet.

America was like a different world. The glimpses I had seen in movies and magazines did nothing to prepare me for actually going there. There was so much of *everything*—people of all types and colors, enormous stores selling more kinds of products than I ever knew existed, highways crammed with cars, and buildings that seemed to touch the sky. When I spoke at a Marian conference, I was amazed at the number of people who recognized me. Many of them said they had been following Međugorje since the beginning.

I was eager to experience America as I had seen it portrayed in the movies. So, as soon as Marko and I had some free time, we went out and tried our first hotdog, and then we went shopping. Upon entering the shopping mall, we stared with wonder at the overwhelming number of shops. When we walked into the first one, a clothing store, the clerk came up to us with a beaming smile. "Welcome!" she said. "How are you today?"

I stood there stunned, and then I whispered to Marko in Croatian, "She recognizes me. Let's go to a different shop."

When we entered the next store, the clerk there greeted us in the same way. "Hi! How are you?"

I finally realized that *How are you?* was just a typical greeting in America, whereas a person in Yugoslavia would only ever pose such a question to someone they knew. Americans clearly had big hearts, and wherever we went, people showered us with kindness, especially at St. Brigitta's parish where Fr. Milan pastored. He arranged for me to be there on February 2, 1990 to experience the monthly apparition. A large crowd prayed the rosary in the church as I awaited Our Lady in an adjoining chapel. When she appeared, she spoke about serious things, and Fr. Milan later told me that I swayed back several times as if a great wind pushed me. I did not recall moving, though.

Our Lady gave me a message for the world, and when the apparition ended, I repeated her words to Fr. Milan in Croatian and he read it aloud in English.

In her message, Our Lady explained that she wished to show us the way to eternal life, and she asked us to be good examples to those who did not believe. *"You will not have happiness on this Earth,"* she said, *"and neither will you come to Heaven, if you do not have a pure and humble heart, and do not fulfill the laws of God."* She also asked us to accept our suffering with patience, adding, *"You should remember how patiently Jesus suffered for you. Let me be your Mother and your connection to God, to Eternal Life. Do not impose your faith on those who do not believe. Show it to them with your example and pray for them, my children."*

I explained to Fr. Milan that Our Lady was referring to the sacrament of confession when she implored us to "reconcile and purify" our souls. Fr. Milan relayed my statement to the crowd, and later he was inundated with requests for confession.

Marko and I headed home to Međugorje on February 5th. Our visit to Portland was the first of many trips to the USA and other far-off places in the world. Knowing how Our Lady cried for everyone in the world who had not come to know God's love, I was eager to share the message of Međugorje with as many people as possible. And it was moving to see the fruits of Međugorje in so many places around the world.

I experienced my next annual apparition on March 18th, 1990. On the same day, communist East Germany held its first and only free election in history. A party called the Christian Democratic Union took power and immediately sought reunification with West Germany. The Berlin Wall had come down only months before, a poignant image for anyone who suffered under communism—including the people of Yugoslavia.

Around the same time, I began to feel strange again. This time was different, though. I suddenly felt tired all the time. My mood would change in an instant and for no apparent reason. Sudden bouts of nausea would overwhelm me and then disappear just as quickly. And, most peculiar of all, I developed an insatiable craving for *ćevapi*, a dish of grilled mincemeat that was popular in Sarajevo—but impossible to find in Međugorje at that time.

When I told my mother how I felt, she shouted joyfully, "That's wonderful!"

I was shocked. "How can you say that? I feel terrible!"

She laughed. "Mirjana, you're pregnant!"

And she was right. When I told Marko, his eyes lit up and he embraced me. "We're having a baby!" he said over and over. For the next nine months, he treated me like a fragile doll, and he reproached me when I tried to do too much. He even drove all the way to Mostar one evening for a ćevapi emergency.

Marko and I never had to discuss possible names for the baby because I already knew what it was going to be. Even before we got married, I experienced a vivid dream in which I gave birth to a girl and named her Marija, the Croatian name for Mary. But during my pregnancy, everyone from grannies to doctors kept telling me that I was carrying a boy. Every time someone told me that, I felt like I had been slapped across the face.

It has to be a girl, I thought. *It has to be Marija.*

Being pregnant in Herzegovina—where old wives' tales were taken seriously—required some extra patience. One tale says that if a pregnant mother has a craving for something red, like cherries or wine, and she touches her skin, then her craving will be forever etched on the baby as a birthmark. I knew it was a myth, but I still found myself keeping my hands to my side anytime I thought about strawberries, which was often.

My family visited us in the days leading up to the due date. When my father saw me with my large pregnant belly, he broke down in a mixture of laughter and sobs. He embraced me carefully so as not to even touch my stomach. "I'm going to be a grandfather," he said, sniffling.

Miro, now 16 and already as tall as our father, said he was looking forward to being an uncle. He, too, seemed certain that the baby was a boy, and he had all sorts of plans to teach him the ways of boyhood. It was as strange for me to think of Miro being an uncle as it was to think of my dad being a grandfather. It seemed like only a short amount of time had passed since I watched my parents bring Miro home from the hospital as a baby.

Marija Soldo entered the world on December 9th, 1990 with a full head of hair. Marko and I had already witnessed many miracles in our lives, but nothing compared to the birth of our daughter. We brought Marija home and embraced our new roles as mother and father. Our lives felt complete and we relished every milestone, from her first laugh to her first tooth.

Our home was filled with peace, but unfortunately the rest of the country was not.

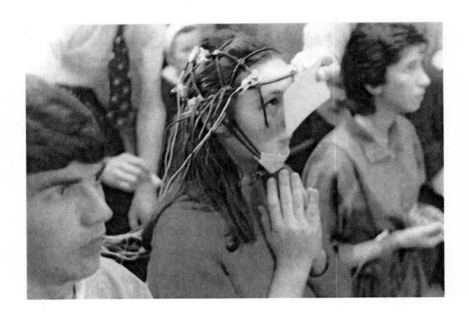

Doctors and scientists came from all over the world to study the six of us. Here, Ivanka undergoes a scientific test during the vision.

CHAPTER 23

"When confronted with an abyss of evil, the only response is an abyss of love."

— *Pope St. John Paul II*

MARY IS THE Mother of the Church, so when she appears on Earth, as she has throughout the ages, the Vatican usually takes notice and investigates.

Our daughter, Marija, was born on the feast day of one of the first visionaries. In 1531, Juan Diego experienced several apparitions on a hill in Mexico. Our Lady of Guadalupe, as she came to be known, proclaimed herself *"the Mother of the true God who gives life"* and left her image on Juan Diego's cloak. When the local bishop saw the miraculous image—which depicted Our Lady with a crown of twelve stars, clothed with the sun, and the moon under her feet as described in *Revelation*—he constructed a church in her honor. As a result of the apparitions, millions of natives converted to Christianity.

In 1555—23 years after the fifth and final apparition—the Church approved Juan Diego's visions. The Vatican has been studying our apparitions from the beginning. The most recent commission, established by Pope Benedict XVI in 2010, completed its investigation in 2014 under Pope Francis. But I never worry about Vatican approval because I know what I see. I trust in God's plan, and I've put everything in Our Lady's hands. I simply focus on my mission.

As Fr. Slavko once said, "Eventually, it will happen, silently as the spring, and Međugorje will be accepted."

In the meantime, Our Lady's plan will keep unfolding.

It's important for the Church to be cautious, as many alleged apparitions turn out to be untrue. Our Lady warned us that there are false apparitions in the world and that people need to be careful not to be deceived. Some alleged visionaries have even come to speak with me. I always wondered why they wanted to tell me about their experiences. If they truly saw Our Lady, what else could they possibly need? Sometimes I could tell that they were lying, but I did not confront them. Instead, I prayed that they might realize they were committing a major sin. Their alleged messages, most of which predicted calamities and horrible times to come, were clearly not from Our Lady.

Jesus, in the Gospel of Matthew (7:15-16), says, "Beware of false prophets who come to you disguised as sheep but underneath are ravenous wolves. You will be able to tell them by their fruits."

When pilgrims ask me about such "visionaries," I tell them to never trust anyone who spreads fear, because faith that comes from fear is not true faith, and Our Lady doesn't want people to love her out of fear.

On August 2, 2006, Our Lady said, *"The way to peace leads solely and only through love."*

Many historic apparitions culminated in some kind of sign left for the world. Guadalupe had the image on the *tilma*. In Lourdes, the miraculous spring began flowing. Fátima had the Miracle of the Sun. And in Međugorje, Our Lady promised to leave a permanent sign.

From the beginning of our apparitions, Catholics around the world were eager for the Church to give a definitive answer about Međugorje. On April 11, 1991, the Yugoslav Bishops Conference finally released a statement with the findings of the commission established to investigate Međugorje. The bishops left the decision about the supernatural character of the apparitions open for further investigation, but they made it clear that people were still allowed to visit Međugorje. They even established a pastoral commission to help guide the parish in its care for the pilgrims.

After years of hypnotizing us, poking us with needles, hooking us up to monitors, testing us with lie detectors, and even asking over a thousand psychiatric questions in one day, various teams of doctors and scientists found that several inexplicable things happened to us at the beginning of each ecstasy. Our eyes all fell on the same point simultaneously, and our eye movements ceased. When we spoke to Our Lady, our larynxes stopped moving and no sound was detected, but other aspects of speech remained intact. And we were virtually impervious to loud noises blasted in our ears and bright lights shined in our eyes.

One neuro-physiologist described those of us he tested as "partially and significantly disconnected from the exterior world" during our ecstasies, and "completely normal, relaxed, well-integrated and happy" when we were not experiencing an apparition.

Another doctor, who had been skeptical when he first heard about the apparitions, concluded in his report that the phenomenon was "scientifically inexplicable." He found no elements of deceit or hallucination and added, "No scientific discipline seems able to describe these phenomena. We would be quite willing to define them as a state of active, intense prayer, partially disconnected from the outside world, a state of contemplation with a separate person whom they alone can see, hear and touch."

Of course, I did not need a doctor to tell me what I was experiencing, or to reassure me that I was sane and honest, but I understood that the medical tests were important for others.

Although the Bishop of Mostar still expressed his doubts about our apparitions, some members of the Bishop's Conference publicly expressed their support for Međugorje. Cardinal Franjo Kuharic, Archbishop of Zagreb, described the commission's findings in a statement. "We bishops," he said, "after a three-year-long commission study accept Međugorje as a holy place, as a shrine. This means that we have nothing against it if someone venerates the Mother of God in a manner also in agreement with the teaching and belief of the Church…Therefore, we are leaving that to further study. The Church does not hurry."

But just as the commission's report opened the door for more pilgrims to visit Međugorje, the mounting conflict in Yugoslavia slammed it shut. Members of the new pastoral commission had planned to meet with the parish staff of Međugorje for the first time on June 27, 1991, but the meeting never took place because Croatia and Slovenia proclaimed their independence from Yugoslavia on June 25, 1991——the tenth anniversary of Our Lady's apparitions. It marked the beginning of a dark period for the region.

Earlier that year, on March 18, 1991, Our Lady may have hinted at the struggles that awaited us when she appeared at 7:30 pm for my annual apparition. I was in Međugorje and many people were present.

During the apparition, she gave me a message to share with the world. She asked us to pray so that we *might be able to spread peace and love to others, because that is now most necessary for you in this time of battle with Satan.* She also added, *"Only by means of prayer will you drive off Satan and all the evil that goes along with him."*

As she ascended into Heaven, I saw three angels waiting for her— something I had only seen once before, in August, 1981. It was a striking apparition, and not only because of the angels; with Yugoslavia on the brink of war, her words about a battle with evil seemed disconcertingly prescient.

This was not the first time our part of the world faced upheaval.

From the early days of civilization, the region surrounding Međugorje has been a crossroads of humanity. Before the Slavs settled from the north in the 7th century, the land was home to Illyrians, Greeks, Romans and various other tribes and peoples. Ancient ruins, Roman aqueducts, and medieval tombs called *stećci* still mark the landscape.

After the breakup of the Roman Empire, the Balkan Peninsula was divided roughly along today's border between Bosnia and Serbia. The western side retained its Roman Catholic roots while the eastern side held fast to the Byzantine Orthodox faith. Later, in the 15th Century, the Ottoman Empire conquered the region and introduced Islam into the mix. When five centuries of Turkish occupation came to an end, the Austro-Hungarian Empire took over.

Several distinct nationalities emerged out of this melee: Croats and Slovenes, who were Roman Catholic; Serbs, who were Orthodox Christian; and Muslims, who are now called Bosniaks. Adding to the complications, the area was also home to Montenegrins and Macedonians. As a whole, the people of the region were called the South Slavs.

The Austro-Hungarian Empire ruled over much of the region until the First World War, after which the South Slavs joined together into what became known as the Kingdom of Yugoslavia. But power struggles between different ethnic groups resulted in conflicts that severely escalated when World War II began. Hitler's bombing of Belgrade in 1941, followed by a German ground invasion, ended in Yugoslavia's surrender.

A resistance group commanded by Josip Broz Tito—who wanted to turn Yugoslavia into a communist state—fought against the Nazis. In the end, Tito's Partisans emerged victorious and established the *Socialist Federal Republic of Yugoslavia*, a communist federation made up of six republics: Slovenia, Croatia, Bosnia-Herzegovina, Serbia, Montenegro and Macedonia. Tito appointed himself president of the country and supreme commander of the military.

Acknowledging the challenges posed by Yugoslavia's diversity, Tito said, "I am the leader of one country which has two alphabets, three languages, four religions, five nationalities, six republics, surrounded by seven neighbors, a country in which live eight ethnic minorities."

While the republic of Croatia was populated primarily by Croats, and Serbia by Serbs, the republic of Bosnia-Herzegovina—in which Sarajevo and Međugorje were located—had a large population of Muslims, Croats and Serbs. In many towns, there were mosques, Catholic churches and Orthodox churches all within walking distance of each other.

Tito's stated goal was to unite the South Slavs, but his communist government was more oppressive than unifying. After Tito's death in 1980, the communists who succeeded him were afraid of losing their grip on the people, and the people feared that the government would persecute them even more. A period of turmoil and economic hardship ensued.

Our Lady began appearing to us a year after Tito's death, forging a place of prayer in a region that some called *The Powder Keg of the World*—at the crossroads of East and West, of Christianity and Islam, of communism and freedom. The apparitions certainly had some effect on the regime.

A large portion of the country embraced Our Lady's messages and citizens from all over Yugoslavia disregarded the government by visiting Međugorje. There were even accounts of communist officials converting and leaving the party.

"Communism collapsed," said Fr. Tomislav Pervan. "It was conquered not by arms or tanks, but by prayers."

In 1990, the communists lost power in the country's first multiparty elections, except in Serbia and Montenegro, where the president of the Serbian Communist Party, Slobodan Milošević, and his allies won. Communism was officially dead in Yugoslavia, but we had no chance to rejoice. In his quest for power, Milošević swapped communism for Serbian nationalism, gaining control of the Yugoslav Army and plotting to turn most of the region into "Greater Serbia," which was to include all of Bosnia-Herzegovina and a large part of Croatia. He warned of "armed battles," which was not a shallow threat—two days after Croatia and Slovenia declared their independence, the Yugoslav Army intervened.

I thought back to one of my early apparitions in Sarajevo, when Fr. Petar asked me to present a question to Our Lady. "Ask her if Croatia will ever be free."

At the time, I did not understand what he was talking about, but I asked Our Lady.

"Yes," she said, *"but only after much suffering and pain."*

Back then I did not give it much thought, but in 1990 it seemed significant.

The period leading up to the war was a strange time. A number of local men and boys who had been called to service by the Yugoslav Army fled to other countries because they did not want to be forced to shoot at their own people. Tanks and armored vehicles paraded about the country. The Yugoslav Army attacked Slovenia first but retreated after 10 days, only to turn their gaze on a bigger prey: Croatia.

In September, 1991, Marko and I decided to take 9-month-old Marija on a week-long visit to see our friend Antonio Cassano at his home in Montemelino, Italy. Bosnia-Herzegovina was still relatively peaceful, but as we made our way towards the Adriatic coast of Croatia to catch the car ferry to Italy, we began to see Yugoslav Army units entrenched in the hills along the Croatian border.

"This doesn't look good," said Marko.

We made it to the ferry safely, but as the ship disembarked from the port of Split, Croatia, we heard there were Yugoslav Navy warships lurking off the coast. The next morning, when we arrived in Ancona, the crew told us that we were either very lucky or very unlucky because our crossing had been the last. The situation in Croatia had become too dangerous for the ferry company to take any more risks.

Marko and I were shocked. We were stranded in Italy with a baby and just one suitcase between the three of us.

As planned, we went to see Antonio. When we told him about our situation, he said, "My home is your home. Don't worry about anything. Stay as long as you need."

We were grateful for his hospitality, but we did not want to burden him for too long. Antonio, who was then in his 50s, had never married and lived by himself in a large, stone house. After all that time, he had gotten used to living in solitude, and in our first few days there, I felt terrible whenever Marija cried at night or made a big mess with her food.

Marko and I considered driving back home the long way

around—through Venice, into Slovenia, and south into Croatia and Bosnia-Herzegovina—but shortly after our arrival, the Yugoslav Army unleashed its fury on Croatia. Driving through a warzone was not an option, especially not with Marija, and we were horrified by what we saw on the news. The city of Vukovar was surrounded and destroyed. Yugoslav planes bombed government buildings in Zagreb. Artillery fire rained down on the old town of Dubrovnik, a UNESCO World Heritage site. In some places, civilians were killed and dumped in mass graves.

Marko and I felt helpless watching the destruction of Croatia from afar, but we could not just sit back and do nothing. We began gathering aid and sending it to Croatia. It started out on a small scale—we'd send a bag of medical supplies one day, a box of clothes the next—but as word spread about what we were doing, the donations quickly increased. Antonio allowed us to use his home as a warehouse for the supplies. The Italians responded generously, sometimes bringing truckloads of supplies to Antonio's house. When people came from distant parts of Italy to donate supplies, Antonio gave them food and accommodation and thanked them in the name of the Croatian people.

In contrast to the unrest back home, the hilltop village of Montemelino was a tranquil refuge. Antonio's house overlooked the hills of Umbria, a rolling patchwork of vineyards, pastures, olive groves, and forests. Marko and I loved taking Marija on evening walks in the cool, fresh country air, and we regularly went to Mass at the nearby *Santuario della Madonna di Lourdes*, the first church in Italy to be dedicated to Our Lady of Lourdes. The plain exterior of the century-old church looked nothing like its opulent, welcoming interior. The blue arched ceiling was speckled with gold stars. Paintings of Jesus, Our Lady and the saints lined the columns and walls.

The most striking feature at the sanctuary was its replica of the Lourdes grotto. A statue of Our Lady gazed out from a niche above the cave, and the light from her crown of stars mingled with the flicker of candles to illuminate the grotto. When I prayed there, I felt an over-whelming sense of Our Lady's presence and a connection to the visionary

Bernadette, whose image hung on the wall. I wondered if Bernadette struggled with feelings of unworthiness like I did.

Three times a day—morning, noon, and sunset—the church's bells tolled the melody of *Immaculate Mother*, the hymn sung during the nightly procession in Lourdes, France. I could hear it clearly at Antonio's house and I always hummed along.

> *Immaculate Mary, your praises we sing.*
> *You reign now in Heaven with Jesus our King.*
> *Ave, Ave, Ave, Maria...*

> *In Heaven the blessed your glory proclaim;*
> *On Earth we your children invoke your sweet name.*
> *Ave, Ave, Ave, Maria...*

> *We pray for our Mother, the Church upon Earth,*
> *And bless, Holy Mary, the land of our birth.*
> *Ave, Ave, Ave, Maria...*

The last verse was especially timely, as the *land of my birth* was in dire need of help from above.

Thankfully, the ill-equipped Croatian forces managed to gain ground against the mighty Yugoslav Army and a cease-fire was announced in January, 1992. At the same time, however, tensions were rising in Bosnia-Herzegovina. They reached a boiling point in late February when the Bosnian parliament declared independence. Croats and Muslims were in favor of the decision, but Serbs wanted to remain part of Yugoslavia—and they had the backing of the Yugoslav Army.

As time went on, my mother yearned to visit us, especially to see her new granddaughter. She was finally able to board a flight from Belgrade to Italy, and Antonio gave her a room right next to ours. It was wonderful to have her there.

My father and brother remained at our apartment in Sarajevo. As conditions in Yugoslavia worsened, I urged them to stay in Sarajevo because I thought they would be safe there. After all, who would shoot at whom? Growing up, I had seen members of all three ethnicities living as friends and neighbors in the city, and everyone got along.

Unfortunately, times had changed.

My dear friends Dr. Vittorio Trancanelli and his daughter, Allesandra.

CHAPTER 24

"My eyes and my heart will be here, even when I will no longer appear."

— *From Our Lady's Message of March 18, 1996*

THE WORD *MEĐUGORJE* means between the hills, an obvious reference to Apparition Hill and Cross Mountain bordering the parish. But in a figurative sense, Međugorje was located between the major ideological mountains of the world as well. In the early part of 1992, those mountains seemed poised to crash into each other.

With the threat of war looming over Bosnia-Herzegovina, I felt an urgency to put Our Lady's messages into practice beyond what I could do alone. During the war she repeatedly called us to pray for peace, so I asked Antonio to help me start a prayer group.

He was enthusiastic about the idea, and he invited everyone he knew to come and pray with us every Wednesday at 11 am. He converted a room at his house into a prayer sanctuary with a small white statue of Our Lady. We expected only a few people to show up for the first scheduled prayer meeting, so we were stunned when the room quickly filled up with nearly 40 people. Those who came later had to pray outside.

Our mission was to pray for those who had not yet come to know the love of God. We always prayed the rosary and read verses from the Bible. Many of the people who came to pray with us had been following Our Lady's messages from the beginning. I was especially impressed by Dr. Vittorio Trancanelli, a local surgeon in his late 40s, and his wife, Rosalia, who went by Lia.

With his caring heart and deep faith, Vittorio provided free medical care to anyone in need. Few people were aware that he suffered from serious medical problems himself because he never complained or let it interfere with what he saw as his mission. He and Lia had a biological son named Diego, but they also accepted many foster children into their home, and they started a community for distressed women who needed a free and safe place to live. They even adopted a beautiful little girl with Down's syndrome, Alessandra, after her mother died.

I felt a bond with Alessandra the first time I met her; I had never seen a child so full of love and so unreservedly happy. She also had a deep and seemingly inherent faith. When I told her that Our Lady had asked me to pray for unbelievers, she vowed to join me in my mission. She even memorized how to say the *Our Father, Hail Mary* and *Glory Be* prayers in Croatian.

Living so close to Assisi, Vittorio and Lia were strongly devoted to St. Francis and St. Clare. Alessandra naturally shared their enthusiasm—so much, in fact, that she disappeared one day and when we finally found her in the bathroom, she had cut her hair as short as possible to look like St. Clare.

Lia used to tell me, "When I bathe Alessandra, I feel like I'm bathing Jesus. She fills me with love and strengthens my faith."

On March 18, 1992, Vittorio, Lia, Alessandra and the rest of our prayer group gathered in Antonio's house to be with me for my annual apparition. An Italian television crew came to record the event. With all the uncertainty of waiting in exile for six months, every meeting with the Blessed Mother gave me strength and hope.

Alessandra knelt beside me and folded her hands exactly like mine as I prayed and waited. Our Lady appeared suddenly at around 1:50 pm. She and I prayed the *Our Father* together three times—once for the sick, once for those who had not yet come to know God's love, and once for everyone present—and then I prayed the *Salve Regina* in her honor.

She also gave me a message to share with everyone. *"Dear children,"* she said imploringly, *"I need your prayers now more than ever before. I beseech you to take the rosary in your hands now more than ever before. Grasp it firmly and pray with all your heart in these difficult times. Thank you for having gathered in such a number and for having responded to my call."*

"Yes," I said, "we will do it, Mother."

After she departed, I scribbled her words on a piece of paper and eventually got the strength to stand in front of the crowd. I glanced out at all the eager faces as I read the message aloud in Italian. When I got near the end, however, I choked up when I recalled the concern on Our Lady's face.

"I can't go on anymore," I said. "I'm sorry."

A while later, the television crew interviewed me in a grassy field beside Antonio's house. "Why couldn't you finish reading the message?" said the interviewer. "What was that about?"

"When I told Our Lady that we would pray," I said, "I had the thought that she was like a pilot who wanted to bring us all up into the skies. She came to show us the route that we should take to get there. I replied on everyone's behalf, 'Yes, we will do it, Mother.' The words just came out of my heart; I said it because I couldn't do otherwise."

"The invitation to pray for peace is repeated many times. Did the Madonna ask you to pray for peace in Yugoslavia or any other ongoing conflict?"

"When Our Lady came to Međugorje eleven years ago, she presented herself as the Queen of Peace. That was a little strange to us because we already lived in peace, like here in Italy, but now we know why. We prayed for peace only a little, no different than we prayed for everything else. But I don't think Our Lady wants us to pray for peace only in Yugoslavia. She wants us to pray for peace on Earth. To her, Yugoslavia, Germany, Italy, and all other countries do not exist. From her perspective, we're all children of the same planet, so we should pray for peace in the entire world."

"For our viewers who do not understand, how does one pray?"

"A prayer only needs to be done with heart. It's simple. We shouldn't think Our Lady wants something from us that we can't do or don't know how to do. First, we should feel God as our father who is always near us and who loves us. Only when we feel this way can we pray. We should start every single day with a prayer, before going to school, work, whatever. Parents should pray with their children. Ask for God's help throughout the day and thank Him for every little blessing you receive. Everything comes from God."

"So, discovering faith is a great victory. One can't just say a Hail Mary and have faith. At what moment can we clearly say that we have faith?"

"When we feel in our hearts that we love God more than anyone or anything on this planet. That's when we can say we have faith. And when we do everything Our Lady invites us to do—when we pray the rosary, when we go to Holy Mass, when we confess our sins every month, when we fast on Wednesdays and Fridays. Then we can say that we have faith."

In response to her message, our prayer group gathered to pray the rosary right after the apparition. On the same day—in Lisbon, Portugal, incidentally not far from Fátima—the three leaders representing the Muslims, Croats and Serbs of Bosnia-Herzegovina met and signed a peace agreement. Some expected the agreement to prevent a war by dividing the country along ethnic lines. But ten days later, the agreement fell apart.

The Bosnian Serb Army, supported by Milošević and the Yugoslav Army, mobilized their forces to secure territory throughout

Bosnia-Herzegovina. Their goal, it seemed, was to inflict as much suffering as possible. The horrors were unimaginable—ethnic cleansing and systematic rape were widespread.

We began directing our aid supplies to Bosnia-Herzegovina, but when the Italian news reported that the Serbs had surrounded Sarajevo, I was struck with fear and could not do anything. Why had I told my father and brother to stay? The Serbian forces—intent on destroying the Muslim Army, which had a strong presence in Sarajevo—launched bombs and rockets into the city from their strongholds in the surrounding hills.

I called our apartment in Sarajevo, but the call would not go through. Imagining the worst, I spent the next three hours pacing, praying and redialing. My father finally answered.

Static muffled his voice. "Hello?" he said, sounding out of breath.

"Oh, Dad!" I said, and I started to cry. "I saw the news. I'm so sorry."

"Don't you be sorry for one second," he said. "No one could have known. Miro and I will be fine."

A series of loud booms drowned out my father's voice.

"Dad? What is that?"

"Mirjana, we have to take shelter. I love you." And he hung up.

I felt like I could not breathe. I looked at little Marija and wondered if she would ever see her grandpa and uncle again.

As each day passed, I watched the destruction of Sarajevo on the TV news. I could not believe what was happening to my city. Every time they showed a body lying in the street, I prayed that it was not my father or brother. I barely even had the strength to hug Marija, but my mother remained surprisingly calm throughout each day; she smiled and played with Marija, and she helped us take care of her. At night, however, I often heard my mother listening to the radio news reports from Sarajevo in her bedroom, and sometimes I heard her crying. She suffered in silence, as she had always done.

I continued calling our apartment every day, but the calls only went through sometimes. When they did, I could hear bombs and gunfire in the background.

Our apartment building was in the center of the city where the worst battles between the Muslim and Serbian armies were taking place. One night, a bomb hit the exterior of our apartment, blasting a large hole in the wall, but thankfully Dad and Miro had started sleeping in the stairwell in the center of the building.

The next time I spoke to my brother on the phone, he sounded exhausted. "It's terrible, Mirjana," he said. "I can't fall asleep."

My heart ached for him. "Because of the bombs?" I said.

"No, because Dad snores so loud! The bombs are quiet compared to him!"

I laughed, but deep inside I knew I had to find a way to get them out of Sarajevo. They would be far safer in Međugorje, which, so far, seemed to be protected from the war. I loved Miro as if he was my own child and I was worried that the Serbian or Muslim Army would take him and make him fight; most of the soldiers in the war were around his age.

My father told me that the Muslim Army had been coming to our apartment almost every day to look for Serb snipers. The soldiers moved our furniture and emptied our closets as they searched, and Miro and Dad would put everything back after they left. But one day they decided not to clean up after them.

The next time the soldiers came, one of them looked at the mess and said, "Why don't you guys tidy the place up a little bit?"

My father smiled. "Because we know you'll just come again and undo all our cleaning!" Even in such dark times, Dad never lost his sense of humor.

It was not long before he and Miro ran out of food. Blockades prevented supplies from reaching the city. It was too dangerous to go out, anyway—snipers killed anyone unfortunate enough to pass in front of their crosshairs. Fasting had taught Miro and Dad how to get by with less, but hunger pangs soon set in. They prayed for help.

Our neighbor, Paasha, who was now quite elderly, came to give my father some canned food one day. "This is for you and your son," she said.

"Thank you, Paasha," said my father, "but we can't take your food."

"Nonsense. Don't you worry about me. Miro is only 17 and he needs to live."

My father reluctantly accepted it, and Paasha continued giving them small amounts of food. Dad and Miro were grateful for her generosity. During a war in which it seemed like everybody was against everybody, Paasha's kindness shone in the darkness. But her sacrifice was even greater than my father and brother knew at that time—sadly, I later heard that Paasha died of hunger during the war.

In contrast to Sarajevo, there was plenty of food in Italy, but I was always too worried about my father and brother to eat. I also felt guilty about eating when people back home were starving. I lost 20 pounds in a few months.

Like any true Italian, Antonio got deeply concerned when he saw that I was hardly eating. One day he sat down to talk with me. "Maybe during the next apparition you should ask Our Lady to help," he said. "Won't she help you?"

"She knows," I said. "And I don't want to be ungrateful for the gift of seeing her. How many others are suffering in Sarajevo? I should pray like everyone else."

And as I was looking at him, I suddenly had an idea. "I know! I will pray to Antonio."

"What can I do?"

I laughed. "Not you. *Saint* Antonio. He's never failed me."

My lifelong devotion to St. Anthony had only become stronger since I was a little girl. Born in

Born in Lisbon, Portugal in 1195, Anthony grew up to become a Franciscan friar. Admired for his insightful preaching, he used simple words to convey deeper truths—not unlike Our Lady's messages. He once said, "What we are before God, we are, and nothing more."

And, like most saints, he had a strong devotion to the Blessed Mother. "Mary provides shelter and strength for the sinner," he wrote.

Anthony earned his reputation as the patron saint of lost people and things after someone stole a book of Psalms from him in Bologna. At the time, books were quite rare and priceless, and he had written his notes and sermons within the pages. Anthony prayed for it to be found, and his prayers were answered when the remorseful thief returned the book.

Anthony died in Padua, Italy on June 13, 1231 and his feast is celebrated every year on the same day throughout the world, including at the St. Anthony Shrine in Humac, about 13 km from Međugorje. Catholics in Herzegovina *love* St. Anthony. We've always joked that he's the only saint you can bargain with.

Every year on the eve of St. Anthony's feast day, people living in the vicinity of Humac leave their homes and walk all night to reach the shrine by morning. I made the pilgrimage with my cousins when I was younger. We went barefoot as an extra penance, and we prayed and sang hymns under the stars. I was not used to walking so much—I always took the train or bus in Sarajevo—and my feet were bleeding by the time we reached the shrine. But I was so happy about making it that I hardly noticed.

Thousands of people walked all night and filled the streets of Humac by dawn. After Mass at the shrine, I prayed the St. Anthony Chaplet while going around his statue in the church, just like many of the other pilgrims did. When I completed the prayer, I felt like my pilgrimage was complete, and I joined everyone in the street to feast on roasted lamb. Knowing we had just done something for God, we were full of joy and free from every worry—except for not knowing how we would get home.

With my father and brother now stuck in a seemingly hopeless situation, I got on my knees and asked St. Anthony to intercede. "Let's make a deal," I prayed. "Please help them come out of this safe and sound. If they do, I'll pray your chaplet every day for the rest of my life, and I'll fast in your honor every Tuesday." And then I added, "But if they don't come out, forget about it."

I had not realized how fitting the St. Anthony Chaplet was for my father and brother's situation until I prayed it that night. The chaplet is like a rosary consisting of thirteen groups of three beads. On each of the three beads, you pray an *Our Father, Hail Mary* and *Glory Be*. And for each of the thirteen groups of beads, you pray and meditate on a specific intention related to St. Anthony:

"St. Anthony, who raised the dead, pray for those Christians now in their agony, and for our dear departed."

"St. Anthony, liberator of captives, deliver us from the captivity of evil."

"St. Anthony, protected by Mary, avert the dangers which threaten our body and our soul."

Days later, Marko's younger brother Stjepan called us. At that time, he was preparing to join other Croats in defending the local villages. Before the war, the Yugoslav Army confiscated all the arms in the region, so young men were going to the front lines with nothing more than small hunting rifles and a few bullets—and rosaries around their necks.

"I know this might sound strange," Stjepan said to me, and then he laughed. "Well, maybe it won't to *you*. A gentleman from Austria recently came to town, saying he had a dream in which the Archangel Gabriel told him to take a busload of people out of Sarajevo."

It did sound strange, but who was I to judge someone else's vision? Maybe the bus trip would be an answer to my prayers. On the other hand, I knew it would have to pass through dangerous Serb checkpoints to leave the city. And how was I supposed to tell my dad to get on a bus with a stranger who claimed to get orders from an angel?

When I called our apartment, my father's initial reaction was as I expected. "Mirjana, that would be like committing suicide! They're killing everyone out there."

But my brother disagreed. "I'm going," he said. "I can't stand it here anymore. I'm hungry."

My father could not let him go alone. "If you go, I go."

Stjepan arranged for the Austrian man to find them, and in June, 1992—around the time of St. Anthony's feast day—Miro and Dad nervously boarded the bus with fifty other people from Sarajevo. As the bus moved through the deserted, war-torn streets of our once-beautiful city, my father gazed through the window and cried. Buildings lay in ruin. Rubble and broken glass littered the streets. Bloodstains marred the sidewalks.

"What have they done?" he said.

When they reached the city limits, a Serb army unit forced the bus to stop at a checkpoint. Grizzled soldiers with scruffy beards and automatic weapons boarded the bus. They looked at each passenger with suspicion and steely-eyed contempt. Miro, trembling, heard a trickle and glanced to his side—the other passengers were so terrified that some of them had lost control of their bladders.

Miro closed his eyes and prayed with all his heart. *Let us live. Deliver us from evil.* When he opened his eyes again, the soldiers were getting off the bus. Moments later, they let the bus pass through the checkpoint.

Just outside of Sarajevo, the bus stopped in a village where smiling nuns waited to greet everyone with food and drinks. But nobody took a bite; instead they just poured shots of *rakija* and toasted to God's goodness. They could hardly believe they had made it out of Sarajevo alive.

When Dad and Miro arrived in Međugorje, my mother bravely left Italy and got back there as fast as she could. The boys were far too thin, my mom said, but she was confident that some homemade food would nourish them back to good health. Still, even my mother's cooking could not erase their traumatic memories of living in constant danger. A violent thunderstorm passed through Međugorje one night while Dad and Miro were sleeping. When cracks of thunder jarred them awake, they ran down to the basement and took cover, thinking they were still in Sarajevo.

On the other side of the Adriatic, I prayed the St. Anthony Chaplet every night.

Sadly, bombed-out houses and orphaned children were common scenes during the war. (PHOTO BY JOE MIXAN)

CHAPTER 25

As they were stoning Stephen, he called out, "Lord Jesus, receive my spirit." Then he fell to his knees and cried out in a loud voice, "Lord, do not hold this sin against them."

— *Acts of the Apostles, 7:59-60*

B Y SEPTEMBER, 1992, the ceasefire in Croatia had brought a tense and fragile peace, but the war raged in Bosnia-Herzegovina. Despite the danger, Marko and I felt drawn to return home to Međugorje. It felt wrong to be separated from our family and friends. We learned that a small ferry started sailing from Italy to Croatia by taking a longer, safer route through the islands of Dalmatia. After praying about it, we decided to return home.

I was sad to leave Antonio. Marko and I had lived with him for an entire year, and he had become like a brother to us. I expected him to welcome getting his solitude back, so I was surprised to see tears in his eyes after I told him we were leaving.

"When you first came," he said, "I must admit that it was difficult to suddenly have a full house. I was praying every evening for God to help me get used to living with a family. But I think I prayed too well, because now I don't think I can live without you three."

"You always have a place to stay in Međugorje." I smiled. "We're just as noisy there so you'll feel right at home."

As we prepared to depart, however, Antonio came to us again. "I'm coming with you," he said.

"Why would you do that?" I said.

"I love you all so much that I can't let you go alone."

Antonio got in the car with us and we set out.

Arriving back in Croatia after the ferry crossing was an eerie experience. People warned us that we should take certain roads to reach Međugorje. It was safest to drive at night, they said, and only with our headlights off.

Was it a mistake to come back? I held tight to Marija and asked God to protect us.

The small roads leading to Herzegovina were winding and dark. We passed a bombed-out house, its charred rafters like the bones of a great black skeleton. We had to stop at several Croatian checkpoints where the soldiers checked our car. But peace washed over me when I saw finally Cross Mountain framed by the twin spires of St. James Church. We were home.

My father cried when he saw us, and he immediately grabbed Marija from my arms. "My granddaughter!" he said, kissing her. "She's so big! How much pasta did you give her?"

Dad's personality was the same, but the stress of the war and his fear for Miro's life had taken an obvious toll on his body. His hair was now completely gray, his eyes weary. Miro seemed healthy, but he was still having nightmares.

Antonio stayed in Međugorje for a while and spent much of his time assessing what types of aid supplies were most needed. He went back to Italy determined to increase his relief efforts.

Everyone was together and I was home, but one thing still concerned me—Dad and Miro had not brought our important papers from Sarajevo, because they were not sure if they would make it out alive. My documents could be replaced, but among them was the parchment that Our Lady had given me ten years earlier. I never imagined that a war could happen in our city, so I thought everything would be safe there in the desk.

Međugorje had not changed much—people had fears and concerns, but overall the air seemed to be filled with the hope that Our Lady would help. By then the village had become a central point for the aid shipments streaming in from other parts of the world. People who had previously come as pilgrims now risked their lives to bring supplies to the region. Americans sent entire freight containers full of aid across the Atlantic, and organizations in other parts of Europe regularly delivered supplies. People from Italy, like Antonio, were especially generous. And a young man named Magnus drove a truck filled with food and medicine all the way from Scotland. This experience led him to start one of the great fruits of Međugorje, a charity called *Mary's Meals* which feeds over a million children around the world.

Fr. Slavko seemed to work harder than ever during the war. Aside from overseeing the church prayer program for the relatively few pilgrims in town, he also wrote books, heard confessions, helped with relief deliveries, and climbed Apparition Hill or Cross Mountain every morning. He was so focused on his work that he never worried about trivial matters, and his humble needs were especially evident in his wardrobe. After getting caught in the rain on the hill one day, he came to our house and borrowed one of Marko's t-shirts. I offered to wash his wet one and bring it to him later, but when he gave it to me, I saw that it was badly stained and worn out.

"You just keep Marko's shirt," I said, "and I'll throw this one away."

His eyes got big. "Are you crazy? That shirt will last me another ten years!"

On another occasion, I met Fr. Slavko at the airport on our way to give a talk overseas. He was wearing civilian clothes instead of his Franciscan robe, and I had to stop myself from laughing when I saw how silly he looked. Only half of his shirt was tucked in, and the hems of his ill-fitting pants ended far above his ankles. I offered to help him buy some new clothes, but he looked at me as if I had said something ridiculous. "I already have clothes," he said. "Why would I need new ones?"

He was only interested in working for Our Lady and spreading her messages, and he did so tirelessly. One day, during one of his frequent visits to our house, he looked especially weary.

"Father, you're going to exhaust yourself," I said. "You need to rest."

"I'll rest when I'm dead," he quipped.

I laughed. "Somehow I doubt that. When do you even have time to sleep?"

"I sleep a few hours a night and that's enough. There's so much work to be done for God."

"Especially now." I poured him a cup of coffee. "You know, Father, I was thinking. I'd really like to help you with the relief effort now that I'm back in Medugorje."

He nodded, rubbing his chin. "I wonder, what can we do together that will help the most people?"

I looked at little Marija playing with a baby doll on the floor. "As a mother, I'd like to help the children."

Fr. Slavko sipped his coffee. "Yes, this war has created too many orphans. Let's think about it and pray for God's enlightenment."

Countless children had lost their parents in the war. The TV showed hungry children of all ages suffering in the streets of Sarajevo, Vukovar, and other places. Why should they be denied the right to a happy childhood because so-called adults could not solve their problems peacefully?

"All grown-ups were children once, although few remember it," said the Little Prince.

Fr. Slavko loved children, too. One day, when Marko, Marija and

I climbed Apparition Hill to pray with the parishioners, he handed the microphone to Marija and jokingly asked if she wished to lead the rosary. He did not expect her to do it, but in her sweet little 3-year-old voice she said, "Do you want me to pray in Croatian or Italian?" Fr. Slavko could hardly stop laughing.

It was clear why Our Lady addressed people of all ages as "dear children" in her messages, but Bosnia-Herzegovina was not a playground—it was a warzone, and the atrocities seemed increasingly depraved, even demonic.

Early in the war, the Croats and Muslims joined together to defend against the Serbs, but in 1992 they began fighting against each other. Much of nearby Mostar was reduced to rubble, its parks converted to sprawling cemeteries and its 400-year-old historic bridge sent crashing into the Neretva River. Fighting destroyed the Franciscan church, Orthodox church and several mosques. The bishop's palace, with its collection of over 50,000 books, was burned to the ground. Bishop Žanić barely escaped.

Fr. Jozo was now the guardian of the Franciscan monastery in Široki Brijeg. He spent much of his time helping war victims. In 1992, he went to the Vatican where he met with Pope John Paul II. According to Fr. Jozo, the pope passionately told him, "I am with you. Protect Međugorje. Protect Our Lady's messages!"

With the front lines just a few miles away, we lost electricity, telephone service and running water. But even though Međugorje was surrounded by war, it seemed like we were in a protective bubble. Missiles and mortar shells were launched into the village but they only landed in the fields. According to a Serbian newspaper, Yugoslav warplanes sent to destroy Međugorje could not drop their bombs because a "strange silver fog" developed over their target.

At times, we felt as though the entire world had abandoned us, but one of my heroes made sure we were aware of his support. During the Angelus prayer at the Vatican on March 7, 1993, Pope John Paul II referred to the war in Bosnia-Herzegovina and said, "How can it happen that in our century—the century of science and technology, able to penetrate the mysteries of space—we find powerless witnesses of gruesome violations of human dignity?"

Then, almost as if he was paraphrasing Our Lady's messages in Međugorje, he said, "We need to return to God, to know and respect His laws! Let us ask the Holy Virgin for this renewed awareness. Her admonishing and maternal presence has been heard so many times, even in our century. It seems almost that she would like to warn us of the dangers threatening humanity. Regarding the dark forces of evil, Mary asks us to respond with the peaceful weapons of prayer, fasting, and charity."

He concluded with a passionate plea: "In the name of God, I invite everyone to lay down their arms!"

Although peace was not forthcoming, my annual apparition of March 18, 1993 brought some momentary comfort. *"Give me your hands,"* Our Lady said in her message, *"so that I, as a Mother, may lead you on the right path to bring you to the Father. Open your hearts. Allow me to enter. Pray, because in prayer I am with you."*

Fr. Slavko constantly urged people in the parish and around the world to pray and fast for peace.

He held the second annual Peace March on June 24, 1993. One year earlier, the first Peace March happened spontaneously when a group of pilgrims walked from Humac to Međugorje to celebrate the anniversary of the apparitions on June 25th. They carried the Blessed Sacrament and prayed for a peaceful end to the war.

Despite the terrible things happening in our country, it seemed like Our Lady was always working behind the scenes to help the victims of the war. One day, Fr. Slavko came over more excited than I had ever seen him. "I was climbing the hill," he said, out of breath.

"When are you ever *not* climbing the hill?" I said, smiling.

"Yes, but this time I got our answer."

"About what?"

"The orphanage we're going to build."

Fr. Slavko told me he climbed Apparition Hill that day specifically to pray for guidance about our desire to help the children of the war. Out of nowhere, a man from abroad came up to him.

"Fr. Slavko," said the man. "Are you building anything at the moment?"

Thinking it a somewhat odd question, Fr. Slavko replied, "No. Why do you ask?"

"Because I want to help you."

The man, it so happened, was quite wealthy, and he had been deeply moved by the suffering he saw in the region. "Why don't you build something for the needs of people?" the man said. "I'll help fund the project."

That was all the confirmation Fr. Slavko needed. He and I immediately started refining our idea. Using Our Lady's messages as a framework, we envisioned a different type of orphanage—one where the children would feel like they were part of a family. Instead of just one large building, it would be more like a community with multiple houses, a school, and a chapel. A group of about eight children would live in each house, accompanied by a nun to serve as their "mother" and caretaker.

Our simple goal was to protect and help children—to ensure they had roofs over their heads, hot meals, and the knowledge that they were loved. From the beginning, Fr. Slavko and I decided against calling it an orphanage because we did not want the children to ever feel like orphans. After all, that's not what they were; each of them had a Mother. We decided to call it Mother's Village because we were sure that Our Lady would be among them every day. But first, we had to decide where to build it, so we began praying for guidance.

Despite the war, Međugorje continued to grow. Rumor spread that a nun from Italy who worked with drug addicts was planning to build some kind of treatment facility in Međugorje. Most people in the village were vehemently against the idea—they did not want drug addicts living in close proximity to their families. But Mother Elvira persevered, and the Cenacolo Community was established in Bijakovići. The idea was simple and had apparently seen great success in Italy: addicts lived together in an environment of prayer and hard work, ultimately changing their lifestyle to focus on God instead of themselves.

"The most effective medicine to alleviate drug addiction is found in the Eucharist," Mother Elvira once said. "There is no pill that can give them the joy to live and find peace in the heart."

The village watched with apprehension as the first community members came to town, but my upbringing in Sarajevo gave me a different perspective—these young men were all human beings who deserved to know God's love as much as anyone. They were no less worthy because they had fallen. In them, I could see my troubled friends from high school, and I could see Jesus. Always smiling and full of love, Mother Elvira had a mission similar to Our Lady's—she wanted to transform despair into hope, hatred into forgiveness, and death into life.

God sent me and Marko a huge blessing during the war—in 1993, I learned that I was pregnant again. With all the uncertainty and chaos around us, it may have seemed like a scary time to be having a baby, but our trust in God's will negated any fears. We loved children and intended to have as many as God would give us. Marija already brought us more joy than we ever thought possible. She was excited about the new baby. She hoped for a little sister, and I think she even prayed for that intention.

I had always wondered how I would explain my apparitions to her, but as my father always said, children are smarter than we realize. One day, when Marija was only a few years old, she was playing in her room with a friend of the same age. I overheard her friend boast in a cute little singsong voice, "Guess what? My mommy drives a car!"

Marija was silent for a moment because she knew I did not drive, but then she said, "Big deal. My mommy talks to Our Lady!"

By that time, Sarajevo was almost unrecognizable in the images

I saw on TV. Most of the buildings were either heavily damaged or destroyed. I thought about the parchment and wondered if our apartment building was still standing.

A battalion of United Nations peacekeepers from Spain were stationed in Međugorje, and one day I met some who were about to leave for Sarajevo. I asked if they could stop at our apartment and bring back my family's personal documents. They happily agreed, so I explained where to find the desk and in which drawer they would find our package of documents. I had long ago learned that only I could read the parchment, so I was not concerned about them seeing something they shouldn't.

My pregnancy progressed and we eagerly awaited the birth of our newest family member, but just after Christmas, we received tragic news—Marko's little brother, Stjepan, had been killed while delivering aid. He was only 22 years old. His death was almost too tragic to comprehend, for us and for everyone who knew him. I thought I had plenty of time to show Stjepan my appreciation for helping my father and brother, but now I could only tell him through prayer.

Marko was devastated. I tried to comfort him by talking about the peace of Heaven and how Stjepan was now with Our Lady, but it was hard for both of us to accept that we would never see him again—at least not during our earthly lives. Stjepan had died within days of the feast of St. Stephen. Like the first Christian martyr after whom he was named, Stjepan's unshakable faith led him to risk his life for the sake of others.

In the face of such a tragedy, all we could do was pray, but it was impossible not to feel bitterness towards those who brought war to the region. I struggled to see Jesus in everyone, as Our Lady asked us to do. It was easy to look at the victims of the war as my brothers and sisters in Christ, but what about the victimizers?

"For if you love those who love you," Jesus said in the Bible, "what recompense will you have?"

I knelt with the intention of praying for Milošević, and for the grace to see him as my brother instead of an enemy. I intended to pray that Milošević would see his errors and be moved to stop the bloodshed, but every time I said his name or thought about him, I was immediately repulsed and could not go on.

"My Jesus," I prayed, "why don't *you* try to see yourself in him?"

Jesus did not start a war. Jesus did not murder innocent people. But I was looking for Jesus in Milošević's actions instead. I should have seen him as a fellow child of God, a son of Our Lady, and a brother of Jesus—albeit one who had wandered into darkness.

I knew that God did not dwell where He was not welcome, and whatever was in Milošević's heart seemed to leave little room for love. But I also believed that if Our Lady had to use just one word to answer every question ever asked of her, it would probably be *"Pray."* Our prayers, she said, had the power to change everything. This was the beginning of one of the most intense inner struggles I've ever experienced: to forgive the seemingly unforgiveable.

On February 4, 1994, 68 people were killed and many more wounded when a mortar attack hit a crowded marketplace in Sarajevo. Seeing my father and brother alive each day in Međugorje felt like a miracle and I constantly thanked St. Anthony for their rescue from the city. As I followed the news, I realized that most of my former classmates probably had not been as lucky. I constantly prayed for them, and for everyone affected by the war—but I still could not bring myself to pray for Milošević and his many accomplices.

My belly was especially large during my annual apparition of March 18, 1994, but I still managed to kneel. Our Lady came surprisingly joyful and her message was filled with hope.

"Today my heart is filled with happiness," she said. She asked us to allow her to lead us, and to pray every day. *"You see for yourselves that with our prayer all evils are destroyed,"* she continued. *"Let us pray and hope."*

On the same day, the leaders of the Muslims and Croats of Bosnia-Herzegovina met in Washington, D.C. They signed an agreement that ended the fighting between them and created the Federation of

Bosnia-Herzegovina. Partial peace had come, but the Serbs vowed to continue fighting.

The remembrance of Christ's sufferings took on a new meaning during Lent. Our 40 days of fasting and abstinence united us with victims of the war who had nothing to eat, and Jesus' wounds were mirrored in the horrible images shown on the news. On Holy Saturday, April 2, 1994, we prayed for peace and took momentary solace in our tradition of making *pisanice*—eggs stained with onion dye and imprinted with tiny leaves from the garden—but Stjepan's absence made it an unusually somber Easter.

On April 19, 1994, two weeks after Easter, I gave birth to our second daughter. Her arrival brought a burst of much-needed joy for our family. I was thinking of naming her after a character in one of the Russian novels I had read—names like Natalja and Nataša sounded so beautiful to me. But when I told Fr. Slavko what I was considering, he said, "Are you sure?"

"Well, what do you suggest?" I said.

Fr. Slavko thought for a moment. "How about Veronika? She was strong, brave, and she comforted Jesus."

"Veronika," I repeated, and I liked the way it sounded. In Catholic tradition, Veronika used a cloth to wipe the blood from Christ's face as he made his way to Calvary. Her deed is recounted in the Stations of the Cross.

"It's perfect, Father," I said. "Her name is Veronika."

Pope John Paul II repeatedly implored the Christian world to pray for an end to the fighting in Bosnia-Herzegovina. Despite the danger, he planned to visit Sarajevo on September 8, 1994, but the trip was canceled out of concern that the Serbs would retaliate against the people of the city. Instead, he celebrated a Mass for peace on that day at Castel Gandolfo, saying "Mary, Queen of Peace, pray for us." When he visited Croatia later that month, he stated that his greeting "goes to Bosnia-Herzegovina, to Sarajevo, the martyred city, that I ardently intended to visit as a pilgrim of peace." His visit brought hope to many in the region.

One day, a UN soldier came to our house. "We found your apartment in Sarajevo," he said, and he handed me a package containing our documents. Among them was the parchment.

"This is an answered prayer," I said, clutching the papers to my chest. "Thank you."

"We're glad we could help. I'm sure they're important."

I smiled. "You have no idea."

During the war, Međugorje became a center for international aide and United Nations humanitarian help. (PHOTO BY JOE MIXAN)

CHAPTER 26

"If there is no peace, it is like there is no sun on the earth."

— *Ancient Chinese Proverb*

"WHY DOES GOD allow war?"

Only those who do not know the love of God can ask such a question. In her messages, Our Lady has called God *"the Great Love."* God does not cause war—we do. God gives every man the freedom to choose how he lives his life and what he wants out of it. Every person must look inwardly and ask himself: *Do I want peace, or do I want to kill my brother?*

God is not to blame for our choices. To suggest otherwise is to deny the gift of free will.

The war brought unimaginable pain to countless victims. As Christians, we should never turn our heads away when we see people suffering. Our presence is the most generous gift we can give. Few people realize that kind words and gentle embraces can change the world. How we treat others spreads exponentially. It affects the future more than anything else.

"God is love," Jesus taught, "and he who abides in love abides in God, and God abides in him."

Fr. Slavko worked tirelessly to make Mother's Village a reality. He acquired a piece of land on the outskirts of the parish. When I first saw the property, I wondered how anyone could build there—the land was rugged, uneven, and filled with giant boulders. But Fr. Slavko reminded me that God would help us, and we continued praying for the project.

At Fr. Slavko's request, the UN soldiers stationed in Međugorje leveled the rocky land with the heavy machinery they had brought for their peacekeeping mission. We needed more funds to start building, though. Later, the government offered to contribute but only on the condition that religious symbols be banned from the facility.

Fr. Slavko refused their offer. "This will be Our Lady's orphanage, so how can we exclude her?"

But other donors—mainly people who had made pilgrimages to Međugorje—helped the dream become a reality. The village also included St. Francis Garden, a beautiful forest park with walking trails, an amphitheater, and a playground.

When Mother's Village opened, Fr. Slavko and I discussed how we might be able to help the orphans even more. We came up with a program that allowed the children to stay with local families during the weekends. Our goal was to let the children see how an ordinary family functioned. Many people in the village received the children, including Marko and me.

The weekend visits were lovely. For the children, spending time with a real family was like a fairytale. Knowing how much they had suffered, Marko and I showered them with more attention than we gave our own children. We laughed with them, cooked their favorite meals, and read them books like *The Little Prince* at bedtime. Marko especially loved playing sports with the boys. But then, after just two days, we had to bring the children back to the orphanage.

Returning them was hard for me as a mother, but it was even more difficult for the children. Fr. Slavko and I finally realized that it was not a good idea after all.

As a visionary, I could relate to how the children felt—after a few minutes with the Blessed Mother, coming back to Earth was excruciating.

A prime example was my next annual apparition, which took place on March 18, 1995. Our Lady came full of sorrow, which was not typical for the March 18 apparitions. She and I prayed together for those who had not yet experienced God's love, for souls in Purgatory, and for the intentions of everyone who had come to my home for the apparition. She also spoke to me about the secrets. Then, in her message for the world, she lamented that peoples' hearts had become hard toward their neighbors' sufferings. *"As long as you do not love,"* she said, *"you will not know your Father's love."* She reminded us that we should never be afraid of anything—not even *"what is to come"*—because *"God is love."* She concluded by saying, *"I am leading you to eternal life. Eternal life is my Son. Receive him and you have received love."*

The apparition lasted ten minutes. After she left, I immediately withdrew to my room and cried. When someone asked me later why I had been so distraught, I explained that every encounter with Our Lady was like a fulfilment of everything—I felt completed.

"For example," I said, "I love Marija and Veronika with all my heart, and like any normal mother, I would give my life for them. But when I'm with Our Lady, even my daughters do not exist. My only desire is to go with the Blessed Mother. When the apparition ends, I feel so much pain—it's like being in a paradise one second and a desert the next. I feel abandoned, even though I know I'm not. Only after several hours of prayer do I understand that I have to stay on Earth and Our Lady has to be in Heaven."

Have you ever loved someone you could not be with? Yearned for a time or place you could never return to? Mourned for someone close to your heart? If so, then you might understand my heartache. Separating from Our Lady feels like a mixture of unrequited love, exile, and grief—and yet it is none of those things.

I go through the same emotions after every apparition. With God's help, I am able to return to living a relatively normal life. Sometimes I wonder if human beings are simply not built to encounter the divine in such an intense way.

Perhaps Our Lady was so sad during my March 18th apparition because she could see that the worst horrors of the war were coming.

On May 25, 1995—President Tito's birthday and Yugoslavia's official Youth Day—Serbs fired a shrapnel shell into the city of Tuzla. In a sad irony, many of the 71 victims were youths, among them a two-year-old child. The attack was like a vile birthday gift from the last remnants of Yugoslav communism. A poem by Bosnian poet Mak Dizdar was later carved into a memorial at the site of the Tuzla massacre:

Here one does not live to live.

Here one does not live to die.

Here one dies to live.

I recalled Our Lady's words about loving our neighbors from my March 18th apparition and prayed that people would begin to see each other as brothers and sisters. But as 1995 progressed, the atrocities became more appalling.

In July, over 8,000 men and boys were killed in Srebrenica, their bodies dumped like trash in mass graves. International observers called the massacre in Srebrenica a genocide, an act of ethnic extermination so terrible that most people never thought it could happen in the "modern" world. But only a year earlier, a genocide also plunged the tiny African country of Rwanda into darkness and bloodshed. Several children in the village of Kibeho, Rwanda reported apparitions of the Blessed Mother in November 1981, just five months after the Međugorje apparitions began, and said she showed them images of the coming chaos.

In Međugorje, Our Lady continued calling for peace. In 1995, she asked people to transmit her messages to the world so that *"a river of love flows to people who are full of hatred and without peace."* She also invited everyone to be her *"joyful carriers of peace in this troubled world,"* and she asked for our prayers, *"so that as soon as possible a time of peace, for which my heart waits impatiently, may reign."*

In early August, Croatian and Bosnian forces launched a major offensive against the Serbs. Later that month, the Serbs launched mortar shells into the same Sarajevo marketplace that had been hit a year before and 43 innocent people died. The world could no longer ignore the massacres. An international coalition launched air strikes against the Bosnian Serb army and a ceasefire was announced in October. The war finally ended with the signing of the Dayton Peace Agreement on November 21, 1995, a Marian feast day shared by two faiths—known as *The Presentation of the Blessed Virgin Mary* to Catholics, and *The Entry of the Most Holy Theotokos into the Temple* to the Orthodox.

In the wake of all the madness, over 100,000 people had been killed in a country merely one-third the size of the US state of New York. The fighting was over, but after four years of war, the wounds were deep and would not heal overnight. Like everyone in the country, I had lost friends and family members, and my heart ached when I looked at all the suffering around me.

Jesus told us to forgive our enemies, but how do you forgive someone who has killed people you love? "You have heard that it was said, you shall love your neighbor and hate your enemy," Jesus told his disciples. "But I say to you, love your enemies and pray for those who persecute you, that you may be children of your heavenly Father, for he makes his sun rise on the bad and the good, and causes rain to fall on the just and the unjust."

If I could not forgive, then how could I call myself a Christian? As someone who saw Our Lady and knew without a doubt that Jesus existed, what excuse did I have to not embrace *all* of his teachings? As I prayed intensely for that grace, I looked back at the war.

From the beginning of the apparitions, Our Lady called herself the Queen of Peace, and she asked us to pray for peace. But back then, I never imagined that she might have been referring to a war in our own country, or that we needed to pray in order to avoid it. I thought she was speaking about peace in our own hearts, because it was unthinkable to me that a war with such hatred and evil was possible in the 20th Century.

I knew little about politics. Our Lady taught me to love everyone, and she said that we were all brothers and sisters regardless of our differences. She never said *Dear Italians* or *Dear Croats* or even *Dear Catholics*—only *Dear Children*. She came as a mother of all people.

Although I was oblivious to most of it while living in Sarajevo, the Croatian people yearned for simple freedoms, such as freedom to express their cultural identity, and freedom to practice religion. For years, the mere mention of their heritage resulted in being interrogated by the police, thrown in jail, or having to flee abroad. On the tenth anniversary of Our Lady's apparitions, they got their Croatian state, but few expected it to come at such a high price.

I've heard it said that people burdened with shame and guilt are often restless on their deathbeds, while people with clean souls tend to pass gently. Perhaps communism could have died gently were it not for its grave sins and all the harm it had caused. Instead, like a wounded beast, it fought ferociously in its final hours to carry everyone down with it. Each battle, each atrocity, was another death throe, increasing in fury until the very end.

In Međugorje, we did not experience the war in the same way as people in Vukovar or Sarajevo. Although we did suffer, we were insulated from the worst of it, whether by luck or by grace—and I suspect the latter. If the Blessed Mother had not appeared here before the war, then who would have known about Međugorje? Despite the dangers, people from the Americas and the rest of Europe brought medical supplies and food, and believers all over the world prayed and fasted for peace.

When I think about the suffering experienced by so many people during the war, my eyes fill with tears. War causes pain and despair and I could never understand those who desired it. When there is no love, and when there is no faith, then the devil takes over. He comes to destroy everything good—life, peace, joy, dignity. We see it happening in places all over the world.

Even when the communists persecuted me, I forgave their violence. I realized that I would be allowing them to victimize me twice if I let their actions steal my peace. Being consumed by hatred harms our relationship with God.

I came to believe that it was not people but satanic forces that ruled in the war. Men allowed the devil to influence them and fill the voids in their hearts with evil and malice. Those who harmed others out of hatred now had to live with their actions, possibly forever. I recalled the story of the soldier who killed the Franciscans at Široki Brijeg in 1945, and how he never got a night's sleep for the rest of his life.

I remembered that Jesus even pardoned those who crucified Him as they were doing it, saying, "Forgive them, Father, for they know not what they do."

Many would argue that Milošević and his allies knew what they were doing, but I came to see it in a different way: if they did not know God, then in reality they knew *nothing*.

Years before, I was deeply disturbed after Our Lady showed me what awaited people who chose darkness over light, so how could I wish that upon anyone? If I wanted my enemies to suffer for eternity, I would be no better than them, and perhaps even worse, because as atheists they did not believe that death led to *anything* eternal.

Perhaps the fact that Milošević's mother, father and uncle committed suicide when he was younger led to his indifference towards life, and maybe his atheism was a result of the communist education system. Does the blame for his conduct fall solely on him or on his environment, or on a combination of things, perhaps? Only God truly knows; only He can judge. But if life seemed meaningless and God did not exist for Milošević, then what incentive did he have to strive for goodness?

In a classroom with an invisible teacher, would every child play nice?

Thinking about Milošević in this way, my anger gradually turned into empathy, and my prayers became stronger. In the end, love prevailed and I was able to see Milošević as my brother in Jesus. I soon found it possible to pray for him with no ill feelings, and I asked God to help him find redemption.

That experience helped me better understand why Our Lady asked us to pray for those who have not come to know God's love. When one knows the love of God, he cannot wage war. I prayed that everyone who had done bad things during the war might discover this love—that they might banish evil from their hearts, and that there might be no more war.

In her message on March 18, 1997, Our Lady said, *"Genuine peace will be had only by the one who sees and loves my Son in his neighbor."*

And on March 18, 2005, she said, *"The way to my Son, who is true peace and love, passes through the love for all neighbors."*

Nothing should prevent us from seeing Jesus in other people—not differences in race, religion, politics, or trivial things like the way someone dresses or what they do for a living. Our Lady asks us to see Jesus in *everyone*. In the homeless man begging for spare change. In the Muslim and the Serb. In the atheist who doesn't believe in Jesus and the Christian who doesn't understand Him. In the newborn baby and in the unborn baby. In your priest, in your bishop, and in the pope. In those who have hurt you and those you have hurt. In the thief. In the drug addict. In the worst sinner you know. And, perhaps most importantly, in yourself. See Jesus in *everyone*.

As human beings, we make all sorts of excuses to circumvent the commandment of loving our neighbors as we love ourselves. *Forgive but don't forget*, some say. Or the Croatian proverb, *The wolf changes his fur but never his temperament.*

True love, however, has no conditions.

From as early as I can remember, my father and I shared a special bond.

CHAPTER 27

"Your lips pronounce countless words, but your spirit does not feel anything. Wandering in darkness, you even imagine God Himself according to yourselves, and not such as He really is in His love."

— *From Our Lady's Message of February 2, 2011*

THE EFFECTS OF the war continued to haunt us after it ended.

My father lived for his children. The stress of taking care of my brother during the Siege of Sarajevo had caused irreversible damage to his health, and one day he suffered a massive stroke. It left him comatose, and the doctors at the Mostar hospital said that he would not survive. I could not comprehend it. How could this man who had been so full of life—a man whose heart was so big that he cried at the mere sight of his grandchildren—leave us?

I knelt beside his hospital bed and prayed with more intensity than ever before. "St. Anthony, thank you for keeping your end of our deal, and you know that I've kept mine. But please ask God to spare my father's life, to give us just a little more time with him."

The war left Mostar Hospital badly damaged and overwhelmed with patients, so Marko immediately started seeking a place that could provide better medical care for my father, and hopefully a second opinion. But the other hospitals in the country were struggling as well.

"Your father is my father," said Marko. "You keep praying and I'll keep looking."

We were finally able to transfer my father to the hospital in Split, which was better equipped to deal with stroke victims. We made the three-hour drive from Međugorje every day just to sit by his bedside. My mother seemed to be preparing herself for the worst, but she never lost hope. Miro stayed silent; I could see the fear in his eyes. Veronika was only a baby, but Marija joined Marko and me in prayer for her beloved *Dida*.

After 21 days in a coma, my father woke up.

It was a moment of joy but also uncertainty. The doctors warned us that my father would never be the same, adding, "You should be grateful if he even lives another year." But they had been wrong before, and their prognosis did not take our prayers into account.

When Dad was discharged from the hospital, he could barely speak. We had to push him in a wheelchair because one side of his body was partially paralyzed. Months of physical therapy helped him learn how to walk again, but he could only manage with a cane that had a special tripod base. With the use of only one hand, he needed assistance with daily tasks. And although his mumbled speech was unintelligible to others, we were eventually able to understand him, in the same way a toddler's vocabulary only makes sense to his parents. But despite all the challenges, he was alive and nothing else mattered.

My mom took care of my dad's everyday needs and never left his side except to attend Mass, and even then she rushed home when it was over. She never complained or said she was tired. Instead, she did everything joyfully. "It's simple," she said. "God willed it, we accepted it, and now we'll pray that He gives us the strength to endure."

Marko, Miro, and I assisted her as much as possible. We always joked with my father and tried to turn every uncomfortable moment into laughter. When he complained that he could not engage in any activities because of his condition, I smiled and said, "Well, you can't use this as an excuse now. You were never a man of action!"

My father laughed knowingly—he had always been cheerful and patient, but never very active.

When my mother needed medical treatment and rehabilitation for her osteoporosis, I got the opportunity to care for my father by myself. Mom worried about leaving him, but I assured her that I could handle it. With a family of my own, I was no longer the Mirjana who could not turn on the washing machine or cook a meal (notice, I did not say a *good* meal). When my mother was away, taking care of my father never felt like a burden. In fact, it was an honor to help the man who had changed my diapers, fed me and raised me. Why should it be difficult to do something for him?

Helping him put on his coat one morning reminded me of one of the many times he had done something for me purely out of love. When I was a teenager, I was not obsessed with shopping like some girls, but I *loved* going with my dad. It was an opportunity to spend time with him, just the two of us. I have to admit that I also liked going with him because he always insisted on buying something for me. One cold day, I saw a beautiful winter coat in a shop. I touched the sleeve and ran the soft fabric through my fingers. It was expensive, especially for communist Yugoslavia, but when Dad saw me staring at it, he said, "Do you like that one?"

"It's gorgeous," I said, "but—"

"Super."

"But it's too expensive."

"Nonsense."

Without even looking at the price tag, my dad pulled the coat off the rack and took it to the cashier. He opened his wallet and took out his money, but when the cashier told him the price, my dad's eyebrows went up. I could see he did not have enough.

"It's ok, Dad," I said. "I'll find a different one."

My dad thought for a moment, but then he shook his head. "No," he said. "A beautiful girl deserves a beautiful coat."

He took out his checkbook and bought it.

Now, as I buttoned *his* coat and tucked his crippled hand into the side pocket, I pledged to show him as much love as he had shown me all my life, and to spoil him with attention. I made dinner and helped him eat, and then I held his hand while we watched television together. Later, when the time came to help him bathe, I felt a little intimidated, but I forced a smile and tried to make him feel comfortable. I think he must have noticed my hesitancy, because he smiled and said, "You think this is easy for *me?*"

We both laughed, and everything became easier.

My father's stroke taught me a valuable lesson—when something bad happens, you can cry for yourself, but tears will not change anything; you'll only be more hurt and hindered. But if you accept your cross, then you'll eventually learn how to carry it, which my mother's endurance and my father's tranquility proved. Through it all, our entire family came closer together.

A simple routine helped us cope. My father wanted us to have coffee as a family every day at 2 pm. I was never late for that coffee, because I always worried that it might be my last one with him.

In the midst of adjusting to my father's ailment, I noticed a small bump on the front of my neck. It felt like a cyst of some sort. I thought about having it checked, but I forgot all about it when I discovered that I was pregnant with our third child. Marko and I were ecstatic. By the end of my first trimester, I had the distinct feeling that I was carrying a boy. Perhaps it was a mother's intuition, or maybe it came from my desire for Marko to have a son, but I was certain enough that I chose a male name—a name I felt Marko would love.

Jakov's wife, Annalisa, was also pregnant. She was from Italy and not fluent in Croatian, so I accompanied her to translate at her doctor's appointment. I had not planned on going to the doctor myself that day, but after Annalisa's checkup, I asked him to check on my baby as well. As he moved the ultrasound transducer over my belly, I thought about my father and how he had used similar equipment in his profession. I waited excitedly to hear the baby's heartbeat for the first time, but there was only silence. I knew something was wrong when I saw the doctor's face.

"I'm sorry, but your baby has died," he said.

The words pierced my heart. "That can't be."

"There's nothing I can do. Your child has been dead for a long time."

I felt dizzy and confused as I left the doctor's office. Annalisa later told me that I started walking in the wrong direction and she had to bring me to the car. I do not even remember coming home, or telling Marko the terrible news. I just wanted to be with our baby.

The next day, Marko took me to the hospital for a second opinion. The doctors there examined me and confirmed that it was true, adding that they needed to clean my womb to prevent infection.

I kept asking, "Are you absolutely sure? Are you certain he's not alive?"

They were, and they had also discovered some medical problems that would make this my last pregnancy.

For the next few days, I was so sad that I could barely get out of bed, but I did my best to carry on as a good mother to our girls. One day, Fr. Slavko came over to visit. I tried to act normal as I served him coffee and chitchatted about life in Medugorje, but he noticed my suffering. We had not yet told him about my pregnancy, let alone my miscarriage, so I was surprised when he leaned toward me and said, "Do you think it was a boy or a girl?"

I looked at him with surprise, wanting to ask him how he knew, but I realized it did not matter. "I think it was a boy," I said, looking down.

"And what were you going to name him?"

Tears filled my eyes. "Stjepan."

Fr. Slavko nodded; the older Stjepan was also one of his nephews. "What a beautiful name," he said, and then he smiled. "It's much better than Natalja or Nataša."

I laughed for the first time in days. Fr. Slavko always knew how to cheer me up, even in difficult moments.

"I know it's distressing," he said, "but try not to be too sad. Now you have an angel in Heaven, an angel who prays to God for you, and who will wait for you. Pray to him and talk to him. He's with Our Lady now, and with his Uncle Stjepan, too."

Fr. Slavko's words helped me immensely. From that moment on, everything got a little bit easier, but my pain never healed completely. As a visionary, I knew that my baby was in Heaven, but as a mother, I could not live as if nothing happened. Anytime I went somewhere and saw a little boy the same age as my son would have been, I was reminded of his absence. Still, I knew he was always near, even if I could not see him or hold him. Praying to my angel in Heaven gave me great comfort.

Now, when other women who have lost babies come to me, I'm able to listen to them, and I understand what they're going through. I can tell them about my experience. I can explain that prayer will help them and I always suggest that they name their unborn child.

"A part of you is missing but not forgotten," I say. "Pray and you'll know that your little angel is safe in the Blessed Mother's arms, and one day you'll meet in Heaven."

Marko and I felt like we needed a respite from all the difficulties, so we took Marija and Veronika on a trip to Italy. Arriving in Umbria, it was wonderful to reconnect with Antonio, the Trancanelli family, and other members of our prayer group, who still met every Wednesday at 11 am to pray.

When we arrived, Alessandra hugged me tightly. "I missed you," she said. "I prayed for you to come back."

I started crying. "I think God heard your prayers."

When Vittorio greeted me, he noticed the bump on my neck. "How long have you had that?" he asked.

"Oh, a few months or so," I said. "I'm sure it will go away."

"Let's set an appointment for me to have a closer look. Just to be safe."

I assumed that Vittorio was just being overly cautious, but after examining me at the hospital, he looked at me with concern. "Mirjana, you need to have surgery. We need to remove your thyroid gland. It might be cancer, and if it's not, it could turn into it."

He warned that it would take at least four days for the lab to determine if the cyst was cancerous once the gland was removed, and he added that my thyroid problem might have caused my miscarriage. Vittorio offered to perform the surgery, and our prayer group met to pray for me.

Alessandra was like my cheerleader. "Don't be afraid. Offer it up."

I smiled. "Good idea. I'll do that."

Lia told me that Alessandra had many health problems, but she accepted her suffering with the patience of a saint. When she had heart surgery, her brother Diego—who had begun to doubt his faith—stayed at Alessandra's bedside all night until her anesthetic wore off and she opened her eyes.

"Alessandra," said Diego. "It's me, your brother."

Alessandra looked at him and smiled. "Diego."

"Are you in any pain?"

"Yes, but I'm offering the pain to God."

"What for?"

"For your conversion, of course!"

Later, the medical staff came to remove the tubes from her body. "This will hurt, Alessandra," said a nurse, "but it's okay to scream."

When they pulled out the tubes, Alessandra bit her lip and remained silent.

"Didn't that hurt?" said Diego. "You didn't even cry."

She nodded towards the crucifix on the wall of her hospital room. "Look how much Jesus suffered," she said. "How can I cry when He's looking at me? I'm offering it for people who do not believe."

On the day before my own surgery, I thought about Alessandra's bravery. I hugged Marko, Veronika, and Marija and made sure they all knew how much I loved them. Just before going to the hospital, I went to confession with a local priest. I wanted to be ready for anything.

I had to share my hospital room with an Italian woman. A few years older than me, she seemed nervous and sad.

"Goodnight," I said, but she did not respond.

I woke early the next morning and tried not to disturb the woman while I quietly prayed. Peace filled my heart as I asked God to let everything happen according to His will. When I finished my prayer, I noticed the other woman watching me, but she quickly looked away.

Later, as I washed my face and brushed my hair, I hummed some melody. Again, I caught the woman looking at me strangely, so I turned to her and smiled.

"I'm sorry," I said, "but is everything alright?"

She seemed startled by my question. "It's just odd to me," she said. "You're about to have surgery but you're in such a good mood."

I laughed. "Well, what should I do? Complain about my luck? Cry? How would that change anything?"

"But what if you die? You're acting like you don't care what happens."

"What will be will be. If I surrender myself into God's hands, what is there to fear?"

We continued talking until a nurse came and took me to the

operating room. I silently prayed as Dr. Vittorio and his team prepped for the surgery.

Vittorio looked into my eyes. "Just know that I'll be praying the entire time."

His words calmed me, although I wished his friendly smile was not covered by a hospital mask. A nurse asked me to count backwards from ten as they administered anesthesia. I was asleep before I got to seven.

I woke up groggy and sore with a breathing tube protruding from my windpipe, stitches across my throat, and IV tubes stuck in both of my arms. A nurse helped me into a wheelchair and pushed me to my room where I would have to spend the next several days recuperating.

Later, I noticed my roommate looking at me again, but this time she had a pleasant smile.

"Did you miss me?" I joked, but I immediately regretted talking because my throat felt like it was on fire.

She came over and sat at my bedside. "I couldn't stop thinking about what you said. Your words and your peace did something to me. I think you reawakened my faith. I even prayed for you."

The next day, a nurse came to me and said, "The doctors want to speak with you."

I felt a sense of dread. *It must be cancer*, I thought.

As she wheeled me into a room filled with doctors and nurses, I prayed for strength and prepared to hear the worst. The nurse positioned me in front of everyone, and after a long silence, one of the doctors smiled and said, "Our colleague Vittorio tells us that you're a visionary. We'd love to hear about that."

I smiled with relief. "Where shall I begin?"

For the next 30 minutes, wearing a hospital gown and sitting in a wheelchair with tubes sticking out of my body, I told them about the love of God and Our Lady's apparitions. That experience made everything worthwhile. If I had not been a patient at that hospital, I never could have shared the message of Međugorje with the doctors and nurses, nor with my roommate. It became yet another confirmation that everything happened for a reason—another reminder to accept my cross before trying to understand its purpose, and to always trust in God's will.

It was precisely this trust that made the four-day wait for the lab results bearable. The doctors finally informed me that the cyst was benign and we were free to return home to Međugorje. I cried as I said farewell to Vittorio, Lia, and Alessandra.

I hugged Vittorio. "Thank you for everything."

"Don't thank me." He glanced up at the sky. "Thank Him."

Back in Međugorje, my mission continued to develop.

In addition to the annual apparitions on March 18th, Our Lady continued to visit me on the 2nd of every month. I usually experienced the apparitions at home surrounded by my family and a few friends. Sometimes, though, I went to one of my favorite places of prayer in Međugorje—a rocky alcove near the base of Apparition Hill and close to our home known simply as "The Blue Cross." People started calling it that after members of a local prayer group erected a plain metal cross and painted it blue to mark the place. Many apparitions had already taken place there throughout the years. In the early days, when the police prevented us from climbing the hill, it had been one of our secret places where we knew we wouldn't be disturbed.

One of my first public apparitions at the Blue Cross took place on March 2, 1997. Several hundred people from all over the world were there, including a group of Native American Indians wearing traditional costumes. As I looked at all the joyful faces, I began to realize how meaningful it was for other people to be present at the apparition.

When Our Lady came, she had a seriousness in her expression, and there were tears in her eyes from the beginning of the apparition to the end. Onlookers told me later that I was in ecstasy for about four minutes. When she departed, I was left so emotionally-drained that I needed a few minutes of prayer before I could convey the message.

"Dear children," she said, *"pray for your brothers who haven't experienced the love of the Father—for those whose only importance is life on Earth. Open your hearts to them and see in them my Son, who loves them. Be my light and illuminate all souls where darkness reigns."*

Our Lady's call to be her "light" seemed as important as ever. Although the war had ended, a dark cloud still hung over the Balkans, especially in areas that had seen the worst fighting. Of the buildings left standing, many had been hit by so many bullets that their concrete facades now resembled the surface of the moon, and fresh graves outnumbered old ones in almost every cemetery. In many places, people lived next door to those they had fought against. Without forgiveness, the sad effects of the war would continue to multiply.

Our Lady once said that to forgive others, we must first forgive ourselves. The secret of this mystery is simply love. If you love, then you will know how to forgive and move on. Without love there is nothing; you are empty and you cannot truly forgive. Only when you love the one who persecutes you can you say that you are on the right path. That is true mercy.

Perhaps nowhere in Bosnia-Herzegovina needed reconciliation more than my former hometown. Sarajevo had suffered the longest siege of a capital city in the history of modern warfare, lasting four years.

The stadium used for the 1984 Olympics later became the venue for several events that heralded a new period of freedom for the people of the region. In 1997, *U2* was the first major band to play in Sarajevo after the war. People of every ethnic group came to the concert. Their song *Where The Streets Have No Name* could have easily described Međugorje.

On April 13, 1997, Pope John Paul II celebrated Mass at the stadium for an estimated 60,000 people, a hillside full of war victim graves visible in the distance. The day's cold wind and heavy snowfall conveyed the bleakness of the decimated city, but the pope's words were like beams of sunlight cutting through the gloom.

"Let us forgive, and let us ask for forgiveness," he said to the crowd, which included Catholics, Muslims, and Serbs. "The hope of all people of good will is that what Sarajevo symbolizes will remain confined to the 20th Century and that its tragedies will not be repeated in the millennium about to begin."

Three days later, during a general audience in Rome, the pope reflected on his visit to Sarajevo and asked everyone to pray for lasting peace in the region, adding, "Pilgrimages of the faithful to the Marian shrine in Bosnia-Herzegovina and in many other parts of the world, especially in Loreto, continued throughout the war to ask the Mother of Nations and the Queen of Peace to intercede so that peace would be restored to that tormented region."

His words seemed like a wink and a smile to all of us here in Međugorje.

In March, 1998, Lia called from Italy and told me that Vittorio had fallen gravely ill. I prayed for God to comfort him just as Vittorio had comforted his patients.

During my annual apparition on March 18, 1998, Our Lady said, *"I call you to be my light, in order to enlighten all those who still live in darkness, to fill their hearts with Peace—my Son."*

Dr. Vittorio Trancanelli had already answered her call—he was one of her "lights" who filled peoples' hearts with peace every day in his work, home, and ministry. He passed away at 54 years old on June 24, 1998, the 17th anniversary of Our Lady's first appearance in Međugorje. As he lay dying, he looked at Lia and his children with tenderness and said, "This is why life is worth living. Even if I had become who knows who, if I had money in the bank, if I'd bought many homes, what would I bring with me now? What would I bring before God? Now I carry only the love I've given to people."

I cried for Lia, Diego and especially my beautiful Alessandra, but not as much for Vittorio—in my mind, he was an angel living on Earth who had simply flown back to Heaven.

Later that year, Jakov and I went to the USA to give some talks about our experiences, and our families joined us. By then, I had begun to accept fewer invitations to speak. After seeing so many pilgrims change their lives in Međugorje, I realized that there was a big difference between people hearing about it and them actually going there. Words could not convey what it was like to climb the hill and feel her presence. Even so, I thought that if my visit to the USA could change just one non-believer, then it would be worth it. In the end, however, I think I was supposed to be there to help my cousin.

On September 11, 1998, Our Lady appeared to Jakov just as she had every day since the beginning. I knelt in another room and prayed in silence. Knowing what he could see, it was too painful for me to be near him.

When the apparition ended this time, however, Jakov came to me with tears in his eyes. "I need to speak with you," he said. "Today was my last regular apparition. Our Lady asked me to prepare myself to receive the tenth secret tomorrow."

My heart broke for him and I started crying as well. "I'm so sorry, Jakov," I said, thinking about the confusion and despair I had felt so many years before. I worried that Our Lady's absence would be even more difficult for Jakov to accept than it had been for me. After his mother died, Our Lady practically raised him. Now, at 27 years old, Jakov would have to face the world without the solace of seeing her every day.

He wiped the tears off his face. "I don't know what I'll do without her."

"Let's pray," I said, and we spent much of that evening on our knees.

Lord, I prayed silently, *help Jakov understand that this is how it must be, that this is your will.*

The next day, Our Lady appeared to Jakov at 11:15 am, much earlier than usual, and she stayed longer than she normally did. Half an hour later, when the apparition ended, Jakov cried and went off to be alone. Later, he told us that Our Lady was sad when she gave him the tenth secret, but then she smiled gently and promised to appear to him once a year on Christmas day. She told him not to be sad *"because as a mother I will always be with you and like every true mother I will never leave you."* She also asked him to be *"an example of the man who has known God and God's love,"* and then she blessed him and thanked him for responding to her call.

Fr. Slavko was shocked when we called to tell him the news. More than a decade had passed since Ivanka's daily apparitions ceased. Everyone in Međugorje was surprised that it happened to Jakov while he was in America and not at home.

I was thankful to be with Jakov in the difficult days that followed. Whenever the regular time of the apparition approached, Marko and I tried to distract him by talking to him, entertaining him, or praying. When we all returned to Međugorje, however, he withdrew from everyone. The Jakov I had known—the one who could not have a conversation without making a joke and whose contagious laugh made everyone else laugh even if they did not know what he was laughing about—seemed to be gone. His depression lasted for many months, but eventually he came to understand what I had already learned: he, like anyone, could still be close to Our Lady by praying with the heart.

*Fr. Slavko Barbarić leads pilgrims in prayer on
Cross Mountain.* (PHOTO BY JOE MIXAN)

CHAPTER 28

"At this great and holy time in which you have entered, pray in a special way for those who have not yet experienced the love of God."

— *From Our Lady's Message of January 2, 2000*

THE FIRST SEVERAL years of the new millennium brought renewed hope—but also the deaths of three people who had each been huge parts of my life.

Pilgrims traveled to Međugorje in growing numbers while the people of Bosnia-Herzegovina worked to rebuild and adjust to the new government. Despite some disagreements, Croats, Muslims and Serbs were coexisting in relative stability.

On Friday, November 24, 2000, exactly seven months before the 20th anniversary of the first apparition, our phone rang. When Marko answered the call, his face turned pale and he threw the phone on the floor. I had never seen him like that.

"That's impossible," he muttered. "It can't be."

"What's wrong?"

He looked at me, tears in his eyes. "Fr. Slavko just died."

How could a man of such vitality die at just 54 years old? He left this world after leading 70 parishioners and pilgrims up Cross Mountain to pray *The Way of the Cross*, like he did every Friday. At the top of the mountain near the cement cross, he sat down on a rock, lay on the ground, and passed away.

The next day, Our Lady acknowledged his passing in her message to Marija. *"I rejoice with you, and I desire to tell you that your brother Slavko has been born into Heaven and intercedes for you."*

Heaven rejoiced, but in Međugorje we were full of sorrow. Fr. Slavko had been our pillar for so many years. We all leaned on him.

Two days later, on the Feast of Christ the King, Marko and I attended Fr. Slavko's funeral along with the other visionaries and 30,000 people. It was strange to see Fr. Slavko's body in the open casket, but the peaceful look on his face gave me consolation. He no longer had to worry about his many commitments. He could finally rest.

Bishop Perić, who succeeded Bishop Žanić—and who maintained the same skeptical approach to our apparitions—presided at the funeral Mass. Although he and Fr. Slavko had been at odds over Međugorje, the bishop's address was full of respect.

"In front of human death," said Bishop Perić, "our death or the death of our dear ones, each one of us stands with a shaken heart, puzzled mind and sad eye. But God has the right to call from this world to Himself, into the eternal home, whomever He wants, whenever He wants, from any place He wants and in the way He wants."

Local Franciscan Fr. Tomislav Pervan spoke next. "Here before us there lies a life that, humanly speaking, filled up not just one, but three life spans," he said. "He passed away just like his Lord did. Not on a couch or a bed, not surrounded by brethren or closest loved ones, but under the cross, on the cold rock of Herzegovina. How many symbols are in that death?"

"Fr. Slavko laid down his life for everyone," Fr. Pervan continued. "Above all, he loved those who nobody else loved, the deserted and the abandoned who had been terribly wounded by sin and human hatred...And therefore he went away too soon because he spread himself out everywhere."

It was true. Fr. Slavko endeavored to live and spread Our Lady's messages in Međugorje and the many other places he visited throughout the world. He authored numerous books about prayer, fasting and conversion, and millions of copies were printed in 20 different languages.

Jakov spoke on behalf of the six of us visionaries. "You often said to us, 'Do you know that I love you?' We felt that love so often and in so many different ways...Thank you for each of your visits to our homes which brought so much blessing and joy into our families...It is now, dear brother, that we say to you what you always said to us: Do you know, brother, how much we love you?"

I was especially touched when the children of Mother's Village gathered on the altar to say goodbye to the priest who had given them so much. A girl named Magdalena spoke for all of them. "Thank you for letting us see that toys have colors, that Nutella is sweet, and that it takes two people to seesaw," she said. "Thank you for making it possible for us to wear a white dress for our First Holy Communion, like other children. Thank you for teaching us how to love Our Lady and how to pray to God. Thank you, because in spite of everything, we've discovered what the word *love* means."

I realized then that Fr. Slavko's legacy would live on through children. Even though he had to end the family visit program years before, that experience inspired him to find other ways to help the children feel less like orphans and more like part of a community. He created a kindergarten named after St. Thérèse, the Little Flower, where the children of Međugorje and the ones who lived in Mother's Village could go to school together. It turned out to be a beautiful thing.

My daughter, Marija, was part of the first generation to attend the kindergarten. Like other local parents, Marko and I were happy because we knew that Marija would be in a safe place where she could learn about God's love through the school's faith instruction as well as by interacting with the less fortunate. As a result, the children who lived in Mother's Village never felt like they were different.

Fr. Slavko's few belongings were given to his family and friends. I only wanted one thing—his alarm clock. It was as plain an alarm clock as any in the world, but to me it was a priceless symbol of Fr. Slavko's inexhaustible dedication to Our Lady. Without it he could not have risen before dawn every day after just a few hours of sleep. Sometimes I put his clock in front of me when I pray, and I can sense that he's near. It's a reminder that my time on Earth, like everyone else's, will one day run out.

With his background in psychology, Fr. Slavko had often heard confessions at the Cenacolo Community, which was now an inseparable part of Međugorje. Because they loved him so much, the young men made a large memorial stone and carried it by hand to the top of Cross Mountain to mark the place where he died. One of the community members even spoke at Fr. Slavko's funeral, saying, "Thank you for protecting life, for radiating peace and love, for always having time for a talk."

After Fr. Slavko's passing, I began to feel in my heart that instead of concealing myself in my room for the 2nd of the month apparitions, I should be in a place where everyone could pray in Our Lady's midst. And I had a realization. How beautiful would it be for Our Lady to appear in the Cenacolo Community? The purpose of the monthly apparitions, after all, was to pray for those who did not know God's love. The young men in the community were once those people and they understood what it was like to walk in darkness. Through prayer, they had been born anew and were learning to live with God as their Father. I could introduce them to their Mother.

The community members were kind and helpful whenever I came. They kept everything orderly and played beautiful music with their guitars as I knelt and waited for Our Lady. Sometimes she came sorrowful, but other times joyful. She often gave a message, and many of her words from those apparitions remain imprinted in my thoughts.

"As a mother invites her children, I invited you and you responded to me." (January 2, 2003)

"Do not allow the false brightness that is surrounding you and being offered to you to deceive you." (October 2, 2003)

"My children, do you not recognize the signs of the times? Do you not speak of them?" (April 2, 2006)

"Through you my heart desires to win—it desires to triumph." (May 2, 2006)

"God created you with free will to comprehend and to choose life or death." (July 2, 2006)

"In these peaceless times, I am coming to you to show you the way to peace." (August 2, 2006)

"Cleanse your hearts and bow your head before your only God." (July 2, 2005)

On June 25, 2001, the parish of Međugorje celebrated the 20th anniversary of Our Lady's apparitions. I had never seen the village so crowded with pilgrims. It was a joyous occasion, but I wished Fr. Slavko could have been there, although I'm certain he was in spirit. It never felt like he truly left us. I hope the Church will declare him a saint one day, but in my eyes, he already is one—an example of God's love, a man of deep faith who died as peacefully as he had lived. Many pilgrims now pray beside his grave in the cemetery behind St. James Church.

The anniversary was always a special time for me. My mother and father wished me well that morning. "Can you believe it's been so long?" said Dad, his voice still slurred from his stroke.

Every time I saw him, I was thankful that the doctors had been wrong. More than six years had passed since they predicted he'd live less than one. Still, anytime I received a call when I was not home, I worried that it would be about him.

Marko, Marija and Veronika bought a bouquet of flowers for me on the anniversary day, which had become their tradition. The girls, now nine and six years old, always amazed me with their deep faith and how patiently they accepted having a visionary for a mom. Although *we* were ordinary, our lives were far from it. Marko always tried to make sure they were not confused about my experiences.

"Sometimes God chooses someone not because that person is the best," he said, "but because He needs that person just as he or she is at that moment. That's probably how He chose your mom."

Marko was an exceptional father from the beginning. Knowing the demands of my mission, he devoted himself to our daughters. He fed them, dressed them, and helped them finish their homework as much as I did, if not more. He and I never discussed each other's obligations. It came naturally. God united men and women to work together, not to have all the burdens carried by one.

These days, people who uphold sacred traditions like marriage and faith are often seen as backward and uneducated. On the contrary, I believe such people are saving the world. When it came to teaching Marija and Veronika about faith, we never preached to them or made them do anything they did not want to do. Even when they were babies, they were with us in the living room when we prayed the rosary. Babies, of course, do not understand, but they do hear. If nothing else, the peace that fills the room during prayer enters into them. Somewhere, deep down, they remember.

We never bought a toy or children's movie with the purpose of just occupying their time. We always played or watched it with them, and Marko was especially active with Marija and Veronika. Perhaps Marko and I had unknowingly become similar to my own parents; he always joked and laughed with the girls, while I was the one who usually set rules and forbade things.

Once, when I got tired of having to raise my voice to get Marija and Veronika to follow directions, I decided to see if emulating Our Lady—the consummate mother—would get better results. Their room was in complete disorder, so when I found them playing there, I closed my eyes and envisioned Our Lady's sweet voice. "Children," I said softly. "Please clean your room."

I came back an hour later and found their room even messier than before. "Children," I said tenderly. "It will make me very happy if you clean your room at this moment."

I did this three times, but when they had not done anything by my fourth visit, I lost my patience. "Girls! Clean your room this instant!"

Five minutes later, their room was spotless.

There's only one Blessed Mother, I thought. No matter how many times she has to plead with us to get "our rooms in order," she never gives up, and she never threatens. Her patience is eternal.

Even so, our home was filled with joy, especially when we prayed together. Prayer seemed to come naturally to Marija, while Veronika was more resistant at first. When Veronika was four or five years old, she'd often say she had to go to the bathroom when it was time to pray the rosary as a family.

"No problem," I would say. "We'll wait for you."

Of course, her face would sink in despair. But we never reproached her, and if she did not want to pray that night, we continued without her. In the same way that Our Lady's messages speak differently to everyone, I learned to talk to Marija in one way and Veronika in another. Instead of forcing Veronika to pray, we tried to make the rosary more entertaining, almost like a competition.

"OK, now who will lead the first decade?" I'd say.

Veronika and Marija would both raise their hands. "Me! Me!"

Soon, whenever we had free time, or if we got in the car to go somewhere, Veronika would be the first to say, "Let's pray!" And as she got older, we often found her praying by herself. She had learned how to see Our Lady with her heart, and nothing could ever take that away.

Although the parish celebrated the anniversary on June 25—the day we first approached Our Lady—for me it always began when we saw her on June 24. On this and every anniversary, I felt similar to how I did in the days before the first apparition. I was filled with a sense of love that I wanted to transmit to everyone, and I often cried at the smallest things. After 20 years, Our Lady's apparitions had become almost normal for some people, especially for those who lived in the parish. But for me, everything was still just as amazing.

"Heaven has come down to Earth for so many years," I told some pilgrims. "How great is God's love that He gives us this gift? That he sends our Mother among us to help us?"

With so many pilgrims coming from all over the world, it seemed like Međugorje was experiencing a renewal after the uncertainty caused by the war. Months later, however, the attacks of September 11, 2001 shook the entire world. I was horrified. I could not stop crying as I watched the devastating scenes I saw on the news. The burning towers, the falling victims, the otherworldly ash cloud, the mountain of rubble—every terrible image was another tear on Our Lady's face, another reason to pray for the conversion of people who, like the 9/11 hijackers, did not know God's love.

As the decade approached the halfway mark, I went to have coffee with my father one chilly November afternoon at 2 pm, just as I had nearly every day since his stroke ten years before. Dad's speech had not improved, nor had his walking, but his cheerfulness made him seem stronger than he actually was.

After we finished our coffee, Mom brought my father some food.

"You can go now, Mirjana," she said. "It's time for him to eat."

I stood up and put my hand on his shoulder. "See you later, Dad," I said.

He grasped my arm loosely. "Don't listen to Mom," he joked. "You can stay a little longer."

Mom smiled. "Excuse me?"

I laughed. "We don't want to start a fight, Dad. You eat and I'll try to come back later."

Later that afternoon, Marko and I were grocery shopping when Jakov called our mobile phone. "Uncle is sick," he said. "I think he's dying. Come quick."

I thought he was talking about our Uncle Andrija, but Jakov explained that he was not talking about *our* uncle—he was talking about *his* uncle, my dad.

Marko and I rushed back to my parent's house. Doctors were already around him when we got there, but there was nothing they could do. He passed within ten minutes, as if he had been waiting for me.

In that moment, everything seemed dark. I felt confused, like I was stuck in a dream. How could my father be gone? I ran into my room and locked the door. The early days of the apparitions had conditioned me to carry my sufferings alone.

I hardly remember his funeral. It felt like I was watching from outside my body—as if someone else was receiving condolences in my place. Days later, whenever afternoon approached, I would start getting ready to have coffee with Dad only to realize that he was no longer there. I wore the customary black clothes for an entire year—and I truly did not feel like wearing any other color.

Seeing Our Lady did not exclude me from grieving like any other human being. Everyone wants to have their loved ones forever near, and I had been so close to my father that it felt like part of me was gone. But as Jesus said, "Blessed are they who mourn, for they will be comforted." (Matthew 5:4)

Through the scope of eternity, it was as if my father and I had been at the ground floor of our apartment building and he took the elevator up first. Before I know it, the elevator will come back down for me—just as it will for everyone—and I'll find him waiting at the top. As Our Lady says, life is as passing as a flower.

In the days after his death, I tried to think about all the happy times with my father in Sarajevo, and how he always made me feel so protected and loved. With a little time and a lot of prayer, my peace was restored.

I never saw my father during an apparition after his death, nor did I ask Our Lady about him, but her apparitions and messages gave me momentary reminders of the paradise which had become his home. On March 18, 2004, Our Lady said, *"watching you with a heart full of love, I desire to tell you that what you persistently seek, what you long for, my little children, is before you."* She promised that we'd *"be able to see"* if we cleansed our hearts and put her Son in the first place.

The 2nd of the month apparitions at the Cenacolo Community continued to draw increasing numbers of people. The apparition I experienced on April 2, 2005, the eve of Divine Mercy Sunday, was both powerful and perplexing. Our Lady appeared that morning at 9:17 am. She blessed the crowd but emphasized that the most important blessing is from a priest. Then, with striking resolve, she said, *"At this moment, I ask you to renew the Church."*

It seemed like an overwhelming request. "How can I do this?" I asked, but just as I did, I realized that she was not just speaking to me—she was speaking to everyone. "How can *we* do this?"

"My children, but I will be with you! My apostles, I will be with you and will help you! First renew yourselves and your families, and then everything will be easier."

"Then be with us, Mother."

It was not a typical message. After the apparition, her words resonated in my mind. *Renew the Church.* What was she trying to tell us?

That afternoon Marko and I went to the wedding of one of our neighbors. We were enjoying the reception when one of my friends informed me that Pope John Paul II had just died. Thinking back on my meeting with him, the image of his piercing blue eyes flashed through my mind.

A saint has died, I said to myself.

I was too emotional to stay at the reception, so Marko took me home. We lit two candles and put one on our windowsill and the other on our living room table, and then we knelt and prayed. Amid the silence and flickering candlelight, God gave me peace and a consoling thought—John Paul had died on Earth, but it was his birthday in Heaven. His mission was now complete.

Two years before he died—on December 8, 2003, the solemnity of the Immaculate Conception—Pope John Paul II read a prayer he had composed for world peace. "Queen of Peace, pray for us!" he said. "Mother of mercy and of hope, obtain for the men and women of the third millennium the precious gift of peace: peace in hearts and in families, in communities and among peoples…"

There were many instances when the pope's words seemed to echo those of Our Lady, as if he and she spoke the same heavenly language. Mothers and sons often do.

On May 1, 2011, Pope Benedict XVI beatified John Paul II, and three years later, on April 27, 2014, Pope Francis canonized him. The kindly man I had met nearly 30 years before was now an official saint of the Catholic Church.

I personally believe that the Holy Spirit gives us the pope we need for the times in which we live. Just as the world needed John Paul II and Benedict XVI, so too does it need Pope Francis now. I pray for the Holy Father every day, that God will protect him and help him carry the heavy burdens of his mission. Like those before him, he leads us and teaches us faith, speaking the same language as his Mother.

Pope Francis' choice of papal name reminded me of how Jesus asked St. Francis to rebuild His church, similar to what Our Lady requested just before John Paul II died. Shortly after being elected on March 13, 2013, Francis asked the patriarch of Lisbon to consecrate his pontificate to Our Lady of Fátima on her feast day, May 13, 2013. He then chose October 13, 2013—the 96th anniversary of the final apparition at Fátima—to consecrate the world to the Immaculate Heart of Mary. At Pope Francis' request, the statue of the Blessed Mother containing the bullet that almost took the life of John Paul II was moved from Fátima to St. Peter's Square for the occasion.

The Holy Father also invited delegations from all the major Church-approved apparition sites, as well as one that was yet to be approved—Međugorje. Our pastor, Fr. Marinko Šakota, led a group of parishioners to Rome for the event. Fr. Marinko is himself a fruit of Međugorje; he credits his priesthood to Our Lady, as well as to Fr. Slavko, who in many ways was his mentor.

In his prayer to the Blessed Mother, Pope Francis said, "With renewed gratitude for your maternal presence, we join our voice to that of all the generations that have called you blessed. We celebrate in you the great work of God, who never tires of bending down with mercy to mankind, afflicted by evil and wounded by sin, to heal and to save it."

Visitors to my home often ask about the pair of elegant leather shoes that I keep in a glass case. I first saw them right before an apparition at the Cenacolo Community, a year or so after Pope John Paul II passed away. In the moments before Our Lady comes, it's as if my mind is in another world, and when I saw this pair of shoes in front of me near the statue of the Blessed Mother, I was confused. People often placed rosaries, petitions, and flowers before Our Lady, but who would leave a pair of shoes? When Our Lady appeared, of course, I forgot about them.

After the apparition, a man who had been a close friend of Pope John Paul II approached me. He asked me not to share his identity— and he was in luck because I'm an expert at keeping secrets. The man told me that John Paul had always wanted to come to Međugorje, but as the pope, he was never able to. So, one day, the man joked with the pope, saying, "If you never make it to Međugorje, then I'll go and bring your shoes there. It will be as if you were able to set foot on that holy ground."

After John Paul II passed away, the man felt a calling to do exactly that. After the apparition, the man gave them to me, and I think about the Holy Father every time I look at them. But the funniest part of this happened even later. An Italian man who makes shoes for the pope in Rome heard about the shoes that were given to me. So, he made a second pair in size 38—my size—and sent them to me. Perhaps he thought I was sad that I could not fit in the pope's big shoes.

But, figuratively speaking, who ever could?

*More than 35 years have passed since I first saw Our Lady, and my
daughter Marija recently got married. (Photos by Foto DANI)*

CHAPTER 29

"It is only with the heart that one can see rightly. What is essential is invisible to the eye."

— From *The Little Prince*

SINCE THE APPARITIONS began in 1981, much has changed in Međugorje, and in my life.

I recently turned 50, although I do not feel or act much different than I did when I was 16. When I see an adult behaving immaturely—or when I realize I'm not acting like the perfect angel some people expect me to be—I think, *No wonder she calls us little children. Look at us.*

When I'm with Our Lady, I'm a child looking up at my Mother. Time stands still, and like a mother to a daughter she speaks to me with gentleness and concern. I doubt I'll ever truly feel like an adult. Age is irrelevant in Heaven, and Our Lady's beauty is not of this world. If people ask me to describe how old she looks, my first reaction is to think, *Is that important?* Still, if I had to give an earthly comparison, I would say she looks to be about 20 to 25—far younger, of course, than her actual age of over 2,000 years. Our Lady has looked the same since 1981. In the way she presents herself to us, she's timeless and ageless.

The people of this region have worked to rebuild since the end of the war. Croatia joined the European Union and is known today as one of the world's top holiday destinations. In Bosnia-Herzegovina, the historic Mostar Bridge was carefully reconstructed, and Sarajevo has risen from the ashes to become the cultured city it always hoped to be. But some scars from the war remain, like the hole in the side of our old apartment building, and the sadness we feel on the feast of St. Stephen every year.

A few years ago, I was invited to speak at the Church of St. Anthony in Sarajevo, where I went to catechism classes as a little girl. I was overjoyed to share my testimony with the people of my former city, but in some ways it felt surreal. Looking out at the crowd, I started to describe Our Lady when I suddenly envisioned the secret police barging into the church to arrest me. I had to stop talking and take a deep breath. *Communism is over,* I reassured myself. *Nobody can take me now. Nobody will hurt me. Now I can talk about God.*

I'm grateful to no longer live under communism. Today we have freedom of faith like people of other democratic countries, and nowhere in the region is that faith more alive than in my adopted hometown, Međugorje.

Marko and I still live within a few hundred meters of Apparition Hill. A large marble statue of The Queen of Peace now stands in the place where we first saw her on the hill. Korean pilgrims donated the statue in 2001.

My mother lives next door and spends her time gardening, cooking, and spoiling her grandchildren. I often think back on how much she suffered in Sarajevo after my apparitions began, and how she supported me despite the constant harassment. Sometimes I wonder if I would be as courageous as she was if Marija or Veronika started seeing Our Lady, and if their claims brought the same level of persecution down on our family. Would I endure, or would I ask my child to keep quiet?

Miro also lives next door with his wife, Svjetlana, and their children—Magdalena, Josip and Robert. Miro and I have a warm relationship. We laugh together and cry together. I still think of Miro as my third child, whether he likes it or not, and I've loved watching my niece and nephews grow. I get to see them every day and we are always together for birthdays and holidays. It's beautiful that we all live so close, although I wish my father was still alive to be part of everything.

Uncle Šimun and Aunt Slava live nearby. My cousins Milena, Jelena, and Vlado all got married, but sadly Vesna passed away on March 3, 2015. I was at her side on the last day of her earthly life. I feel blessed that I had the opportunity to comfort her in those tender moments. I caressed her face, kissed her forehead, and assured her that she would soon see the beauty that I had tried to describe so many times. I recalled our time together as little girls, running and laughing in the fields, whispering late into the night. Back then, adulthood seemed like a thousand years away.

Our Lady is right, I thought. *We are only here a short while.*

Aside from my role as a visionary, I live a somewhat ordinary life. I usually wake up early because I like to start my day with a prayer to ask for the gift of love. Without love, I would not be able to function in Međugorje. Like other mothers and wives, I cook, clean, wash and iron clothes, and serve lunch to my family. When everything calms down in the afternoon, I pray again. At least once every day, I recite the St. Anthony Chaplet, just as I promised to do more than 20 years ago. After that, Marko and I might spend time alone or visit with some of our friends—like Violeta and Antun, or Julijana and Mladen—whom I've shared an unbreakable friendship with for some 30 years. Then, in the evening, I pray one more time.

When I look back, I see how I've changed and grown since the early days of the apparitions, and what I have learned. For example, I used to wonder how a loving God could allow suffering.

Bez muke nema nauke is an old Croatian proverb that translates to *Without suffering there is no learning.* It's now clear to me that every hardship in my life contributed to who I am today—every sorrow refined me as a messenger of God's love and gave me a better education than any school could have offered. Now, as an apostle of Our Lady, I'm able to answer difficult questions by drawing on my own experiences.

Only when you experience suffering can you truly understand the suffering of others. You can relate to what they're going through and help them cope, either with words, prayers, or just your presence. After carrying my suffering in silence for so long—so used to hiding my pain in order to protect others from it—I've learned how to share my feelings. Perhaps this book is part of that.

Life with Marko has been everything I had imagined it would be, but one thing I never could have foreseen is the excessive number of dogs we've accumulated. Perhaps Marija and Veronika inherited my empathy; they fell in love with every stray puppy they ever saw, and, like my father, Marko could never say no to his "little princesses." But after the girls started going to college in Mostar, we've taken care of their pets. The smallest one loves to sit on my lap, and Marko enjoys taking the bigger ones for walks every afternoon. When Marija got married recently, I joked that her wedding gift from me might start barking.

Our Lady continues to appear every day to Ivan, Marija and Vicka wherever they are in the world. Each has received 9 of the 10 secrets.

Ivan married an American and spends half the year in the USA and the other half in Medugorje, Marija married an Italian and divides her time between Italy and Medugorje, and Vicka married a local and they live near the village.

As for those of us who have received all ten secrets, Jakov only sees Our Lady on Christmas and Ivanka on June 25, while I'm blessed to see her 13 times a year—on the second of every month and once on March 18. All six of us visionaries have children, many of whom hang out together.

Jakov lives in a house across the street with Annalisa, their son, and two daughters. His humor only gets more mischievous as he gets older. One day, he was walking his dog, Bimba, when some American pilgrims stopped to greet him on their way to my house. One of them asked, "What's your puppy's name?"

Jakov smiled and said, "Her name is Mirjana!"

When the pilgrims came to my house, one of them remarked, "It's so sweet that Jakov named his puppy after you."

I laughed. "Is that what he told you?"

Later, they saw one of our dogs and asked, "Did you name your dog Jakov?"

"No," I said. "I love my dog far too much!"

When Jakov and I get together, we usually laugh and joke more than we talk, and I often think: *If only all the people who are so afraid of the secrets could see us visionaries and how much we laugh!* After all, if we who know the future don't let fear darken our lives, then why should anyone else?

As Međugorje grows, so does my responsibility, but Our Lady has sent people to help me in my mission—people who I can rely on without even having to ask. My friend Damir, who runs a local photography studio, always ensures that I have a microphone when I speak to large groups of pilgrims. My friend Miki, fluent in English and Italian, translates for me when I speak to groups. He's also always next to me during every apparition to write down the message and translate it for pilgrims.

I love interacting with the pilgrims who come to Međugorje. Together with my brother we built a guesthouse next door to our home, and I work there serving food, cleaning, and making sure the pilgrims have what they need. People come from all over the world, and every time I talk with one of them, I get to see the Međugorje experience from a pilgrim's perspective. Plus, I do not have to travel the world to learn about different cultures, because the entire world comes here. Sometimes I think I learn more from the pilgrims than they do from me—seeing the changes in people from the time they arrive to when they leave is a testament to the transformative power of this place.

Because I'm a visionary, some think that I should not work, but I always joke that those same people would probably call me lazy if I did not have a job. Marko and I work hard to support our family. If I did anything else, I wouldn't be able to interact with pilgrims as much as I do now, and aside from being a wife and mother, sharing Our Lady's message is my top priority. Work is a necessary part of life, and having an honest job that glorifies God in some way is essential for the wellbeing of our souls. By serving pilgrims, I can show them that I'm not different or above anyone. We are all equal before God, and our Mother loves us all the same.

One day I was walking up Apparition Hill to pray and I saw a group of pilgrims from Italy in front of me. They were taking turns carrying a handicapped boy on their backs. The steep, rocky terrain is difficult to climb, especially with the extra weight of another person. But they carried him with love, and everyone was smiling, including the boy. After a while, an American group climbing the hill caught up to the Italians. One of the Americans simply said "switch," and began carrying the boy up the hill. In the same way, pilgrims from Australia, Poland and elsewhere took turns carrying the boy, and he reached the top in the hands of the entire world. They saw in him a brother who needed help, regardless of his nationality, language or disability. This, to me, was the embodiment of Međugorje.

When I speak to groups of pilgrims, the main thing I ask of them is to simply be a pilgrim. "Even if you don't believe that Our Lady is appearing," I say, "somehow you ended up here, so what do you have to lose by trying to live the messages for a week? At least then you'll be an *educated* non-believer."

Few people leave here with doubts, though. In fact, by the last day of their pilgrimage, most people say they do not want to leave.

In the early days, I was deeply hurt whenever someone accused me of making everything up. I always wanted to ask them, "Why would I invent such a lie? What would I gain by lying?"

I would have to be an extremely troubled person to lie about such a thing, especially during communist times. Before the apparitions, I had a beautiful life. I lived with parents who cherished me, and I went to one of the best schools in Sarajevo. Why would I want to turn my life upside down? Why bring turmoil and agony into an otherwise pleasant situation? Only an unstable person would do that. But I was not the only one; there were six of us, including a ten-year-old boy who much preferred playing soccer over praying.

These days, I only feel sorry for those who can't see that Our Lady has been offering her hand for all these years to lead them to salvation. And I pray for them. A just person never makes conclusions about someone they do not personally know. Only if you know me, if you have talked with me, can you form an intelligent opinion about who I am and what I claim.

Pilgrims sometimes ask, "Why have the apparitions been going on for so long? Why so many messages?"

I tell them as much as I can. Our Lady is preparing us for everything that's going to take place in the world. She is training us for victory. When the events in the secrets begin, everything will be clear. You will see, for example, why she chose to appear to me on the 18th of March every year, and why I experience the other apparitions on the second day of every month. You will understand the importance of these dates, and you will realize why she's been appearing for so long. Every mother knows that children need constant guidance. Through her messages, Our Lady persistently reminds us to stay on the right path.

When I'm with Our Lady, I have no sense of time. I never know the actual duration of an apparition until people tell me later. I am always shocked at how such a seemingly timeless experience only lasted five or ten minutes for observers. But earthly time is nothing like God's time, which is why some people question how Our Lady can appear so many times over so many years. As the Bible tells us, "With the Lord, one day is like a thousand years and a thousand years like one day." (2 Peter 3:8) In the scope of eternity, these 35 years are barely a flash.

On July 2, 2012, Our Lady said, *"I implore you to stop for a moment and to reflect on yourselves and on the transience of this your earthly life."*

In many ways, it's nice to be a visionary now. Sure, there are hardships—people always stare, and it's impossible to go outside when there are many pilgrims in town. But I'm used to living this way now, and I'm never bored. I've always preferred curling up with a good book instead of going to parties, and when people ask if I have a favorite type of music, I say "silence." I enjoy spending time with family and friends, and every ten days or so, Marko and I have coffee together in Mostar. That's enough for me.

Still, I always make time to share my testimony. When I talk to pilgrims, I feel an immense love for them, and I'm often moved to tears. Perhaps it's no surprise that my friends have nicknamed me "the crybaby." Meeting with pilgrims—many of whom traveled long distances to come here—is a beautiful union in front of the Mother we all share in common. I did not choose my role as a transmitter of the messages; for whatever reason, I was chosen. But I feel incredibly blessed every time I get to share what I know about the love of God.

The parish trains local guides to make sure visiting pilgrims are given correct information. Mornings begin with Mass in different languages at St. James Church, and during the day pilgrims might listen to a talk from a visionary or a priest, or they may climb Apparition Hill or Cross Mountain. I always encourage pilgrims to stay on the hill after they climb with the group, or to go alone later—find a nice, flat rock to sit on, I tell them, and talk to Our Lady about everything in your heart. Leave your pain and suffering behind, or pray for the strength to carry your cross back down.

Late afternoon in Međugorje is wonderful. The Evening Prayer Program—established by Fr. Jozo in the first days of the apparitions and developed further by Fr. Slavko—has evolved into one of the main highlights for many pilgrims. It begins around sunset. The first hour is reserved for the rosary. In nice weather, a priest leads it from the outside altar, and pilgrims pray along from the benches. At the same time, priests gather in and around the confessionals on both sides of the church, and it's common for each priest to have a line of ten or more people waiting to confess. Many priests have told me that hearing confession is the highlight of their pilgrimage here, and that they've never experienced confessions of such magnitude or beauty anywhere else. Some refer to Međugorje as "the confessional of the world," and Cardinal Schönborn called it a "superpower of mercy."

After the rosary comes the international Mass. Although it's celebrated in Croatian, pilgrims use headset radios to listen to live translations in their own languages. Broadcasts include English, Italian, Polish, German, French, Spanish, Arabic, Korean, and more, depending on the pilgrims in town at the time. Seeing priests of different nationalities together on the altar also shows how the message of Međugorje has spread throughout the world. On alternating nights, Mass is followed by a holy hour of gentle music and reflection with Adoration of the Blessed Sacrament or Veneration of the Cross. By then, the sky is full of stars.

Many initiatives have developed into annual traditions. The Peace March from Humac to Međugorje, established during the war, still takes place every year on June 24th. Thousands of pilgrims and locals take part. Every Christmas, the Cenacolo Community puts on a live Nativity play in front of St. James Church, complete with real farm animals and a life-size crèche. Throughout the year, the parish hosts seminars for married couples, doctors and nurses, priests, disabled people, and others.

The widespread fruits of Međugorje show how Our Lady's plan to "renew the Church" is developing. Over the years, countless people who came here with lukewarm faith, or no faith at all, departed with a newfound belief in God. People who had never prayed before discovered how to pray with their hearts, and those suffering from addictions conquered them here.

Many terminally ill people look for healings in Međugorje and some are always near me during the apparitions. I cry when I see them suffering, especially the youngest ones, and I pray for them. When

God intervenes, I usually only hear about it later, because Our Lady is my only focus during the apparition.

A few years ago, an Italian doctor and his wife brought their ten-year-old son, who was dying of stomach cancer, to Međugorje. Every specialist at home told them nothing could be done to save the boy's life. The boy and his family came to an apparition and kneeled near me. They prayed intensely.

The parents told me later that when Our Lady came, the boy held his stomach and winced. "Mommy, Daddy," he said. "My stomach is burning."

When the family returned to Italy, the specialists discovered no trace of cancer.

I know many similar stories, but most ailing people who come to Međugorje return home with the same illnesses. Why some get healed and others do not is a mystery of God. Perhaps the most difficult thing to understand is the passing of a child. How can a loving God allow such misery? It's natural to ask that question. Living in a temporal world, we're conditioned to think in terms of years and lifetimes. When people die "too young," we wonder why God couldn't have let them live full lives.

But remember—we do not die.

Our Lady knows what it feels like to lose a child, but she was reunited with Him in Heaven and has been with Him ever since. We're destined to see our departed loved ones again, but it's not always easy to understand God's will.

Who's to say that a short life is less valuable than a long one? If "a day is like a thousand years" to our eternal God, the difference between a decade and a century is infinitesimal. Why can't a person fulfill his mission and learn all he needs to know—or teach others what they need to learn—in a short time?

Our Lady has shown me that Heaven is devoid of suffering. I see abundant truth in the statement heard so often at funerals: "They're in a better place now." Our true home is with God. We are like pilgrims on Earth, here for a brief sojourn on our way to an eternal reality that transcends time, space and death. Your pilgrimage might end today, tomorrow, or in twenty years, but you are going to meet God, whether you're aware of that or not. Was your walk guided by humility and sacrifice, or arrogance and greed? It's better to contemplate this question now instead of at the end of your journey.

People who think that the existence of suffering disproves the existence of God misunderstand their *own* existence. If the world were devoid of sorrow, could we recognize joy? If sickness did not exist, would we cherish good health? In many ways, a pilgrimage to Međugorje is a metaphor for life. The pilgrim endures the pain of long-distance travel and the exhaustion of climbing the hills, but in the end he realizes that all the suffering opens a doorway to love.

I always tell people who come to Međugorje that a spiritual healing is infinitely more valuable than a physical one. Only one kind of healing leads to *eternal* life. A man can enter Heaven without an arm or a leg but not with sin in his soul. Still, Our Lady cannot heal people; only God can. But she does intercede for us. She prays with us—and for us—if we ask her to. If you suffer physically, the most important step is to ask God to help you. Jesus showed by example that the person who tries to carry his cross alone will fall down under its weight.

I went to St. James Church for Mass one morning and sat in a pew near the statue of the Blessed Mother. Moments later, an Italian woman came in and knelt in front of the statue. She started crying and I heard her whisper, "Why, God? Why me?"

She cried throughout the entire Mass and kept repeating those words. I didn't know why she suffered so terribly, but I cried along with her.

As Mass ended, she suddenly stopped crying. Her look of sorrow changed to joy. "Why *not* me?" she said. "Yes! Why *not* me?"

I went to her after the final blessing. "Hello," I said.

The woman seemed embarrassed. "Pardon me," she said. "I hope I didn't disturb you during the Mass."

"Don't worry. If anything, you made me pray harder."

She smiled and looked up at the ceiling of the church. "Oh, this place! I think this is the best day of my life. May I tell you?"

"You don't have to ask permission. Tell me."

"Well, I have three handicapped children back home. I came to Medugorje to beg God to heal them, and I wanted to know why He gave me this cross. But now I understand! It hit me when I was praying. Why *wouldn't* God give me this cross? It means He sees that I can carry it! He trusts me and I have to trust Him. He'll help me when it gets too heavy. I can't wait to go home and kiss my children. I'm so blessed to have them."

I started crying again. "And they're blessed to have you."

The woman looked at the statue of the Blessed Mother. "You know, it's funny, I didn't even ask God to heal them like I planned on doing. And guess what? I don't think I need to anymore."

Visiting with Cardinal Christoph Schönborn, the Archbishop of Vienna.

CHAPTER 30

"What is so beautiful about my memory to be preserved? Only my tears and my prayers, because they have been pure."

— *Tin Ujević, Croatian poet (1891-1955)*

THE FRUITS OF Međugorje go far beyond our pomegranates and grapes.

One of the greatest fruits of Međugorje is the large number of religious vocations. Cardinal Christoph Schönborn, the Archbishop of Vienna, once said that if not for the apparitions, he'd have to close down his seminary since nearly all the candidates received their calling to the priesthood through Međugorje. I met with Cardinal Schönborn when he visited Međugorje. I thought I was looking at John Paul II for a moment. The cardinal's eyes, facial expressions, and even the way he rested his head on his hand reminded me of the pope.

"This is my first visit," he said, "but since I became a bishop in 1991, I've noticed the fruits of Međugorje."

In the Gospel of Matthew (7:16-18), Jesus says, "Can people pick grapes from thorns, or figs from thistles? In the same way, a sound tree produces good fruit but a rotten tree bad fruit. A sound tree cannot bear bad fruit, nor a rotten tree bear good fruit."

Many are drawn here by the fruits they see. But among all the good coming out of Međugorje, there have been a few unfortunate situations.

For example, words that I never said have been attributed to me. People who have come here on pilgrimage naturally want to share what they've discovered, and some have written books. Despite their good intentions, many books contain errors and rehash the same falsehoods that have been going around for decades.

As it says in the Book of James, "Not many of you should become teachers, my brothers, for you realize that we will be judged more strictly, for we all fall short in many respects."

I am only called to transmit the message. Like anyone else, I have to interpret Our Lady's words for myself. Prayer is the key to unlocking each message and understanding how to integrate it into our lives. Even though Our Lady speaks simply, her messages have sometimes been misinterpreted, often when people ascribe their own ideas and agendas to the messages through lengthy commentaries. I always say that the messages do not need to be explained. Our Lady speaks in a simple way so that all of her children can understand.

For example, Our Lady has said, *"I am giving you my motherly blessing"* and she has asked us to be her *"extended hands."* Some people misunderstood this to mean that they should go and bless others, but I do not think that's what Our Lady meant. Instead, she wants our life to be a blessing for other people. I can bless my children at night, but that is merely my motherly blessing.

On the contrary, Our Lady has taught us that the blessing of Jesus only comes through a priest. *"Their hands are blessed by my Son,"* she said, and she often repeats that our priests do not need our judgment; they need our prayers. Many people abandon or reject faith because they find fault in a priest, but this is only an excuse. God will judge priests on how well they carried out their missions and He will judge us on how well we treated them.

St. Francis of Assisi held a similar view. When parishioners from a nearby village complained to Francis that their priest was living in sin, he went with them to their village. The residents expected Francis to admonish their wayward shepherd, but instead Francis got on his knees and kissed the priest's hands. "All I know and all I want to know is that these hands give me Jesus," said Francis. "These hands have held God."

I wish I could divulge more about what will happen in the future, but I can say one thing about how the priesthood relates to the secrets. We have this time that we are living in now, and we have the time of the triumph of Our Lady's heart. Between these two times we have a bridge, and that bridge is our priests. Our Lady continually asks us to pray for our shepherds, as she calls them, because the bridge needs to be strong enough for all of us to cross it to the time of the triumph. In her message of October 2, 2010, she said, *"Only alongside your shepherds will my heart triumph."*

Never is this "bridge" more evident in Međugorje than during the annual Youth Fest, another legacy of Fr. Slavko. It's common to see over 500 priests concelebrating the evening Mass and hundreds more hearing confession. Every year, thousands of young people brave the summer heat during the first week of August to celebrate their faith with prayer and song. During the opening ceremony, delegates from nations near and far take part in a procession and introduce their homeland on the outside altar. Flags from the USA, China, Australia and beyond wave in the crowd, but in reality everyone is united under the banner of God.

When young people ask me for advice, I usually say, "Don't be afraid to follow Jesus. Instead of looking for peace in drugs, alcohol and things that will kill you, find it in faith and prayer, and then you'll have more fun. *Real* fun."

Many of them think that everything will be forbidden if they follow Jesus, but faith cannot be reduced to a set of rules. I tell them that if they like to go out, to socialize, to dance, then why not? But dance with Jesus—just like everyone does at the Youth Fest.

I often hear older pilgrims complain that their children are doing things wrong; like the "angry God" of my catechism classes, some parents constantly point out mistakes. But I always try to tell these mothers and fathers that the way our young people turn out depends on us—what we tell them, how we guide them, and especially the example they see in us. Our Lady has said that we as parents will have to answer for how we raise our children. The measure by which we'll be judged, I believe, is love.

Speaking about Our Lady's messages is easier than living them, but the rewards of striving to live according to God's will are priceless, as Marko and I have seen in our own family. Marija and Veronika have grown into beautiful, faithful young women. Now that they're older, I never wonder if they're praying, going to Mass or helping those in need. It just comes natural to them, because Marko and I instilled it with our example. If we chose to stay home from Mass on rainy days, then they would have adopted the same attitude later in life. Instead we even went in the worst weather. Or if they never saw Marko and me praying, they would think that it was not so important. Instead, we tried to say at least one rosary together every evening. Children see much more than we think they do. They need to observe that God comes before anything else for their parents. Every good mother, as long as she lives, constantly worries about whether or not she's done enough for her children. It's the same for Our Lady, but she never tries to force anyone to listen to her.

What I love most about my girls is their joy. They smile, they radiate peace, and they know how to joke, which, I believe, is the result of a healthy faith. As Pope Benedict XVI once wrote, "Where joylessness reigns, where humor dies, the spirit of Jesus Christ is assuredly absent."

Still, Marija and Veronika worry about me because I'm often occupied with pilgrims. They're afraid that my health will decline if I exhaust myself, a concern that might stem from the death of our beloved Fr. Slavko. If they see me tired and in pain after a long talk to pilgrims, they bring me water and remind me, "You also need to think about yourself sometimes. We need you, too." It's as if I have two angels at my side.

Thankfully, though, they understand my mission. We've always told them that people come to Međugorje seeking peace. It's our job—as people who are privileged to know God's love—to help them find what they're looking for. We can't keep the graces of Our Lady's apparitions to ourselves. They're to be shared with everyone, now and in the future.

At this moment, according to Our Lady, we are living in a time of grace. After this will come the time of the secrets, and the time of her triumph. God-willing, you will hear from me then. Of course, there's no guarantee that I will be alive when the secrets are revealed. When people ask me about the end of the world, I ask them why that even matters to them. The end of *my* world can happen at any time, just as it can for anyone. That is the only "end" we need to prepare for. By keeping our souls clean, we are ready to stand before God at any moment.

A few years ago, Marko and I traveled to the USA to speak at a prayer gathering, and a few friends from Međugorje joined us. They were all afraid of flying. As our airplane was about to take off, one of them gripped the armrests of her seat and said, "Let's pray that this plane doesn't crash."

Our other friend closed his eyes. "Please let us make it there alive," he said.

But another interjected, "Wait a minute, what are we talking about? Mirjana's with us and she can't die; she has the secrets! We'll be fine."

I laughed. "I have the secrets *written*, which means I don't have to be alive!"

They all suddenly got nervous again, but of course we arrived in America safely.

I've kept the parchment in a secure place ever since the UN soldier unknowingly returned it to me. I could even have it sitting on my living room table and you wouldn't know what it is. When the time comes, those who need to read it will be able to.

It's possible you're reading this book after the secrets have been revealed, but if not—if the events foretold by Our Lady have yet to take place and the permanent sign has yet to appear—then I urge you not to wait. Abandon yourself to God today.

The secrets always come up in questions when I speak to pilgrims. During one talk, a young man from Naples repeatedly asked me about the secrets. I was a little disappointed because I always prefer to talk about God's love.

"Don't waste your time worrying about the secrets," I said to him, "because you don't know when your own secret will happen. What if I say that the first secret will happen ten days from now, but you're going to die tomorrow?"

The young man got a strange look on his face. Without a word, he turned and hurried away. Afraid I had hurt his feelings, I ran after him. "What's wrong?" I said.

He looked at me with fear in his eyes. "How can you ask me what's wrong? You said I'm going to die tomorrow!"

"Oh, no!" I could not help but laugh at the misunderstanding.

"You think it's funny!?"

"I'm sorry. Perhaps my Italian didn't come across right. I don't know when you're going to die. Hopefully not for a long time. I was trying to tell you that it doesn't matter when the secrets will be revealed. All that matters is being ready to stand before God."

One day, though, that young man *will* die. So will I, and so will you. The future is up to God and no one else. What if today is your last? It will be for many, and it already was for Grandma Jela, Vesna, Vittorio, Stjepan, Fr. Slavko, my dad, Pope John Paul II, and the billions of other human beings who have lived and died on this planet. Just think about all the people in my life who have passed on and realize that God might call you at any moment. If you knew you were going to die tomorrow, would you go on living the same way you have been, or is there something you'd change? If there's someone you haven't forgiven, or someone you have wronged, or a sin you haven't confessed, do not wait until tomorrow to make restitution. You do not know if tomorrow will come.

When I visit with the other visionaries, we might talk about our families or our missions, but we never discuss the secrets. The six of us do not even know if all the secrets we've been given are the same. Some people wonder why there are secrets at all, but it was not Our Lady who decided to have it this way. Everything will happen according to God's will, not mine. People used to ask me why I did not choose Fr. Slavko to reveal the secrets. He was Marko's uncle, after all, and we became quite close to him. But Father Slavko died. God's plan always supersedes our own.

Again, secrets are secrets, and women know how to keep secrets.

A man visiting Medugorje from Argentina came to me one day. He looked at me with somber eyes and said, "Before I came here, I didn't believe in God. My life seemed meaningless. But now I know He's real and I want to tell people about Him."

By the look on his face and the sad tone of his voice, I thought he was about to tell me he was dying, but he was perfectly healthy. I told him the same thing I tell everyone: If you want to be an example to unbelievers—if you desire to show that you have faith—then you have to smile. To know the love of God is to know joy. If Marija and Veronika are sad about something, then naturally I feel sad, too. So it is with Our Lady. Her heart cannot triumph if her children are unhappy.

I still experience thirteen apparitions every year—one on March 18th, and the others on the second of every month.

In 2009, Bishop Perić—still skeptical about our experiences— requested that the apparitions no longer take place at the Cenacolo Community. Initially, I was sad about his decision. It felt so natural to be among the community members when Our Lady came to pray for those who did not believe. Each of the young men reminded me of the lost son in Luke's Gospel who "was dead and has come to life again." As a Catholic, however, I accepted my bishop's decision respectfully. I continue to pray for him every day. If he were to ask me to walk a hundred miles just to meet with him, I would do it without hesitation. No matter what, he's my bishop and I love him.

Many times, I've thought about writing him a letter. *Dear Father Bishop, I'd like to tell you everything that's in my heart.* But I've never been able to put a pen to paper.

With Cenacolo no longer an option, I struggled to decide what to do. Should I go back to experiencing the apparitions at home, or should I find a new place to be in public?

I was tempted to stay home as I've always enjoyed my solitude. I remembered how peaceful it had been when Our Lady came to me in my room. There was no commotion, crowds, or cameras in my face, and I could focus more on praying as I waited to see the Blessed Mother.

But I thought back to one time when I was returning to Croatia on a ferry from Italy. I saw a multitude of pilgrims coming on the ferry to be in Međugorje for my next apparition, but they did not recognize me. Their faces were joyful but full of suffering as they struggled to push their suitcases across the deck. Tears filled my eyes. These people left the comfort of their homes and traveled for days, all to answer Our Lady's call. Any difficulties I might have to endure by experiencing the apparitions in public were nothing compared to their sacrifices. When I thought about all the pilgrims who had been coming to the second of the month apparitions—and all the conversions I had seen and heard about—I knew that I would be neglecting my role as a messenger if I shut myself off from the world. After many hours of prayer, I decided to go back to the base of the hill where it all began.

When I climbed up to the Blue Cross for my next apparition, I finally saw God's hand in the bishop's decision. Previously at Cenacolo, the apparitions took place in a small auditorium which could only hold a few hundred people. At first, there was plenty of room, but as more people began coming to the apparitions, it became far too small, and the vast majority of pilgrims had to stay outside. Thousands of people could gather on Apparition Hill. Everything had come full-circle, back to those early days when the hill was full of pilgrims and Our Lady appeared to us in the harsh splendor of nature. She comes in the chill of winter and the scorching heat of summer, among believers and non-believers alike—her dear children, her apostles of love, all drawn together from every corner of the world.

A statue of Our Lady marks the place of her first apparitions on Podbrdo (IMAGE FROM THE FILM APPARITION HILL).

CHAPTER 31

"Only with total interior renunciation will you recognize God's love and the signs of the time in which you live. You will be witnesses of these signs and will begin to speak about them."

— *From Our Lady's Message of March 18, 2006*

FTER EXPERIENCING HEAVEN for all these years, I believe I can finally answer the question that burned inside my heart for so long—the same one that burns in every human heart:

What's the meaning of life?

Many people expect a complex answer. My answer, however, is the shortest sentence in this book.

Love.

Our Lady has said the word *love* over 400 times in her messages on the second of the month and March 18. God is love. Jesus is love incarnate. The Blessed Mother leads us to love. And everything happening in Međugorje today originates from that love.

On March 2, 2007, Our Lady appeared with particular conviction and gave me the following message. *"Today I will speak to you about what you have forgotten: Dear children, my name is Love. That I am among you for so much of your time is love, because the Great Love sends me. I am asking the same of you. I am asking for love in your families. I am asking that you recognize love in your brother. Only in this way, through love, will you see the face of the Greatest Love. May fasting and prayer be your guiding star. Open your hearts to love, namely, salvation. Thank you.*"

Problems arise among people, nations, and religions when they forget the fundamental truth that God is the *Greatest Love*. Our Lady doesn't simply say that God *has* love; she says that He *is* love, and furthermore she tells us that her name is Love. It's clear to see how the Blessed Mother is synonymous with love, but was she also speaking literally? Scholars believe that *Miriam* (מִרְיָם), the Hebrew name for Mary, likely comes from the Egyptian word for *love*.

My prayer mission, too, is rooted in love. On July 2, 2015, Our Lady asked us to transmit faith *"to those who do not believe, who do not know, who do not want to know. But for that you must pray a lot for the gift of love, because love is the mark of true faith and you will be apostles of my love."*

The message of the Queen of Peace mirrors the message of her Son. In *The Gospel of Matthew*, Jesus said, "You shall love the Lord, your God, with all your heart, with all your soul, and with all your mind. This is the greatest and the first commandment. The second is like it: You shall love your neighbor as yourself."

Just as meeting the inhabitants of different planets ultimately taught the Little Prince about himself, our lives are shaped by the people we encounter.

When I was still just a shy little girl, I never would have believed that my adult life would be intertwined with so many people from all over the world. Sharing my testimony has taken me to big cities, lovely communities, and even remote islands like Réunion and Mauritius where the locals brought me to tears by learning and singing *Gospa Majka Moja*, a Croatian hymn about the Queen of Peace.

I travel less frequently now, perhaps because I don't have to actually leave my home to see the world. The world comes to Međugorje. But I still go to Italy occasionally to visit Lia, Alessandra, Antonio, Anna Maria, and others.

Lia has become one of my dearest friends, and Alessandra, now in her forties, continues to pray for "those who do not yet know God's love." She says she has three mothers—Lia, the Blessed Mother, and me. Stories about her father's exemplary life spread throughout Italy after his passing, and today Dr. Vittorio Trancanelli is revered as "the saint of the operating room." The Vatican opened his beatification process and Vittorio is now officially known as a Servant of God.

Antonio was diagnosed with Parkinson's disease and is now confined to a wheelchair, but the prayer group still meets at his house every Wednesday at 11 am. I join them whenever we visit. As always, we still pray the rosary and read verses from the Bible, but now we also recite a special prayer for Vittorio's intercession.

Looking back at June 24, 1981, the first time we ever saw Our Lady, I often wondered why she chose to appear with a baby. Years later, I came to believe that she wanted to symbolically tell us, *"I come to bring you my Son."*

By bringing her Son to us, she gives us everything. She gives us peace. For more than 35 years, she's been offering us this peace through her messages.

Dr. Fr. Ljudevit Rupčić, the priest who used to visit me in Sarajevo, died on June 25, 2003, the 22nd anniversary of the apparitions. Known as one of the most prominent Croatian theologians of his generation, he earned recognition for translating the New Testament into Croatian and writing several books about Međugorje, among other things.

Fr. Rupčić wrote, "We can say that Our Lady's messages underline that peace is the greatest good, and that faith, conversion, prayer and fasting are the means by which we can attain it."

True peace comes from God alone. Some people come to me thinking that I can solve their problems, but I am just a human being who must pray like anyone else. Others treat Our Lady like she's some kind of deity who grants wishes and heals the sick, but she, too, must pray to God to attain anything.

"I lived your earthly life," she said during her apparition on September 2, 2015. *"I know that it is not always easy, but if you will love each other, you will pray with the heart, you will reach spiritual heights, and the way to Heaven will be opened for you."*

And on February 2, 2016, she said, *"I know you. I know your pain and sorrows, because I also suffered in silence."*

Through her recent messages, Our Lady seems to be trying to come closer to us. She understands what it's like to live on Earth because she was one of us. She dealt with many of the same pains, joys, fears, and hopes. She smiled and rejoiced, and she suffered through grief and hardship. The problems we face are nothing new for her, and we should never be afraid to ask for her help, even with something we feel embarrassed or ashamed about.

In the early days of the apparitions, I wanted to know more about her life because so little of it was written in the Bible. When Our Lady showed me scenes spanning from her early childhood to the death of her Son, I wrote down everything in a notebook. I will be able to release the story of her life when the events she foretold start to happen.

After Our Lady showed me her life, I experienced my faith in a much deeper way. For example, after I saw glimpses of what we now call The Nativity, I'm always emotional around the holidays. I cry a lot on Christmas Eve because I think about the suffering she endured and the fear she felt when giving birth at night in an unfamiliar place. But I'm filled with joy on Christmas Day because I think of Mary coddling her infant Son, beaming with the love of a new mother and soothed by the realization that she had done everything God asked from her.

Hers was a simple life. The most important thing for her was love—a complete surrender to God. She asks us to strive for Heaven by living in a similar way, and by practicing our faith instead of just theorizing about it. *"Do not waste time deliberating too much,"* Our Lady said during the apparition on August 2, 2015. *"You will distance yourselves from the truth. With a simple heart accept His word and live it... The more you love, the further away you will be from death.*"

I don't think she was speaking of earthly death, which is inevitable for everyone. Instead, I believe she was speaking of *eternal* death, which we each have the power to avoid. *"This is a time of decisions,"* she once said. Our Lady has also called this a time of grace, and whoever accepts this gift will find that death is only a transition to a better life.

Fr. Rupčić wrote, "Conversion is another one of Our Lady's frequent messages. This presupposes that she noticed either a weakness or a complete lack of faith in humanity today. And without conversion it is impossible to achieve peace."

Conversion begins when you admit that you are lost. Ancient Christians called on the Blessed Mother with the title *Stella Maris*, or Star of the Sea, because they saw her as a guiding light for wayward "mariners" navigating the stormy waters of life. She invites you to embark with her on a journey. She's already plotted the course, so all you have to do is cast off the lines and set sail for the "New World" like a modern-day Christopher Columbus crossing the ocean with the *Santa Maria*.

In her message of December 2, 2011, she invited each of us to *"become a seed of the future, a seed that will grow into a firm tree and spread its branches throughout the world."*

And through her apparitions, Our Lady has created a "garden" of conversion. Many pilgrims feel a profound force in Međugorje, one that softens their hardened hearts and inspires them to change their lives. Our Lady's reach, however, is not restricted by geography. Some people feel her call from afar, maybe while reading a book about the apparitions, watching a documentary, or hearing a testimony. Yet most pilgrims agree that her presence is the strongest in Međugorje, as if the air is infused with her love. And once they breathe her in, their lives are never the same.

One day, six Italians came to stay at my family's guesthouse in Međugorje. All in their sixties, five of them were strong believers and one was not. When I greeted them, the one who did not believe in God immediately said, "I'm not interested. I just came to be with my friends."

"No problem," I said, smiling. "If you ever need to talk—"

"I won't, thank you."

I could sense a deep sorrow in the man, but he guarded it with his gruff exterior. Over the years, I've been able to sense things about some people, though not all. Perhaps being in close contact with Our Lady has heightened my sensitivity to the point that I sometimes "see" spiritual suffering. When I do, I feel an overwhelming desire to talk with such people, to help them heal their wounds. I cannot remove their pain, but I can listen to them and help them understand that they are not alone, that God loves them. But I can only wait for them to open up. Trying to pry open a clamshell only makes it close tighter.

In her message of June 2, 2010, Our Lady said, *"Free yourself of everything from the past which burdens you, that gives you a sense of guilt, that which previously led you astray in error and darkness. Accept the light."*

Occasionally I also feel evil breaking out from people, radiating around them like an invisible cloud of dread. When I encounter such a person, chills run down my spine. I fear for him, and I pray intensely, because he doesn't realize that the devil has a chokehold on his soul.

But suffering and evil are very different things, and I did not sense evil in the Italian man. I only sensed hurt. And I knew that he, like others who have declared their disbelief upon arriving, would not leave the same.

The next day, I found him crying on the couch like a child. It pained me to see a 60-year-old man so distraught. I sat beside him and said, "Is it my cooking?"

He smiled, took a breath, and wiped his eyes. "Can you write down the *Hail Mary* prayer for me?" he said. "I don't know the words and I want to go to the hill and pray to her."

"Of course I can."

"I've wasted so much time," he said, sobbing again.

I put my hand on his shoulder. "You didn't waste a second. Few people are ever fortunate enough to feel what you're feeling right now."

He spent much of that night praying on the hill.

Another time, a group of Americans stayed at our house. I greeted them when they arrived. One by one, they smiled as they entered, but the last one came in frowning.

"Let's make this clear," he said. "I'm a Protestant."

I was a little stunned by his emphasis on it, but I smiled and said, "So what? You're a Protestant, I'm a Catholic. All I want is for you to feel welcome."

He stayed here for seven days, climbing the hill with his friends, taking walks through the fields, and experiencing the Evening Prayer Program at St. James Church. Whenever I served dinner, I would go to his table and say, "I'd like to give you this food, but only if you don't protest about it."

He laughed every time, and one day he asked me, "Do you even know what a Protestant is?"

I smiled. "I just know that you constantly protest about things."

We laughed and talked for the entire week, and I was sad when it was time for him to leave. With his suitcase in hand, he hugged me at the same door at which he'd met me.

"Thank you," he said. "This trip has changed my life. I came to know my Mother."

He had recognized the same thing that the original Protestant, Martin Luther, once wrote: "Mary is the Mother of Jesus and the Mother of all of us."

Why does anyone run from Our Lady? No family on Earth is truly complete without a mother, and it's the same for our heavenly family.

Excluding the Blessed Mother from your life and ignoring her messages is to exclude and ignore love. She personifies—and speaks—love.

"Immeasurable is my love," she said on January 2, 2013. *"Do not be afraid."*

A young woman from Milan once brought her fiancée here. At first, he was upset to be in Međugorje, but by the time he left, he seemed happy. A few months later, he came back.

"I didn't believe in God for most of my life," he told me. "He simply couldn't exist. When my fiancée said that she wanted to visit Međugorje, I only came because I loved her. I would have gone to Hell for her, not that I believed in Hell. When we arrived, I wanted to turn around and go home, but on our second day here, the Madonna took me in her arms. I can't describe what I felt in my heart, but I'd never felt anything so wonderful. It knocked me off my feet. When I got back to Italy, I met my longtime friends at a café. I didn't say anything about my trip, but I noticed that my friends all looked at me in a strange way. I asked if something was wrong. 'You're different,' they said. 'Normally you're so loud and arrogant. What's going on with you?' I couldn't believe they noticed. I smiled and told them, 'I came to know God.' They were shocked. I've come back to Međugorje to give thanks. The Madonna is helping me become a new person."

On March 18, 2008, Our Lady said, *"Dear children, today I extend my hands towards you. Do not be afraid to accept them… Fill my heart with joy and I will lead you towards holiness. The way on which I lead you is difficult and full of temptations and falls."*

I've heard countless testimonies similar to the young man's. It's important to remember that no one can ever truly say "I'm a convert," because conversion is a lifelong process. Even the holiest among us can always be better. Our Lady calls us to conversion, not only to help us save ourselves, but to save all mankind and the planet we live on. We hurt each other and destroy nature, and then we say "why, God, why?" when disaster befalls us. God gave us free will to choose how we want to live, but today we try to have everything without thinking about the future.

With its unusually large church named after the patron saint of pilgrims and a mountain already capped by a cross, it seemed as though Međugorje had been prepared as a shrine long before Our Lady first appeared. Some people believe that one local man actually predicted that Our Lady would come to Međugorje, years before she actually did.

Mate Šego, born in 1901, claimed that Međugorje would be a holy place and that hundreds of stairs would lead up Podbrdo. Everyone laughed at him, but today the path up the hill is so worn and polished by the feet of countless pilgrims that it resembles a marble staircase. The village would change dramatically, Mate said, and so many foreigners would come that locals would not be able to sleep at night, which reminds me of Jakov's answer when someone asked him what it's like to be a visionary.

"Imagine being woken at 2 am by pilgrims outside your window singing to you," he joked.

Mate even said that he would not live to see his predictions come true. He died in 1979. When the apparitions began two years later, people in the village reconsidered what they had dismissed as the ramblings of an old man.

The Međugorje of today barely resembles the one of Mate's time. The hamlets of the parish have virtually melded into one town, and U2's song no longer applies here—our streets were given names in 2014. *Pope John Paul II Street* leads into the main part of town, *Fr. Slavko Barbarić Street* circles the rotunda and extends past the school, and *Queen of Peace Street* passes through Bijakovići along the base of Apparition Hill. Thankfully, despite all the development, the surrounding hills and most of the fields remain relatively untouched.

Just as Mate predicted, people come from all over the world, making Međugorje like a *United Nations* of prayer. In addition to all the Christians who visit, I've encountered pilgrims of many beliefs including Muslims, Buddhists, Hindus, atheists, and agnostics. People who have been searching all their lives often seem to find what they're looking for here.

In her message on July 2, 2014, Our Lady addressed us as *"Dear Children"* and said, *"I, the mother of all of you gathered here, and the mother of the entire world, am blessing you with a motherly blessing and call you to set out on the way of humility."*

Just as the village changed and grew, the apparitions made me stronger. As a tender and withdrawn child, it was difficult to suddenly be the focus of attention in the first days of the apparitions. I still remember crying out of fear when Fr. Jozo asked me to stand at the altar and address the congregation. But through all my experiences, both good and bad, I now hardly recognize that shy little girl who used to hide in her room whenever guests came over.

On a recent trip to Italy, I stopped to pray at the 700-year-old Basilica of Saint Anthony in Padua, where Anthony's body is interred. I knelt in one of the pews and thanked him for his help in my life. I felt like St. Anthony was there with me, listening to my prayers and consoling me like an older brother.

As I started praying the St. Anthony Chaplet, which I had done every day since the war, an older woman and her two grandsons sat down in the pew behind me.

"You lead the *Our Father*," the woman said to one of the little boys.

"But I don't want to, Grandma," he whined.

The woman raised her voice. "You must!"

The boy finally started praying and I tried to reconnect with my own prayer. Moments later, however, the woman instructed her other grandson to pray the *Hail Mary*.

"But this is boring," he said.

"Pray it now!" the woman said sharply.

When something disturbs my peace in church I usually ignore it, but this time I felt like I had to say something. I turned to the woman and said, "Ma'am, forgive me, but if you force them to pray, then they'll just hate praying when they grow up."

"Oh? And what makes you an expert?"

I was tempted to say *Well, I see the Virgin Mary,* but instead I replied, "I'm not an expert, but I am a mother."

After I turned back around, the woman remained quiet and I was able to pray in peace.

Our Lady never demands anything from us—she only invites.

Pilgrims await Our Lady at the Blue Cross where she appears to me on the second of every month. (PHOTO BY FOTO ĐANI)

CHAPTER 32

"You will be my light-bearers of God's love. You will illuminate the way for those who have been given eyes but do not want to see."

— From Our Lady's Message of October 2, 2012

"THE MOST BEAUTIFUL things in the world cannot be seen or touched—they are felt with the heart."

This line from *The Little Prince* could almost describe Međugorje. It's difficult to find the right words to describe all the beautiful things that I see and feel with my heart during the apparitions, but I am always determined to try.

If you experience something for most of your life, you usually get used to it. But I've never gotten used to seeing Our Lady. Every apparition feels like the first, and I cry whenever I speak about it. Even today, it's hard for me to believe that it's been happening for such a long time.

Looking back at August 2, 1987, when the second of the month apparitions began, I see the Blessed Mother's patient and gentle hand in the way everything has evolved. Beautiful things have happened, and will happen, on the 2nd of August. The Church celebrates August 2 as the feast day of Our Lady of the Angels, which is connected with St. Francis and Assisi. It was on this day in 1981 that Our Lady allowed the villagers to touch her dress. And when the things Our Lady has spoken to me about start to happen in the future, the world will understand why she chose August 2 as her first apparition for those yet to know God's love.

There were only a few people with me during the 2nd of the month apparitions in the beginning, but now the entire village fills up with pilgrims a few days before each one. I was intensely moved by Our Lady's message of May 2, 2009 when she said, *"From the depth of your heart cry out for my Son. His name disperses even the greatest darkness. I will be with you. Just call on me: 'Here we are, Mother. Lead us.'"*

Now, I see her words written on some of the buses coming from Italy before each apparition:

Eccoci Madre! Here we are, Mother!

Towards the end of every month, I begin to pray and fast more intensely, which helps me feel closer to the Blessed Mother. An enormous excitement builds in my heart. I get little sleep on the night before the apparition. I toss and turn in bed. Anticipation steals my breath and makes me feel like I'm suffocating. But when I pray, I feel as if God gives me strength, as if He whispers to me, *"You can do it,"* and only then am I able to wait patiently until morning.

Usually by around 3 am, I start hearing faint voices and songs coming through my window from the hill. Some pilgrims spend the entire night waiting there on the cold, sharp rocks, praying and singing hymns. I think to myself, *Could there be any sound more beautiful?*

As the first glimmer of dawn brightens my room, I rise with the eagerness of a child on her birthday. As I get ready, I am in constant prayer. I gaze out my window and see the base of the hill around the Blue Cross covered with pilgrims. Their songs, now accompanied by guitar, resonate through the village, competing with crowing roosters and barking dogs.

In the past, I only knew that she'd appear to me at some time on the 2nd. But these days, I know that Our Lady always appears to me a little before 9 am.

I usually spend the first part of the morning praying in my living room. By then, I can feel the love building in my heart—I can feel the moment drawing near—but it's not yet time.

I look at the clock and know that my doorbell is about to ring. Before every apparition, without fail, Damir arrives at 7:30 am. Afraid I'll be hungry after so much fasting, he brings a few loaves of bread even though I always tell him it's not necessary. Even before he comes to my house, he and his team have already been to the Blue Cross to set up speakers so that everyone can hear the prayers and message. Damir has been filming during the apparitions for many years, both to keep a historical record and provide pilgrims with memories to take home. I used to hide from cameras but I've had to get used to them over the years. I still never watch Damir's videos, though—it's too painful to see myself experiencing what I wish I could experience at every moment of my life.

There was never any concerted effort to organize the morning; everything just kind of fell into place, and now there's a familiar rhythm. Miki usually comes to my house at around 8 am, and before I know it, it's time to leave. From the moment I step outside my door and breathe the cool morning air, I feel like I'm someone else. Mirjana the housewife—the one who likes historical novels, scented candles, and joking with her friends over coffee—is still at home. I'm now Mirjana the visionary.

There's always a crowd of pilgrims waiting for me outside my house. I smile at them, but deep down I wonder why they're not on the hill. After all, I'm *nobody*. I want them to be excited about Our Lady, not about me.

By now, I'm beginning to experience the feeling of Heaven, and I can sense Our Lady's presence and hear her faint voice in my heart. That's when I'm able to encourage myself.

I can do it, I think. *See, she does love me. I'm not such a sinner that she won't come.*

But as my consciousness drifts farther into Heaven, I comprehend less of what's going on around me. For example, I invited an American friend to come with me to the Blue Cross for one of the recent apparitions. When we met in front of my house that morning, I greeted him and asked him how he'd been, but he did not reply. I told him to stay close to me when we walked up so that we wouldn't get separated in the crowd, but he looked even more baffled. Finally, he politely said, "Mirjana, I'm sorry, but I don't speak Italian."

Of course, I knew he spoke English, but my thoughts were so jumbled before the apparition that I even forgot which language I was speaking. Some people even get offended when they tell me something and I do not respond, but it's difficult to explain that I'm already halfway in another world.

Marko and the girls set out first, usually accompanied by some of our friends or family members. Marko's mother always comes to the apparitions. My mother does too, although she prefers not to be too close to me. She cannot watch me cry without being able to comfort me.

"Your tears hurt me too much," she says.

Some local men always wait for me at my gate to escort me through the crowds. They wear yellow shirts and call themselves *Association Kraljica Mira*, Croatian for *Queen of Peace*. They also help pilgrims who need assistance. My brother Miro joined the group to help protect his big sister.

Protect me from what? The best answer I can give is simply too much love.

The *Kraljica Mira* volunteers escort me down the street, and I stop to greet people if I feel compelled to do so. At this point, my heart is bursting with love for everyone I see on my way. Usually when we reach the base of the hill, the crowd of pilgrims is so large that it blocks the entire street. Thousands more wait on the hill. In the past, we had to squeeze through the crowd to make it up to the Blue Cross, but Miro and his friends now keep an open pathway to make it easier.

Italian people are known to be blessed with passionate temperaments, and some of them think it's necessary to touch me, as if I'm some kind of saint or miracle worker. One time, I even caught a woman trying to cut off a lock of my hair as a keepsake.

When I was on my way to one apparition, a disturbed woman in the crowd grabbed my arm so forcefully that it dislocated my shoulder. Intense pain shot through my entire body, and I cried as I held my injured arm with my other hand. When I finally reached the Blue Cross, I was in agony and my body trembled. I prayed in silence, *Blessed Mother, please come quickly. I can't withstand this pain much longer.*

When Our Lady appeared, the throbbing instantly vanished. In Heaven, there is no pain. There is only love. Damir later told me that I was moving my injured arm normally during the apparition. But when Our Lady departed, I immediately felt the pain again, and it took several doctor visits and months of physical therapy to move it properly again.

I know it's out of love, so I never get angry when people grab me or try to touch me. I can understand why people might think there's something special about a person who sees the Blessed Mother, even though I do not necessarily agree with them. What I don't understand is when they confuse me for Our Lady. I'm a human being, no better than any of her children. I simply have a different mission in life. Thankfully, the majority of pilgrims who come are respectful and kind.

It's a strange feeling as I navigate the steep, rocky path leading to the Blue Cross. Thousands of eyes are on me. People shout my name and snap photos. The little girl within me wants to run and hide, but I know I must be strong.

The alcove in front of the Blue Cross is mostly reserved for priests, the infirm, and those who for many years have led pilgrims in prayer and song. My heart breaks as I see people suffering with cancer, paralysis, and other serious ailments. I kiss them, hug them, and silently pray for them.

It's uplifting and beautiful to hear thousands of people singing local hymns like *Gospa Majka Moja (Our Lady, Our Mother)* and *Zdravo Kraljica Mira (Hail Queen of Peace)*. Between songs, pilgrims pray the rosary together, switching to a different language after each decade. *Hail Mary, full of grace... Ave Maria, piena di grazia... Zdravo Marijo, milosti puna...*

The cross that gives the Blue Cross area its name is embedded in a rocky ledge behind a small statue of the Blessed Mother. On the morning of the apparition, the ledge is covered in flowers, religious articles, and folded prayer requests written by pilgrims or brought for loved ones who could not join them on the pilgrimage. Still, I always say that the most powerful way to deliver a prayer isn't on paper or even on the lips—it's from the heart. When you pray with your heart, God not only listens, but He speaks as well.

What does it mean to pray from the heart? For me, it's when I *feel* everything I want to say instead of merely thinking it, when every word passes through my heart before it comes out of my mouth. When I say *Hail Mary*, I try to feel like I'm truly greeting Mary with love. When I say *full of grace*, I marvel at how much grace Our Lady gives everyone. I talk with her in prayer—it's not that I see her or hear her, but I can sense her voice within. When I reflect on Mary's Assumption into heaven, for example, I ask her how she felt and what she thought in that moment. Prayer never seems like repetition to me because I always feel new and different things. "With prayer and fasting we can turn from all material things that bind us to contemplating God," said Fr. Slavko. "The more we contemplate God and Our Lady, the more we become like them. And the more we become like them, the easier it becomes to open our hearts to them."

It takes practice, perseverance, and a clean soul to feel God's presence when you pray. If you don't know what it means to pray from the heart, consider trying this: confess your sins and give everything over to God. Fast on bread and water. Pray the rosary and then speak to God in your own words, as if you are talking to your closest friend or loved one. Continue with your fasting and prayer. Soon you will discover what it means to pray from the heart. You will recognize God's unmistakable presence when you feel it, and you will never want to stop.

As I kneel on the flat rock, facing the Blue Cross, I feel as if I'm losing my breath. My heart is awash with a maelstrom of emotions. I'm waiting for the moment when Paradise comes to Earth, and I always feel unworthy. Marko and Miki kneel behind me, and Damir is in front of me with his camera. Friends or family members are usually beside me—sometimes even Lia, Alessandra, or Antonio whenever they visit from Italy. Since Antonio is now confined to a wheelchair, the young men from Cenacolo carry him up to the Blue Cross before the apparition, just as the *Kraljica Mira* volunteers carry other pilgrims who cannot climb on their own.

I join in with the crowd praying the rosary, and as the time of the apparition approaches, I feel increasingly breathless, and I think, *Our Lady is about to come!* I would probably hyperventilate or pass out if not for the calming effects of prayer.

The feeling builds to a crescendo. I put my hand over my chest as if to prevent my heart from jumping out. I gasp for air. Suddenly it's as if someone flips a switch—the world disappears and I'm encompassed in a great, unending blueness. Our Lady is before me in the middle of it all. Every pain and fear disappears. I'm comforted. I'm loved. I'm *complete.*

"Praised be Jesus," she says.

Wonderstruck, speechless, it takes me a moment to reply. "May He always be praised, my dear Mother."

But with the floodgates of my heart now open, a river of love spills out of my mouth. "Oh, thank you, Gospa! How beautiful you are!" I cannot control what I say in those first breathless moments. "Oh, my dear Mother! I missed you so!"

I'm no longer on Earth. The pilgrims see me there—my lips moving inaudibly and tears streaming down my face—but I'm not aware of anyone or anything around me. I'm not even on the hill anymore. Everything is concealed by the blueness, which itself is difficult to describe. I might compare it to the color of the sky on a cloudless day in springtime, but it's really nothing like the sky. In fact, it's more than just a color. It's like a place and a feeling at the same time. It totally envelopes me and Our Lady.

The only times I ever see some of the people around me are the rare instances when she prays over people. Somehow I do not have to turn my head to see them. When she prays for a particular individual, she raises her hand in his direction, or she simply looks at him with an expression of care, concern, or sorrow, but never with anger. She does not tell me why she prays over certain people, but after the apparition I usually try to tell the person what occurred.

When Our Lady looks directly at me—as she does for most of the apparition—I see no one else, even though I'm surrounded by people. They can be praying, talking or even shouting, but I can't hear them. Sunlight might shine directly into my eyes, but I can't feel it. I'm experiencing Heaven in that moment. I'm experiencing God's love and I'm filled with a joy that I've never felt on Earth. My mind is distinctly calm and devoid of trivial thoughts, and I have only two desires in my heart— for the moment to never end, or for Our Lady to take me with her.

I see her like I see anyone else—as a tangible, physical being, in no way transparent or spectral.

Her beauty, however, is clearly not of this world, and when she speaks, it's like music from Heaven. But her voice is more than a sound. If I had to compare it to something, I would say that her voice is *love*. It sounds like love and it feels like love. I hear her voice with my ears but also with my heart—with my entire being. One time, an acoustic engineer came from New York with the goal of identifying what Our Lady's voice was like. He brought recordings of many different types of voices. With headphones on my ears, I listened to all of them, but nothing came close.

Our Lady usually gives me a message halfway into the apparition. She doesn't forewarn me, but I know she's about to start when her gaze moves from me to the people and she says, *"Dear Children."* She looks at me again and says what she wishes to tell the world. Sometimes I get concerned that I won't be able to memorize the message, especially if she says some words that I never personally use, and I've even asked her, "Will I be able to remember all this?"

She responds with a gentle smile, as if to say that I needn't worry. When she gives me the message, she doesn't always speak in the same continuous way that I dictate it later. Instead, she connects certain parts of the message with what has happened and what is supposed to happen in the future. I cannot share specific details about this yet, but, for example, if Our Lady's message asks us to forgive, then she might explain to me that if we do not forgive, then this or that will happen.

After the message, Our Lady sometimes speaks to me about things that I cannot share publicly yet, and we pray together. We recite the special prayer for those who have not come to know God's love, which she taught me many years ago. One day, I'll be able to share it with everyone.

When we pray, she extends her hands towards me, but she doesn't always use the same gestures the rest of the time. When she speaks to me, for example, sometimes she puts her hands together palm to palm as if she's in prayer. Likewise, she doesn't always have the same expressions on her face; just like our expressions, hers vary according to what she's talking about. But unlike people on Earth, she doesn't express her emotions by laughing, shrugging, or—like I always joke with the Italians—making excited hand gestures.

Occasionally I ask a question on behalf of someone, usually about a special intention or a serious matter such as a terminal illness or family problem. In the early days, Our Lady allowed us to ask more questions, perhaps so we could know her better. Later, she still allowed questions, but somehow I knew what I should and shouldn't ask her even before I opened my mouth.

Sometimes she even gives me a message to relay privately to someone who I don't know and did not ask about.

Towards the end of the apparition, she gently raises her hand and says, *"In the name of my Son, I give you my motherly blessing."* She puts a slight emphasis on the word *motherly*, and in her messages she stresses that the blessing of a priest is the blessing of her Son, so I always ask all the priests at the Blue Cross to also bless the crowd and everyone's religious articles after the apparition. Unlike the way a priest gives a blessing, Our Lady does not make the sign of the cross; she only raises her hand.

She usually concludes by saying *"Pray, pray, pray,"* and then she rises slowly into the blueness, almost as if being vacuumed away.

On rare occasions, I see some kind of sign off in the distance as she goes. On August 2, 2006, for example, the blueness opened and I saw the silhouette of a cross in front of the sun. Other times I've seen a beautiful warm light behind Our Lady.

On June 2, 2009, I saw a large, golden cross. Emitting a beautiful light, it took my breath away. At the intersection of the beams of the cross was something like a heart—vibrant and beautiful and surrounded by a crown of thorns.

Exactly one year later, on June 2, 2010, a white dove appeared as Our Lady departed. The tips of the dove's feathers shone a golden color and something like a luminous dust emanated from it. I assumed the dove was meant to represent the Holy Spirit, but I have to reflect on its meaning like everyone else. Our Lady never explains these signs to me and I'm always surprised when I see one.

Our Lady rises just a short distance before she disappears, and the blueness immediately recedes with her. Suddenly back among the pilgrims, I'm assaulted by a cacophony of sound, as if people are shouting in my ears and blasting harsh noises through a megaphone. In reality, though, everyone is quietly praying. Even a whisper sounds like a scream in the moments after I leave the peace of Heaven.

Someone helps me to my feet and I sit on a nearby stone bench. I feel completely broken, lifeless, and I need a moment to readjust. Sometimes I can't stop crying. I've just experienced a brief moment of love in its purest form and lost it just as quickly. To know Heaven and live on Earth is more painful than anyone can imagine. I want to go home and lock myself in my room to pray, but there's one more thing I have to do.

My state of mind is far too turbulent after the apparition for me to pick up a pen, so Miki sits beside me with a notebook to transcribe Our Lady's message. Over the years, he's filled multiple notebooks. I can only remember the message clearly for a few minutes. Later, I can recall what it was about, but I cannot repeat it exactly. So, knowing how imperative it is that I transmit the message immediately, I force myself to speak. As I dictate to Miki, I feel as if I can hear Our Lady repeating the message, but I hear her words in my heart, not with my ears. I don't even have to be focused on Miki in that moment—while he's writing one sentence, I can turn and say something to the priest next to me, and then pick up again where I left off. It's as if there's a temporary recording of the message within me, and I can pause it and continue playing it as needed. I believe Our Lady somehow conveys the message to me until it's documented.

Miki reads the message to the pilgrims through a microphone, first in Croatian and then as a rough translation in English and Italian. He tells everyone that a more precise translation of the message will be available later, and after the apparition, he and several language experts meticulously check every translated word to ensure the message is released in its purest form. In the past, the messages traveled slowly, but with modern technology, they reach every part of the world in numerous languages on the same day they're given.

I see Our Lady's messages as a call to conversion and an affirmation of God's existence. In simple terms, she gives us the tools we need to connect with God, including prayer, fasting, confession, Holy Mass, and the Bible. But the overall emphasis is on love. God desires us to see a brother in *every* person we meet, to love them without condition or exception, and to reject the temptation to hate and judge.

"If you judge people, you have no time to love them," said Mother Teresa.

I'm in a daze as I make my way down the hill after the apparition. Our Lady's love is still so strong within me. I look at people but I don't see them. I listen but I don't hear what they say. It feels like someone else has taken my place again.

Sometimes I'm compelled to stop and speak with certain people, almost as if I'm guided to them. After one apparition, I felt a strong feeling within as I was coming down from the Blue Cross. I knew that I had to say *something* to *someone*, but I did not know what or to whom. There were thousands of people on the hillside, but my eyes fell on a young woman in the crowd. I instantly knew she was the one, and as I approached her, I also knew that I had to speak to her in Italian. "I have to tell you something, but I have no idea what."

The young woman's eyes filled with tears. "Yes, but I know. Thank you!"

She beamed as if a thorn of anguish had been plucked from her heart. Crying, she receded into the crowd. I had never seen her before, nor have I ever seen her again.

As I continue down, I'm often moved to give away the rosary I was holding during the apparition. But when people thank me, I quickly redirect their gratitude. "Thank God and Our Lady, but not me."

As soon as I reach my house after coming down, I go to my room. I pray. I cry. I ask God to help me understand why I have to stay on Earth. Through this prayer, I begin to feel God gently nudging me forward. I comprehend that my earthly quest must start again—that I have to carry my cross and search for God's love just like everyone else in this world; that I have a duty as a wife, mother, and messenger; and that I cannot yet go with Our Lady and she cannot stay here with me. Finally, after two or three days, I have enough strength to face life as a typical person—at least until I taste Paradise again next month.

Even after all these years, time seems to stand still when I'm with Our Lady. (PHOTO BY FOTO ĐANI)

CHAPTER 33

"My Son could have won with strength, but He chose meekness, humility and love. Follow my Son and give me your hands so that, together, we may climb the mountain and win."
— *From Our Lady's Message of July 2, 2007*

CARDINAL SCHÖNBORN ONCE said, "Millions of people around the world read the messages of Međugorje and in them they recognize the call of the Mother of God in their lives."

As our teacher in "the school of love," the Blessed Mother gives us a curriculum through her messages. Her "lessons" aim to help us come to know God's love. These include the "five stones" identified by Fr. Jozo: prayer, fasting, Holy Mass, confession, and the Bible.

Our Lady doesn't demand that we embrace these things. Instead, she encourages us, and she presents a map that will lead us on the path to love. Through her messages, she reminds us that the means for living Heaven on Earth—and *after* Earth—are at our fingertips, available freely to everyone.

"Many false truths are being offered to you," she said on January 2, 2015. *"You will overcome them with a heart cleansed by fasting, prayer, penance and the Gospel."*

PRAYER

Everything begins with prayer, and Our Lady emphasizes its value in almost every message she gives me during the apparitions.

"Only a pure heart, filled with prayer and compassion, can feel the love of my Son." (December 2, 2005)

"Dear children, my motherly heart begs you to accept prayer, because it is your salvation! Pray, pray, pray, my children." (January 2, 2005)

"By your surrender and prayer, ennoble your body and perfect your soul." (April 2, 2010)

"Pray that you can be apostles of the divine light in this time of darkness and hopelessness. This is a time of your trial. With a rosary in hand and love in the heart set out with me." (March 2, 2012)

"Dear children, proper prayer comes from the depth of your heart, from your suffering, from your joy, from your seeking the forgiveness of sins." (February 2, 2011)

A short prayer from the heart is more powerful than a long one comprised of words with no feeling. God speaks to us through love, so love is the language He understands.

Having seen Our Lady over 700 times since 1981, I never get bored while praying the rosary because I can envision her every time I say a *Hail Mary*. Still, I remember being a little girl and feeling impatient whenever Grandma Jela led the evening prayers. It's not always easy to focus, but Our Lady says that nothing unites a family better than praying the rosary together.

If your thoughts begin to wander when you are praying, then put the rosary aside and speak directly to Our Lady as a child talks to his mother. Tell her why you can't be still. Tell her what's burdening you.

Give her whatever you have in your heart and she will give you what's in hers—the peace of God.

After having to hide my faith from the communists, I still pray the rosary on my fingers. Even when I have a rosary, I usually end up giving it to someone I meet, and if I'm asked to lead the rosary in a group, I prefer to use my fingers because I'm afraid of miscounting the beads.

FASTING

Our Lady almost always mentions prayer when she speaks of fasting. The two are linked. Fasting should always be accompanied by prayer.

"It's important to know that when we pray and fast, it is to open ourselves to God and to what God gives us," said Fr. Slavko. "Often when people pray and fast, it becomes an exchange of action. We pray and fast, then wait to get something back. When we do not get what we are praying or fasting for, then we stop praying. It is important to remain open to receive everything that God wants to give us. Graces come when we remain open through prayer and fasting."

The fasting Our Lady invites us to is meant to open our hearts. When I fast, I prove to myself that I'm the boss of my own body. Even though it seems like a small sacrifice, I'm showing God that I will do anything for Him. Fasting also strengthens my prayer.

"The great love of God sends me to lead you to salvation. Give me your simple hearts, purified by fasting and prayer. Only in the simplicity of your hearts is your salvation." (September 2, 2007)

"Today I call you with prayer and fasting to clear the path in which my Son will enter into your hearts." (June 2, 2010)

"Do not resist hope and peace. Along with your prayer and fasting, by His cross, my Son will cast away the darkness that wants to surround you and come to rule over you. He will give you the strength for a new life." (March 2, 2013)

"My children, pray and fast that you may be able to recognize all of this which I am seeking of you." (December 2, 2013)

"I desire that by fasting and prayer you obtain from the Heavenly Father the cognition of what is natural and holy—Divine." (February 2, 2014)

Our Lady asks us to fast on Wednesdays and Fridays. The best form of fasting, she says, is on bread and water. In this way, we forgo the pleasure of food and drink without depriving our bodies of sustenance.

Fr. Stanko Ćosić, a young priest serving in Međugorje, says, "You can only taste the flavor of bread and water in the desert."

CONFESSION

Our Lady asks us to confess our sins at least once a month, and for Catholics, of course, she means through the Sacrament of Reconciliation with a priest.

"My children, only a pure heart, unburdened by sin, can open itself, and only honest eyes can see the way by which I desire to lead you." (December 2, 2011)

"Dear children! In the great love of God, I come to you today to lead you on the way of humility and meekness. The first station on that way, my children, is confession. Reject your arrogance and kneel down before my Son." (July 2, 2007)

"...I desire to help you to be free of the dirtiness of the past and to begin to live anew and differently. I am calling you to resurrect in my Son. Along with confession of sins, renounce everything that has distanced you from my Son and that has made your life empty and unsuccessful." (May 2, 2011)

Our Lady said that there isn't a man in the world who doesn't need to go to confession at least once a month. When I relate this to pilgrims, I always smile and add, "Notice that she didn't mention women. Our Lady knows that we have enough crosses to bear!"

When Jakov hears me say that, he says, "Yes, it's true that men should go to confession monthly, but women need to go every day!"

A heartfelt confession cleanses you from past transgressions, lifts the weight of sin from your shoulders, and allows God to fill you with His peace.

"A pearl that falls in mud is still a pearl," says Fr. Stanko Ćosić, "but you can only see its beauty after you clean it off. So it is with our souls in confession."

MASS

During the apparitions, sometimes Our Lady tells me things besides the message. I often remember it later when I pray.

She once said something which touched me deeply. I had the feeling that it was something of great importance, but I've never shared it until now.

"I was the first Tabernacle," she said. *"The Holy Body grew within me first."*

From the beginning of the apparitions, Our Lady emphasized the importance of Mass. She told us that if we ever found ourselves having to choose between attending Mass or seeing her in the apparition, we should always choose Mass.

"May the Mass, the most exalted and most powerful act of your prayer, be the center of your spiritual life." (August 2, 2008)

"...In the Eucharist my Son gives Himself to you anew." (April 2, 2015)

"I am calling you for the Eucharist to be the life of your soul." (August 2, 2014)

When I receive Communion, I feel that my God and I are one. I feel as if I've become his keeper, that He lives in me. When I kneel and pray afterwards, I ask Him to stay with me as long as possible so that I can continue to feel the love and fullness that only He can give.

THE BIBLE

Our Lady asks us to return the Word of God to our homes. Do not let it sit in a dusty corner like a decoration, but put it in a place of honor where it will be seen and touched.

> *"With a simple heart accept His word and live it. If you live His word, you will pray. If you live His word, you will love with a merciful love; you will love each other." (August 2, 2015)*

> *"My children, to live my Son means to live the Gospel." (December 2, 2014)*

She did not specify how much of the Bible we should read every day, but a few sentences are better than nothing. The most important thing is to open it regularly.

ANSWERING THE CALL

On July 2, 2012, Our Lady said, *"I am praying that the light of the love of my Son may illuminate you, so that you may triumph over weaknesses and come out of misery."*

If prayer is not already a joy for you, then start slowly. If you force yourself, you are more likely to succumb to weakness, get discouraged, and give up. Faith should be nurtured like a delicate flower and given time to grow.

Our Lady taught us by example. The first thing she asked from us was to pray the *Apostle's Creed* and seven *Our Father* prayers, *Hail Mary* prayers, and *Glory Be* prayers every day. Later, she asked us to pray one rosary and to fast every Friday. When we finally got used to that, she asked us to add another rosary, and later a third rosary, and to also fast on Wednesdays.

I always joke that I hope she will stop at this, but in truth prayer has become a joy for me. By starting slowly and doing everything from the heart, anyone can attain the treasure that Our Lady tries to lead us to. Hers is a gentle call. She never makes demands.

Our Mother comes every month to pray for *"those who do not feel the love of God yet"* because, to her, even one lost child is one too many. Her vast love for us practically forces her to intervene. Look at the world around you to understand her concern.

On July 2, 2011, I saw an especially striking sign as Our Lady was leaving. To her right was a beautiful cross shimmering with golden light. The light seemed to emit a sense of joy and victory. But to her left a darkness appeared unlike anything I had ever seen—a murky void emanating a sense of desolation. Moving and undulating, it filled me with fear.

Her message that day was a strong call to conversion. *"Dear children,"* she said, *"today I call you to a difficult and painful step for your unity with my Son."* She beseeched us to purify ourselves, explaining that an impure heart *"is not an example of the beauty of God's love to those who surround it and to those who have not come to know that love."*

After the apparition, Veronika asked with concern if she'd been kneeling on the good side or the bad side, but I assured her that she needn't worry. Our Lady did not explain the image to me, but in my opinion it revealed the difference between a pure heart and an impure one, as if to illustrate her message by showing that our hearts will be full of light if we choose the path of virtue. Like Jesus said, "Blessed are the clean of heart, for they will see God." (Matthew 5:8)

If we reject Him, however, then we'll walk in darkness, confused about who we are and where we are going.

Thankfully, the difference between light and darkness is merely a choice. No one can say that his heart is entirely pure, but it's crucial that we try. I'm afraid of anyone who claims that he does everything perfectly.

The apparition of October 2, 2011 is another one that stands out in my mind. In her message, she called us to seek a close relationship with God, saying *"the Father is not far away from you and He is not unknown to you."* She explained that God revealed Himself to us and gave us life through Jesus, adding, *"Do not give in to temptations that want to separate you from God the Father."* She asked us to pray so that our hearts *"may be flooded by the goodness which comes only from my Son,"* and she implored us not to judge our shepherds, lest we forget that God called them.

Our Lady showed me something during that apparition which I cannot speak about, but what shook me the most was the intense sadness on her face. I've seen women on Earth who were suffering, but nothing compares to the pain on Our Lady's face. In a way, I envy those who have never witnessed her sorrow. It hurts her most when she sees that we haven't even tried to change, when our hearts remain hard and indifferent, when we've chosen a path of ruin rather than salvation. She has so much love and patience, and she does so much for us, but we are often deaf to her call and reluctant to take even the slightest step forward.

Imagine a mother here on Earth whose son has fallen into the wrong crowd and lives in darkness. He doesn't talk to his mother anymore because he knows how much he's disappointed her. Think of that mother's pain. Now, multiply that pain by a billion and imagine looking into her eyes. That's what it's like to see Our Lady when she prays for her countless children who have gone astray. Or consider the indescribable grief of a mother who has lost a child. Our Mother in Heaven grieves for every child she loses.

After the October 2, 2011 apparition, I collapsed in tears. The image of Our Lady's suffering was burned into my mind. Looking at all the people around me, I felt like the apparitions were in danger of being taken for granted. People were chatting and snapping photographs. Some were there just to look for visible signs and would only talk about what they saw. Others would hear the message but forget it just as quickly. I usually never gave my own comments after an apparition, but this time I had to say something.

"Are you aware, brothers and sisters, that the Mother of God was with us?" I said. Miki relayed it through the microphone. "Each of us should ask ourselves, 'Am I worthy of this?' I'm saying this because it's difficult for me to see her in pain. Each of us is looking for a miracle, but we don't want to work a miracle in ourselves."

I was ill for three days after that apparition. Our Lady's sorrowful face remained before my eyes. I thought I was going to die. Through prayer, however, God gradually eased my mind. I emerged believing that with perseverance we could wipe away Our Lady's tears and lessen her pain.

Our Lady doesn't always appear sad, though. If she tells me something of great importance, for example, she does so with a look of determination. My favorite moments are when she's joyful. Anytime she speaks about her Son, she has the most beautiful smile on her face. Her joy affects me deeply and I feel less pain when the apparition ends. But seeing her sad stays with me the longest.

When I described Our Lady's sorrow to a group of pilgrims, one woman shook her head and said, "When will this world change? When will people understand?"

"That's not what we should be asking," I said. "Instead, we need to ask ourselves 'When will I change? When will I understand?' We cannot put the blame on others. We need to start with ourselves, and only then can we help others."

The only soul I need to scrutinize is my own. When it's my time to stand before God, He won't ask me about you. He'll only ask how well *I* answered His call.

Still, Our Lady believes in you—even if you don't yet believe in her. Her love is unconditional. She loves the sinner as much as she loves the saint. She loves the atheist as much she loves the believer. She loves *you* and all her children as much as she loves me.

Our Lady was once an ordinary woman who experienced human suffering. You can turn to her with all your difficulties and needs. She is your true Mother, even more than the one who gave birth to you. She knows and understands you more than you know and understand yourself.

If you feel lost, if you're struggling to understand your mission or find your place in the world, just look—Our Lady is extending her hands to you. Take them. She will lead you to peace.

If you're hurting, if something has stolen the light from your heart, just listen—Our Lady is calling to you. Talk to her. She will fill you with the light of her Son.

Our Lady has started a great movement through these apparitions on the second of each month. Many people throughout the world have answered her call by establishing prayer groups, spreading the messages, and living as examples of those who know God's love. Our Lady cannot triumph without us, and we cannot triumph without her.

"Help me," she says. *"Set out with me."* And on January 2, 2014, she said, *"Dear children, for you to be able to be my apostles and to be able to help all those who are in darkness to come to know the light of the love of my Son, you must have pure and humble hearts."*

Through her example of purity and humility, she comes on the second day of every month and shows us how to pray *"for those who do not comprehend love, who do not understand what it means to love."* She has confidence in us and repeatedly asks us to join her. *"I am calling you to be my apostles of light who will spread love and mercy through the world,"* she said in one message. And, *"I will make use of you, apostles of love, to help all of my children come to know the truth."*

Through prayer and fasting, she says, we can be her *"river of love"* flowing out into the world, and she urges us to comprehend that we don't have to be perfect to work for Heaven, saying, *"Do not waste time thinking about whether you are worthy to be my apostles."*

Do you understand that she's talking to you? Whatever you do during your short "blink" on Earth will affect you for all eternity. If you had to spend a relatively short amount of time doing something difficult in order to guarantee yourself everlasting joy, wouldn't you do it?

But Our Lady wants us to strive for more than that. She calls us to join the fight here on Earth by helping our brothers and sisters come to know God's love. Evil yearns to deprive us of our eternal reward by luring us with temptations and then destroying us from within. More darkness on the planet equals more souls lost forever.

"As individuals, my children, you cannot stop the evil that wants to begin to rule in this world and destroy it," she said on August 2, 2011. *"But, according to God's will, all together, with my Son, you can change everything and heal the world."*

Our Lady told me many things that I cannot yet reveal. For now, I can only hint at what our future holds, but I do see indications that the events are already in motion. Things are slowly starting to develop. As Our Lady says, look at the signs of the times, and pray.

I can compare it to spring cleaning. If I want my home to be spotless, I know that I have to first turn everything upside down. I move the sofa, I stack the chairs on the table, I open all the cupboards—nothing remains in its place. My home is thrown into chaos and disorder. It's unrecognizable to my children and the peace is gone. But then I clean under everything. I wipe away all the grime. I put every piece of furniture back to its rightful place. In the end, my home is more immaculate than ever.

This is how I see all the confusion in the world today. This is how I see Our Lady's apparitions and God's plan. A truly clean house starts with a big mess. Will you be like most children who stand back while Mom cleans, or will you *not be afraid* to get your hands dirty and help her? Like Our Lady said in one of her messages, *"I desire that, through love, our hearts may triumph together."*

May the triumph of her heart begin with *you.*

THE END

ABOUT THE AUTHOR

Mirjana Dragičević-Soldo was born in Sarajevo, ex-Yugoslavia, on March 18, 1965. Her life was dramatically changed in 1981 when she and five other young people experienced an apparition of the Virgin Mary in a small village called Međugorje. *My Heart Will Triumph* is her first book.

LEARN MORE AND STAY CONNECTED

Visit the book's website, *MyHeartWillTriumph.com*, for:

- Additional photos and online videos.
- Free eBook containing the Međugorje messages.
- Free eNewsletter featuring the latest news from Međugorje.
- Forum to discuss Mirjana's book with others.
- Bulk discounts for multiple copies and/or wholesale orders.
- Links to the book's Facebook and social media pages.

A SIMPLE SOLUTION TO WORLD HUNGER

A portion of the proceeds from *My Heart Will Triumph* supports *Mary's Meals*, a charity that feeds more than a million children in schools around the world. Visit MarysMeals.org to learn more.